Israel

1967
- Massive military build-ups by the neighbouring Arab states and an Egyptian blockade of the Straits of Tiran result in the Six Day War, as Israel launches a pre-emptive strike to protect her borders, June 6–11.
- Jerusalem officially reunited under Israeli control.
- The Golan Heights are taken by Israel after fierce fighting against attacking Syrian forces.
- Judea, Sumaria, Gaza, and Sinai peninsula come under Israeli control.

1984
- Shimon Peres becomes prime minister.
- Operation *Moses* brings Jews from the ancient Jewish community of Ethiopia to Israel.

1990
- Operation *Exodus* begins, bringing mass immigration of Jews from the Soviet Union to Israel.

1995
- Prime Minister Yitzhak Rabin is assassinated by a Jewish extremist at a peace rally.
- Shimon Peres begins second term as prime minister.

1996
- Operation Grapes of Wrath against terrorist bases in Lebanon is launched.
- Benjamin Netanyahu becomes prime minister.

1978
- Camp David Accords, constituting a basis for peace between Israel and Egypt and a basis for peace in the Middle East, are signed by Israel and Egypt.
- Prime Minister Begin and Egyptian President Sadat are awarded the Nobel Peace Prize.

1985
- Israel withdraws from Lebanon, retaining a narrow security zone to protect northern Israel.

1992
- Yitzhak Rabin begins second term as prime minister.

1974
- Yitzhak Rabin becomes prime minister.

1979
- Peace Treaty signed between Israel and Egypt.

1983
- Yitzhak Shamir becomes prime minister.

1980

1990

1993
- Continued Katyusha attacks on northern Israel.

1994
- Israel-Jordan peace treaty is signed.
- Rabin, Peres, and Arafat are awarded the Nobel Peace prize.

1998
- Israel celebrates its 50th anniversary.

1970

1972
- Eleven Israeli athletes are murdered by PLO terrorists at the Munich Olympic Games.

1976
- The IDF frees hostages held captive in Entebbe, Uganda, with a daring air-rescue mission.

1982
- Operation Peace for Galilee is launched against PLO terrorist strongholds in Lebanon used for attacks against northern Israel.

1987
- Palestinian uprising (intifadah) begins in the West Bank and the Gaza Strip.

1991
- Israel is attacked by Iraqi Scud missiles during the Gulf War.
- Operation *Solomon* brings most of the Jews remaining in Ethiopia to Israel in a massive airlift.

1977
- Menachem Begin becomes prime minister.
- Egyptian President Anwar Al-Sadat visits Jerusalem.
- Project Renewal initiated to improve the quality of life for inhabitants of distressed urban neighbourhoods and towns.

1986
- Anatoly Sharansky, well-known refusenik in the U.S.S.R., arrives in Israel as a new immigrant.
- Yitzhak Shamir begins second term as prime minister.

1973
- The Yom Kippur War begins on the Day of Atonement, the holiest day of the Jewish year, when Egypt and Syria launch a co-ordinated surprise attack on Israel. They are repulsed by Israel after fierce fighting and heavy losses, October 6 – November 11.

Voices from the Heart

A Community Celebrates 50 Years of Israel

An informal lesson at the kibbutz, 1920s.

Voices from the Heart

A Community Celebrates 50 Years of Israel

Edited by Bonnie Goldstein & Jaclyn Shulman

Canadian Cataloguing in Publication Data

Main entry under title:

Voices from the heart: a community celebrates 50 years of Israel

Includes index
ISBN 0-7710-3398-2

1. Israel – History.   2. Jews – Ontario – Toronto.   I. Goldstein, Bonnie.
II. Shulman, Jaclyn.

DS126.5. V64 1998   956.9405   C98-931686-6

Previously published works are reprinted by permission.

We acknowledge the financial support of the Government of Canada through the Book Publishing Industry Development Program for our publishing activities. We further acknowledge the support given by the Canada Council for the Arts and by the Ontario Arts Council for our publishing program.

Design by K.T. Njo

Map by Visutronx
Historical timeline illustration by Andrew Judd
Film work by Rainbow Digicolor Inc., Toronto

Printed and bound in Canada

McClelland & Stewart Inc.
The Canadian Publishers
481 University Avenue,
Toronto, Ontario
M5G 2E9

1 2 3 4 5 6   02 01 00 99 98

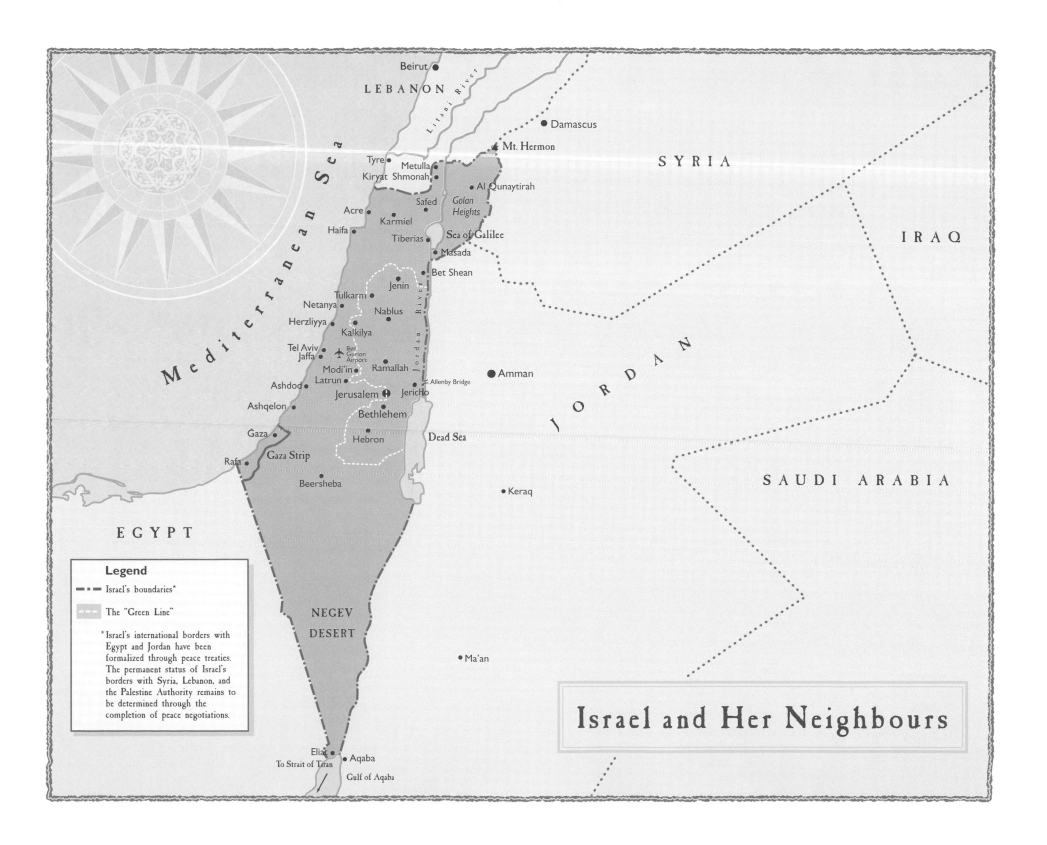

Beirut

LEBANON

Litani River

Damascus

Tyre
Metulla
Kiryat Shmonah

Mt. Hermon

SYRIA

Al Qunaytirah

Acre
Safed
Golan Heights

Karmiel

Haifa

Tiberias
Sea of Galilee

IRAQ

Masada

Bet Shean

Jenin

Jordan River

Tulkarm
Netanya
Nablus

Herzliyya

Kalkilya

Tel Aviv
Jaffa
Ben Gurion Airport

Modi'in
Ramallah

Amman

Latrun
Allenby Bridge

Ashdod

Jerusalem
Jericho

Ashqelon

Bethlehem

JORDAN

Gaza
Hebron
Dead Sea

Gaza Strip

Rafa

Beersheba

Keraq

Mediterranean Sea

EGYPT

SAUDI ARABIA

Legend

— ·· — Israel's boundaries*

‑ ‑ ‑ The "Green Line"

*Israel's international borders with Egypt and Jordan have been formalized through peace treaties. The permanent status of Israel's borders with Syria, Lebanon, and the Palestine Authority remains to be determined through the completion of peace negotiations.

NEGEV DESERT

Ma'an

Eliat
Aqaba
To Strait of Tiran
Gulf of Aqaba

Israel and Her Neighbours

Hongkong Bank of Canada is proud to support
this commemorative book celebrating 50 years of Israel.

Hongkong Bank of Canada

Member HSBC *Group*

For the community of Toronto — a gift of treasured memories.

B. G. and J. S.

CONTENTS

FOREWORD

This year, Israel and I both turned fifty. A man of fifty may begin to show signs of ageing, but when he is surrounded by youth, he himself feels young. One feels strong and imbued with energy. This is how I feel every day of my life in Israel. As a nation, Israel is in its adolescence – an age when some experience doubts and fears of what they can do and what is to come. But it can also be an age when one begins to appreciate one's uniqueness and the fact that one is master of one's future.

This is what we are celebrating when we rejoice in the fiftieth year of the independence of Israel. We have returned to the land where our forefathers prayed, our prophets preached, and our kings ruled. The founders of the State of Israel did not struggle and sacrifice so that Israelis would have a state, but rather so that the Jewish People would have a home.

Many of us have begun to take this cherished independence for granted. Most Jews alive today do not remember a world without Israel, many having grown up after Israel had achieved its historic victory in the Six Day War. They know only a strong and mighty Israel. But not to recognize the significance of our present freedom would be to turn our backs on thousands of years of Jewish history, when our freedom was determined at the whims of a czar, king, or kaiser.

I consider myself fortunate to have lived a life that allows me to appreciate every minute of freedom. Before my physical incarceration, Zionism had set me free. The Soviet State had sought to strip the individual of every facet of identity, severing ties to religion, heritage, and culture. It was the feeling of connection to the thousands of years of history, to the millions of Jews throughout the world, and to the State of Israel, that gave me the courage and stamina to join the struggle for human rights in the Soviet Union. So, even when in solitary confinement, where my world was reduced to the area within four stone walls, I knew myself to be free.

Beneath the sound and fury of our daily lives, a subtle change has occurred. For fifty years the Jewish People worked to shape the State of Israel, and now Israel is beginning to shape the Jewish People. We live in an exciting period in the next phase of Israel's history, discussing and voting on issues that will influence our people for generations to come. The conflicts we face are the conflicts of a society struggling with its identity. With diligence and patience we have reclaimed our land. We now work to strengthen the nation for whom Israel exists.

Voices from the Heart is a collection of stories of the struggle, commitment, and devotion evoked by the land of Israel. This book is a valuable and unique addition to the educational archives documenting the birth and growth of the State of Israel. Writing this foreword is particularly meaningful for me because of the special link I have to the people of Toronto. Shortly after my arrest in Moscow in 1977, my name was recognized by my cousin Noah Landis as he was reading a newspaper in Toronto. "I think he is family," he said to his son. This kinship was soon confirmed through letters to my father, *Olov Hashalom*, and the struggle for the rights of Soviet Jews entered a new phase in Canada.

The Jewish community of Toronto deserves a special mention at this point, for they too said to themselves, "I think he is family," and joined the campaign to set me free. They also deserve special recognition for their ceaseless efforts and tireless work during those dark years when we had to fight for the release of every one of our brothers and sisters who sought to leave the Soviet Union. And their continued involvement in helping to overcome obstacles, as well as in celebrating the victories of Israel, points to the great strength of the community – and to the central force which binds together all our communities, the Jewish State of Israel.

Anatoly Sharansky
Minister of Industry and Trade,
Jerusalem, June 1998

Voices from the Heart is a collage of words and pictures that represent the precious, never-to-be-forgotten memories of their contributors. The stories in this commemorative book honouring Israel's fiftieth anniversary express the many different ways members of our community have found or created a special link to the land of Israel.

To be a Jew has always meant being married to two concepts, Israel and the Diaspora, and seeking a harmony between the community in which we live, work, and contribute, and the inextricable ties that bind us to our ancestral, historical, and spiritual homeland. The individuals in this book have all, in their own unique ways, found that harmony.

It is with great admiration and profound respect that I pay tribute to Bonnie Goldstein and Jackie Shulman, who have devoted a great part of their waking hours to ensuring that the words and memories in this book will be a source of reading pleasure and, above that, a treasured record and resource.

Julia Koschitzky
Toronto, June 1998

ACKNOWLEDGEMENTS

When we launched into the making of this book, we were uncertain if it would generate any interest. We took the risk – and the response was overwhelming. The Toronto community took this project to heart, immediately responding with great feeling. Indeed, so many individuals assisted us in this effort that it is a challenge to thank each one personally.

Julia Koschitzky, chair of Israel at Fifty, and Karen Morton, chair of Israel at Fifty Showcase, presented us with the opportunity and privilege of doing this project according to our own vision, of capturing the community in all its richness and diversity. Thank you for your encouragement and confidence, and for letting us "run with it." We thank the Hongkong Bank of Canada for their extremely generous support of *Voices from the Heart*, allowing the book to be more accessible to the community at large.

To Avie Bennett, who knew how impossible this task would be to complete on time and still said "yes," we offer our personal thanks. On their behalf, we express the gratitude of the Toronto community to McClelland & Stewart and its staff for publishing this book as a public service.

We thank each member of our advisory board for their creative brainstorming, their direction, and their wisdom: Irving Abella, Steve Ain, Charlie Diamond, Saul Edell, Marty Goldberg, David Goldstein, Mark Gryfe, Gerry Halbert, Ben Kayfetz, Bryan Keshen, Jehudi Kinar, Julia Koschitzky, Allan Offman, Rabbi Gunther Plaut, Sam Sable, Rosalie Sharp, Michael Shulman, Ted Sokolsky, and Kurt Weinberg.

Sherry Kaufman and Shaindy Nathanson put their personal lives on hold in order to help turn this concept into a reality. With great care, they matched up interviewees with just the right interviewer, kept track of who's on first, and made sure no one went missing. Susie Mogil, with great skill, took us onto the computer, and we bless her for that. Paula Draper dropped everything to train the interviewers, who dropped everything to get us the story. Our thanks to these intrepid interviewers, writers, and transcribers: Lani Alexandroff, Pearl Banks, Marlene Berkowitz, Judy Breuer, Vicki Campbell, Ellen Cole, Deborah Dalfen, Roz Davidson, Paula Draper, Phyllis Feldman, Lilly Fenig, Maxine Granovsky Gluskin, Judy Godfrey, Susan Goldberg, Fran Goldman, Jeanette Grosman, Penny Gross, Judy Gwartz, Sherry Kaufman, Lorri Kushnir, Sheila Lancit, Cecily Levine, Judy Magder, Shaindy Nathanson, Rachel Nisker,

Susan Organek, Esther Peters, Myrna Riback, Helaine Robins, Freida Sherman, Audrey Taerk, Dorothy Tessis, Melanie Unger, and Yaffa Wise.

To Stephen Speisman, the director of the Ontario Jewish Archives, who made his archives and knowledge available to us at a moment's notice, our many thanks, as well as to Brooky Robins, Howard Markus, and Miriam Beckerman.

Many others helped with the ingathering process. Thanks to Dora Singer of the Canada Israel Committee, Claire Adams, Sheila Mandel, Paul Morton, Joyce Goldstein, Nancy Goldstein, Syd Charendoff, Pnina Zilberman of the Holocaust Education and Memorial Centre of Toronto, Stan Solomon, Mel Fenson in Israel, Monte Mazin, Amy Rotman, Lisi Tesher, Jill Offman, Harold Troper, Mordechai Ben-Dat of the *Canadian Jewish News*, Michelle Levy, and Cynthia Gasner.

A special thank you for excellent research and writing to Dianna Roberts Zauderer, Francesca David, Eric Goldstein, as well as to Elisa Morton Palter, Rabbi Frydman-Kohl, and the Israel at Fifty office, who helped to spread the word to the community at large.

Thank you to the professionals in the community who gave of themselves and their time far "above and beyond." You are professionals in every sense of the word. Your commitment to this project reflects your deep attachment to the community you serve. We thank Bryan Keshen, director of Israel at Fifty, for his constant encouragement and for helping us formulate a strategic plan to see the project through. Whenever we needed historical research or clarification we called in our modern-day "Hillels" – David Goldberg, director of research and education at the Foundation for Middle East Studies, and Erica Simmons, media liaison at the Consulate General of Israel, Toronto – both of whom reviewed our initial manuscript in its entirety and assisted us with our glossary. Eli Rubenstein, director of young leadership development at the United Israel Appeal, was a continuous source of creative energy, writing articles, researching information, and generally taking us under his wing.

Fay Rotman always made herself cheerfully available to face the administrative challenge. Also, thanks to Helen Mak and Rosaline Lau, as well as to Yael Kinar and Greg Ginsberg, for helping us process the masses of material that crossed our desk on a daily basis.

We thank Joel Rose for introducing us to our generous sponsor, the Hongkong Bank of Canada, and for also, with Owen Duckman, providing us with valuable legal advice.

A very special thanks to David Goldstein, who provided us with his administrative staff and office equipment, and with his boardroom as our permanent home. We thank him for his positive attitude and for sharing his commonsense approach. Despite the inevitable disruption caused by a project of this magnitude, everyone in the office was always supportive.

Many thanks to Barbara Hehner, our senior editor, whose sensibility allowed us to expand our creative horizons. She gave us the confidence to respect our own skills and instincts. She has the singular talent of bringing out the voice of the author while improving the flow and clarity of the story. There were interviews in need of becoming stories, and stories that needed to be refined. With great skill, Barbara made that, and more, happen. Thanks also to Eric Zweig, Ruth Chernia, and Maryan Gibson for their editorial assistance under the great pressure of time, and to Patricia Buckley, our knowledgeable and efficient photo researcher.

Rochelle Diamond, Lisa Levitan, and Jamie Shulman read our manuscript with a critical and fresh eye, and we thank them for their suggestions. We thank Russell Goldstein, whose computer expertise was helpful to the project, particularly on a not-to-be-forgotten, suspenseful, all-night vigil, when he retrieved a host of stories lost in cyberspace.

For helping to turn our vision into a beautiful book, we were fortunate to have the expertise of Alex Schultz. He is our thoughtful and valuable McClelland & Stewart editor. Through his wise advice, clear thinking, and meticulous search for accuracy, our finished product gained in consistency, form, and overall readability. Our thanks to Kong Njo, McClelland & Stewart's talented art director, whose imaginative design helped bring the contributors' many voices and cherished photos to life as part of a unified whole.

We thank our families and friends who have been lost to us for much of the time it has taken to prepare this book. Their understanding allowed us the space to pursue this great adventure, which often took away from our valued time together. We're glad you are back in our lives.

Our children, Jennifer and Jamie, Laurence, Lesli, and Russell, have each, in his or her own way, provided us with valuable moments of insight into this endeavour. Each one has come forward just when most needed, and we thank them for that.

To our husbands, David and Michael – you have our love, gratitude, and more. We will always appreciate the respect you have for us as individuals, as well as the respect you have given our work.

To the many we have been unable to acknowledge here, we are deeply grateful. And above all, we thank the hundreds of people who took the time and effort to send us their stories, reflecting the variety and richness of their experiences of Israel. Thank you for helping us create *Voices from the Heart*, and for allowing us into your homes and your hearts.

INTRODUCTION

Archives are the gift of one generation to another . . .

V*oices from the Heart* was born from the Toronto community's wish to commemorate Israel's fifty years of statehood and give expression to its profound sense of connection to Israel.

As the editors, we felt that an anthology of personal stories and recollections of a nation in the making, highlighted by cherished family photographs, would create a treasury of oral history for future generations. We hope this book will become a valuable educational resource, an archival record portraying, in words and pictures, the great breadth and diversity of our community's ties to Israel. The stories here are representative of the thousands of similar stories which can be heard in communities across the country.

Voices from the Heart began with a simple idea, and then, like many creative enterprises, it developed a life of its own, involving many people.

We were assisted, especially in the early stages, by our Israel at Fifty advisory board, composed of members of all ages, and representing the makeup of the Jewish community. Their job was a crucial one: to suggest, from so many possibilities, those pioneers in our community who would be representative of the rest.

And then *our* challenge began! We reached out to the community, seeking stories that would reflect its rich diversity. Through newspaper articles and advertisements, fliers and synagogue announcements, word of the book travelled. We created story guidelines, since most of the narratives were to be written by the contributors themselves. Other stories were the result of interviews conducted by newly trained volunteers, who made themselves available at a moment's notice to become part of this exciting project. These interviews resulted in the "conversations" that appear throughout the book.

The community took this quest for personal histories to heart, and their response to our call was overwhelming. For earlier generations, the Land of Israel was first a dream, then a hope, and finally a wonderful reality. For many of their children, Israel was often regarded more as a political entity. Our community felt that now was the time to show them the way it was.

At first we had barely dared hope to receive 150 stories, but almost 500 submissions were sent in without delay. Since we had only a few months to gather and give structure to these stories, we often had to work into the small hours of the night. And by the time we realized how impossible this all was, we were almost finished!

The stories arrived in random order, but as we read through them, obvious groupings emerged. We saw that the stories, arranged within a roughly chronological framework, provided multifaceted views of both the great and ordinary events in Israel's history, and of our community's involvement with them. Often, the decision was made to use only a portion of a story, which, when grouped with others, would provide a vivid picture of a time or an event. Gaps in history, or areas of the community not yet represented, revealed themselves by their absence. And so the research began again.

Our modest office space became a repository for treasured possessions of the contributors. Military medals, passports, vintage photographs, identity cards, and other cherished items were entrusted to us. We were obsessive about their care; every document and original story was copied in triplicate so that we could keep the originals under lock and key. The volume of paper alone was almost overwhelming, and we quickly learned the art of cross-referencing.

We were determined to make this book as accessible as possible to every reader. To provide a historical context for the personal stories, we researched and created timelines. We consulted experts to help form background notes on crucial historical events. Indeed, one of the greatest rewards of this project was that, in the course of our research, we learned so much ourselves. Additionally, each time a Hebrew or Yiddish term was introduced, we decided to include an English translation. Just try to find general agreement on a single proper transliteration of a Yiddish or Hebrew word. It isn't easy! It's like gefilte (or is it gefulte?) fish – everyone's recipe differs. Yet despite all this, our glossary was compiled.

The need to clarify details and solve inconsistencies put us in constant contact with contributors. Why didn't the date mentioned in the story match the date noted on the reverse side of the photograph submitted? Was that village in Poland or Russia? Many queries arose, too, from the typed transcriptions of the interviews, which often included words or phrases foreign to the transcriber. Our helpless laughter from some of these guessed-at words made it easier to get through the marathon phone calls and research needed to pin the corrections down.

Although computers were given a mighty work-out during this project, we more often turned to the editor's traditional tool – the pencil – as we corrected manuscripts, proofs, revised proofs, and so on – sometimes it seemed the process of checking and refinement would never end.

In reading these stories, extraordinary events unfolded before us, producing shivering goosebump moments, admiration, laughter and tears. At other times there were moments of surprising coincidence. We would discover, for example, that several people had been at the same place at the same historic moment, each unknown to the others. One man wrote of taking part in a huge effort in Toronto to gather clothes for new arrivals in the infant State of Israel. And then we received a story from a woman who, as a little girl, had been given a treasured red coat from that clothing drive – along with a photo of herself wearing it!

Many contributors told us of the wonderful emotional journeys they had taken as they looked through old photo albums and shared life experiences with their families and friends while preparing their submissions. These stories are history as the authors lived and remembered it.

We hope that those people whose stories could not be included also enjoyed that journey of recollection and sharing. Copies of *all* submissions, including photographs, will, after publication of this book, become part of the permanent collection of the Ontario Jewish Archives.

Creating this anthology has been extremely rewarding for us. We feel enriched by the stories, by the background and character of the authors themselves, and we feel privileged in having had a hand in preserving their individual voices. Though each life is unique, these pages explore the rich and varied links which, together, create a story that is universal. We have assembled this book, but the story is yours.

Bonnie Goldstein and Jaclyn Shulman
Toronto, June 1998

The opening of the Hebrew University of Jerusalem on Mount Scopus, 1925. Attending the ceremony were Chaim Weizmann and Lord Arthur James Balfour, author of the Balfour Declaration, who is seen here addressing the crowd.

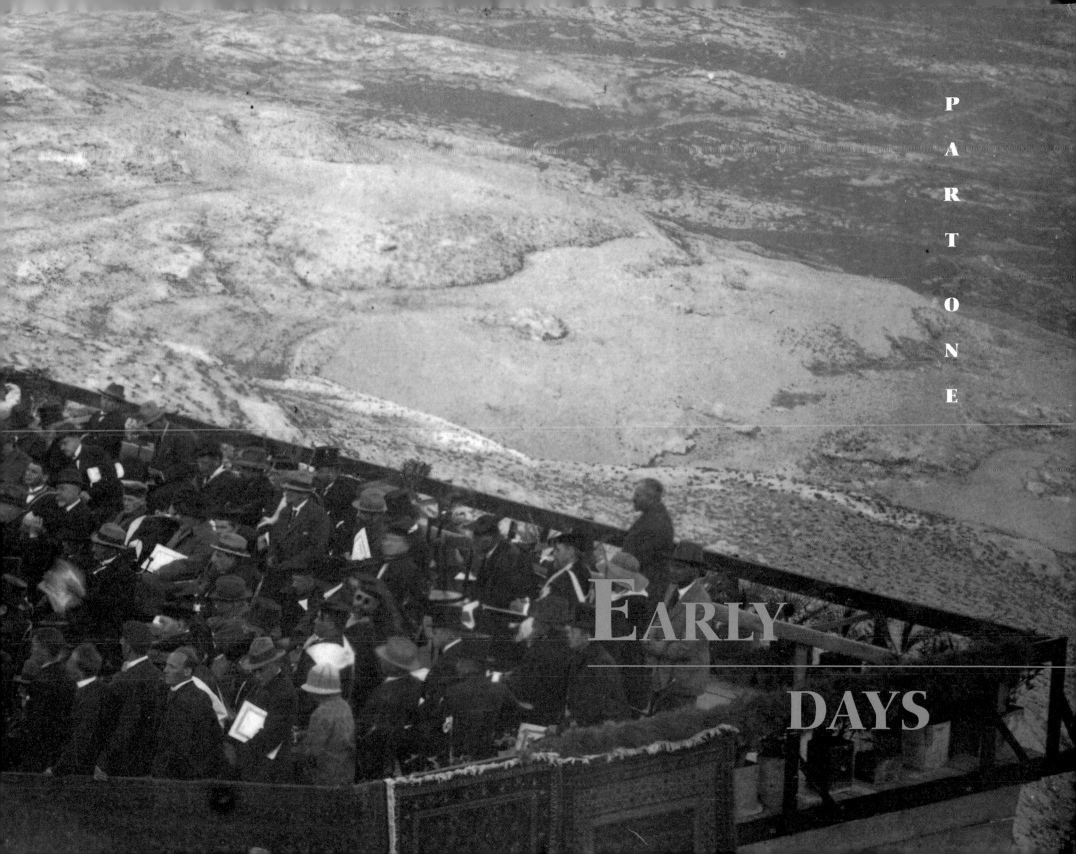

PART ONE

EARLY

DAYS

Samuel Goldenhar of the "Jewish Legion"

BY DAVID H. GOLDBERG

During World War I, Vladimir (Ze'ev) Jabotinsky and other Zionist leaders petitioned the British government to establish a Jewish-only military unit that would serve alongside other British forces in liberating Palestine from Turkish rule. In August 1917, after several delays, Britain finally approved the formation of such a unit, known officially as the 38th Battalion of the Royal Fusiliers. After training in England and Egypt, the battalion arrived in Palestine in June 1918 and was assigned to active front-line duty. Two additional Jewish battalions of the Royal Fusiliers were subsequently formed, composed primarily of volunteers from Palestine, the United States, Canada, Latin America, and Europe.

By early 1919, the three Jewish battalions stationed in Palestine numbered more than five thousand men, about one-sixth of the entire British Army of Occupation. At the end of the Palestine Campaign, and in gratitude for the battalions' efforts in several important battles against the Turks, the name of these units was changed to the "Judean Regiment" or "Jewish Legion." The Legion took as its insignia a menorah emblazoned with the Hebrew word *kadima* ("forward"). Among

the prominent volunteers to serve with the Jewish Legion, in addition to Jabotinsky, were David Ben-Gurion, destined to become Israel's founding father and first prime minister, and Yitzhak Ben-Zvi, Israel's second president.

One of the lesser-known members of the Jewish Legion was my maternal grandfather, Samuel Goldenhar. From a tiny *shtetl* in the vast Pale of Settlement in Russian-controlled Poland, Samuel Goldenhar was of the generation of Eastern European Jewry that, in the late nineteenth century, came to view Jewish nationalism – Zionism – as the only response to czarist oppression and other forms of anti-Semitism. In the early part of World War I, Samuel Goldenhar made his way to Great Britain, where he volunteered for service in the Royal Fusiliers. He served with the Jewish Legion in Palestine between 1917 and 1919.

Above: Private Samuel Goldenhar of the Royal Fusiliers (Jewish Legion), Palestine, c. 1919. Note the "Magen David" on his pith helmet. Facing page: The founding of the city of Tel Aviv, 1909.

After the Turks had been defeated and British control consolidated, units of the Jewish Legion were demobilized, and many of its members left Palestine. Samuel Goldenhar returned briefly to Poland, but then emigrated with his wife and son to Toronto, where my mother, Shirley, was born. His commitment to Zionism was passed down to his daughter, who was an active member of Hashomer Hatzair (a Zionist youth movement), and his son-in-law, Solomon Goldberg, who served with the Canadian forces that liberated Nazi camps at the end of World War II – and through them to me, his grandson.

—————

Below: Members of the Royal Fusillers, Jewish Legion, Palestine 1919. Private Samuel Goldenhar standing second from right. The Hebrew sign is a phrase from Leviticus 19:23 "... and you shall come into The land and plant it ..."

The Balfour Declaration

The British government's Balfour Declaration of 1917,
issued by the then foreign secretary Lord Arthur Balfour, announced:
"His Majesty's government view with favour the establishment
in Palestine of a national home for the Jewish people...."

Kibbutz

The term *kibbutz* is derived from the Hebrew word for "group"
and is used to describe collective agricultural communities established
by Jews throughout Palestine, beginning in the early decades of the
twentieth century. The earliest kibbutzim were founded by Eastern
European immigrants who sought to integrate the ideals of Jewish
nationalism (Zionism) and socialism – the goal being to create a new
kind of society for a new kind of Jewish people. The first kibbutz,
Degania, was founded in 1909.

These members of the Jewish Police Force, shown lined
up for inspection, were trained and armed by the British,
and were under the authority of the British Mandate.
This force was formed as a response to Arab attacks
on Jewish settlements that occurred between 1936 and
1939. Before that time the British did not formally allow
the Jewish settlers to protect themselves. In later years
the Jewish Police Force became the Haganah, Israel's
earliest defence force.

On Israel's First Kibbutz

BY MAX SHARP

When I was fifteen, I decided to leave my home in Poland and work in Israel as a farmer. I trained with a Zionist youth group, Hashomer Hatzair, waited a year in Austria for a visa, and arrived in the newly mandated British territory of Palestine in 1920. I had just turned eighteen.

After a short stint on guard duty during the Arab riots in the Galilee, I was sent to Degania, a pioneer outpost in bleak, swampy hill country just east of where the Jordan leaves Lake Kinneret – a place now celebrated as Israel's first kibbutz.

Life on a collective farm was austere, sometimes even harsh. There was no modern equipment. People slept three or four to a room on straw-filled mattresses. We didn't have any clocks, but relied on the sunrise at 4:30 AM to get us up for work. Then we ploughed or planted in sun-scorched fields, or broke rock with a sledgehammer, or worked with pick and shovel, planting eucalyptus trees, which in time would dry up the wetlands through their huge intake of water. After working all day on the farm, I baked bread at night to earn some extra money.

It was a constant struggle with nature – scorpions, snakes, bugs, drought, and heat – as well as with Arab bandits who made sporadic attacks. Every evening at dinner in the communal meeting hall, our limited range of rations was supplemented by malaria medicine. But despite this, many died.

I met some kibbutzniks who were learning the building trades, and followed them in becoming a professional plasterer and tiler. Two years later, I was one of the ten builders who created the town of Hadar HaCarmel in the Galilee.

After five and a half years, I left to join my brother, who had emigrated to Canada. But my involvement with Israel has never stopped. Before the Six Day War broke out, I organized a syndicate to build the first condominium hotel in Netanya, with the condition that Four Seasons Hotels (the family business) manage it. This was the first building under construction following the Six Day War, and when it was completed, it encouraged the growth of tourism in the country.

Above: Max Sharp, in the canoe he built at Degania, 1921.
Facing page: Max and his wife, Lil, in Toronto in 1930 with their daughters, Edie and Bea. Their son, Issy, is born a year later.

Yochaved Horovitz, My Mother

BY HONEY NOVICK

Yochaved Horovitz was born in Jaffa in 1910, the seventh of nine children born to a North African father and an Austrian mother who were Zionist pioneers. Yochaved was orphaned at age seven, when both her parents died of consumption. She and her younger brother and sister, Pesakh and Esther, were placed shortly afterwards in an orphanage, where she learned to nurse the babies and younger children.

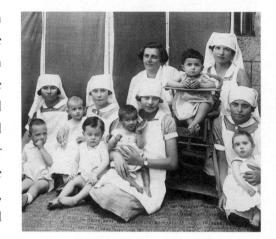

Meanwhile, Yochaved's older brother Chaim had enlisted in the British Army during World War I and had become friendly with another soldier named Sam Stern. In peacetime, Sam was an upholsterer, living in Toronto. Chaim had with him a picture of another of his sisters, Leah. Sam fell in love with the picture and arranged for Leah to leave Palestine and marry him in Toronto. Leah told fortunes with tarot cards until she earned enough money to get Yochaved out of the orphanage in Palestine and finally bring her to Canada. Yochaved's passport was finally issued in Jerusalem on November 21, 1928.

Postscript: Yochaved's brother Pesakh eventually settled in Toronto, while her sister Esther remained in Israel, where she raised her family.

Above: Yochaved Horovitz at the orphanage with some of her charges. She is the nurse's aide on the far left.
Below: Some of Honey Novick's family, outside of Jerusalem in the early 1920s.

Members of the Jewish Settlers Defence Corps, with iron fence-posts in hand, set off to erect a barbed-wire barricade in the upper Western Galilee hills to guard the most daring venture of the "Watchtower and Stockade" period, the founding of Hanita, Palestine, 1938.

Ben Miller, left, a former member of the Haganah — the force established to protect Jews and their property from Arab attacks — sent this postcard from Palestine to his family in Poland. It shows the port of Tel Aviv under construction in 1936. He recalls, "It was needed because it had become too dangerous for Jews to come into the Arab-controlled port of Jaffa. Before the port was built, ships had to stop five to six hundred metres out — it was the middle of the ocean — and little boats would come out to them. This situation forced the British to let the Jews build a proper port at Tel Aviv, then just a small suburb of Jaffa."

Laura Kaplan Silver writes, "My father, Philip Kaplan, took this photograph in 1926 in Szczuczyn, Poland. He titled it "Chalutzim" ["Pioneers"]. Szczuczyn was a training ground for future pioneers to Palestine, and all the young people in the photograph were working on farms in preparation for kibbutz life. Each of them received a copy, carefully hand-tinted, to take with them to Palestine. Later, my father and his brother, Kaye Marvins, emigrated to Canada. Kaye, himself a renowned photographer, on a trip to Israel met the "Szczuczyn Club" and was gratified to learn that each of these people from that small Polish town had carried this picture with them to Israel. We felt that this linked us in Toronto, in a small but unique way, with our landsmen [compatriots] in Israel."

A small sports car being used to rush victims to hospital after an Arab bomb spread death and terror through the Jewish Agency building in Jerusalem, 1948.

Struggle for a Homeland

Destination Israel

Saving Lives with the Bricha

FROM A CONVERSATION WITH JERRY BENGALL

After World War II, I risked imprisonment and death, again and again, to help Jews escape to Palestine. I was one of the founders of the Bricha – derived from the Hebrew word *barach* ("escape") – a secret organization that brought as many Jews as possible from Eastern Europe into Germany and Italy. We placed these Jews in displaced persons' camps, with the ultimate goal of sending them to the Holy Land.

I was born Yuri Venglishevski, in Piotrkov Tirbunalski, Poland, in 1921. As a teenager, I was involved in Zionist movement activities. After I escaped from a concentration camp in 1941, I somehow managed to fool soldiers and guards; I didn't have any money, and I was hungry, but I told officials whenever they stopped me that I was a good Pole. It helped that I could speak fluent Polish and German, as well as Russian and Lithuanian. And I looked like an Aryan.

I lived the life of a fugitive, always on the run. Using a list of assumed names, I managed to drift through Eastern Europe, working whenever I got the chance, sometimes as an electrician. But there was

never enough food, and there was never a safe place to rest.

At one point I was even arrested and tortured by the Gestapo (the Nazi police). They kept me imprisoned for a long time, because they thought I was a spy. Eventually, they set me free. I must be one of very few people to have escaped their clutches alive.

When the war ended, I no longer had a home to go to. My parents and brothers had all perished in the Holocaust. Along with many other Jewish survivors, I felt there was only one route to take, and that route led to Palestine. Only there could we imagine starting our lives over again, and at the same time, building a Jewish state.

Above: Jerry Bengall in Israel, 1948.
Left: Using a false identity, Jerry Bengall worked as an electrician in Lithuania in 1943.
Facing page: Jews who volunteered to fight for the survival of the new State of Israel are shown leaving a displaced-persons' camp near Frankfurt, Germany, enroute to Israel, 1948.

I was in Budapest when I met a man who persuaded me to go to Vienna to organize an office that would help people get to Palestine. At this time, European borders were still changing, and the idea was to get as many Jews as possible out of Eastern Europe before the borders closed permanently, leaving them to face an uncertain future behind the Iron Curtain. And so I became Vienna's Bricha leader. Our network was organized in Poland, Slovakia, Hungary, Austria, Italy, and Germany.

My first task was to recruit suitable people to train as Bricha group leaders. These leaders then travelled on foot to Poland and Russia, for example, and brought people out. There were always borders to cross and British, Russian, and American soldiers to deal with. About forty or fifty people were working for me, day and night, to carry out this operation. In all, hundreds of thousands of Jews were smuggled out of Eastern Europe because of the Bricha.

On one occasion, I remember, I went to the French military command in Vienna, and I told the officials that I had Jews returning to France who needed permits. We then forged names on these documents, and two leaders used them to take a hundred people from Vienna, where they were in a Bricha camp, to safe territory. Then two more leaders used those same documents to bring another hundred people out. And so on. The result was that thousands came through. It was a well co-ordinated organization. In other cases, the Bricha was able to manufacture false visas.

The Bricha sent the older refugees to the American occupation zones in Germany, where the American transit camps took care of them until they were strong enough to travel to Palestine legally. Many waited in such camps for up to three years. Younger Jews were sent to Italy, on overland journeys that were physically challenging and dangerous. They had to cross rivers, clamber over hills and through gullies, and hide in fields and forests to get to their port of embarkation. Then, under the auspices of the Haganah, they sailed illegally to Palestine, where they could build and defend what would one day become the Jewish state. It was rather like the underground railroad before the American Civil War, except that we were dealing with groups of fifty or more.

The Bricha was also in charge of providing transportation and food for the refugees. The Jewish Agency managed to provide the organization with ten thousand dollars, and that money was handled through the Jewish Brigades in Italy, Holland, and Belgium.

Wherever I travelled in my work with the Bricha, danger always loomed. I was arrested by Russian soldiers and, on another occasion, by the Austrian police. But while there were dire risks when dealing with Eastern European soldiers and police, there was also silent support for the Bricha, sometimes from surprising sources. The Polish consulate gave me money, supposedly to help send Polish Jews back to Poland after being in concentration camps and prisons during the war. Of course, I used the money to get those Jews to Italy and

Above: Jerry with his daughter, Nira, in Jerusalem, May 1948.

Germany, and the Polish government turned a blind eye to this. They knew it would look good in the eyes of the international community if they supported an effort to return Jews to their home, while the anti-Semites among them could be pleased that these Jews were in fact headed elsewhere.

I arrived in Palestine just in time to fight in the War of Independence in 1948. The memory that most haunts me from those days is the sinking of the *Altalena* [see page 67]. Although I was, by then, with the Haganah, and we had been ordered to shoot at the ship, I felt that this was one order I could not fulfil. I could not shoot at my own Jewish brothers.

Eventually I got married and we had two daughters while living in Jerusalem. I worked for the ministry of industry. But we decided ultimately to leave Israel for Canada, to be closer to relatives who lived in the United States. And so I started my life over in yet another country. I did everything I could in order to pay the rent. I was a bookkeeper, an office manager, and a travel agent. I'm still a travel agent, making a living because people know they can trust me.

– based on an article by Stephen Gardner, Jewish Tribune, November 24, 1994.

Background: During the summer, the Haganah gave high-school graduates military training. They are pictured here at the end of their survival training in mountain and forest areas, c. 1947.

The British Mandate

Before World War I, Palestine, and indeed much of the Middle East, was ruled by the Ottoman Empire. With the defeat of the Turks, the political fate of the peoples of these areas was taken up by the League of Nations, which in turn divided administration among the victorious European powers. Great Britain was granted a mandate over Palestine, and another over Iraq, while France was left to administer Syria and Lebanon. Initially, the League of Nations mandate incorporated all of historic Palestine, including both sides of the Jordan River.

In September 1922, the League of Nations and Great Britain decided that the provisions for setting up a Jewish national home would not apply to the area east of the Jordan, which constituted three-quarters of the territory included in the Mandate and would eventually become the Hashemite Kingdom of Jordan. After the United Nations General Assembly adopted the resolution to partition Palestine on November 29, 1947, Britain announced termination of its Mandate, to take effect May 15, 1948.

The White Paper

The MacDonald White Paper was issued by the British government on May 17, 1939. Reacting to widespread Arab rioting in Palestine, the White Paper recommended restricting Jewish immigration quotas to a maximum of seventy-five thousand over the next five years, after which time no Jewish immigration would be permitted without the consent of the Arab community in Palestine. It also recommended severely limiting Jewish land purchases in Palestine. The Zionist leadership viewed the White Paper as Britain's capitulation to Arab pressure, and as a complete repudiation of Britain's commitment, in the 1917 Balfour Declaration, to support the establishment of a Jewish homeland in Palestine. Following the MacDonald White Paper, there was a significant upswing in illegal Jewish immigration to Palestine (Aliyah Bet). The Zionist leadership also reassessed its policy of avoiding direct confrontation with the British mandatory authority.

A typical illegal ship arriving in Palestine, listing under the weight of new immigrants.

The Haganah

The Haganah was founded in 1920 as a small underground force to protect Jewish life and property against attacks by Arabs; the term "Haganah" is Hebrew for "defence." Initially, the Haganah was mandated by the Zionist leadership only to defend Jewish settlements. As the frequency and ferocity of Arab attacks grew, however, the role of the Haganah was expanded to include daring retaliatory raids on villages serving as bases for Arab terrorist groups. As British policy became decidedly more anti-Zionist, the Haganah joined the Irgun in operations designed to accelerate the end of the Mandate. The Haganah also took the lead role in organizing illegal Jewish immigration (Aliyah Bet) to Palestine both before and after the 1939 MacDonald White Paper. During the Mandate, the Haganah maintained caches of weapons in Jewish settlements throughout Palestine and secretly trained the settlers in the use of the weapons. This advanced preparation was instrumental in Israel's victory in the War of Independence, as were the heroic activities of the Haganah's elite strike force, the Palmach. The Haganah was officially transformed into the Israel Defence Force shortly after independence was proclaimed on May 14, 1948.

The Irgun

The Irgun (Irgun Zva'i Leumi – national military organization, with the acronym of Etzel) was, effectively, the underground paramilitary wing of the Revisionist Zionist movement founded in 1925 by Vladimir (Ze'ev) Jabotinsky, who had broken with the World Zionist Organization over its conciliatory policy toward Great Britain. Reacting to the anti-Zionist recommendations of the MacDonald White Paper of 1939, the Irgun, under the leadership of Menachem Begin, initiated a campaign of terror against British institutions in Palestine, including the bombing of the King David Hotel on July 22, 1946. The Irgun also waged an offensive campaign against Arab terror factions in Palestine and the local villages believed to be offering them safe haven. Units of the Irgun fought separately in the early part of the War of Independence, rejecting David Ben-Gurion's call to integrate into the Israel Defence Forces. However, shortly after the *Altalena* incident of June 1948 (see page 67), the Irgun agreed to disband and have its forces placed under central military command.

Out of the concentration camps and into the War of Independence, 1948.

The Patria – and Afterward

BY HENRY WELLISCH

In March of 1938, when the Germans occupied Austria, my father lost his business and I was forced to leave high school. We learned that Zionist organizations were planning to send "illegal" ships to Palestine, and my father paid a sum of money for our family to be included.

We sailed down the Danube to Romania, and there transferred to three Greek ships, the *Atlantic*, the *Pacific*, and the *Milos*. My parents and I were on the *Atlantic*, an old wreck of 1,400 tons with 1,829 people packed onto it. The *Atlantic* left Romania on October 7, 1940, a few days after the other two ships. Conditions on board were terrible, and several people died at sea. When we arrived at Heraklion, in Crete, on October 16, we had run out of coal. Eventually, with the help of the Greek Jewish community, we obtained more coal and left Heraklion on November 8. But somehow the captain managed to use up all the coal – there were even rumours he had thrown it overboard – and he wanted to return to Greece. Instead, the transport committee arrested him and we continued our journey, using the decks, masts, and even furnishings for fuel. We were in sight of Cyprus when our engines stopped for good.

After a few hours, a tugboat approached and towed our ship into Limassol. British police came on board, and after we were supplied with coal and a British escort, we set sail for the Promised Land. With the sunrise next morning, we saw Mount Carmel and we sang *Hatikvah*. It was a moment I will never forget.

When we arrived in Haifa harbour, we were told by the British police that, because of overcrowding in the refugee camps, we would be temporarily accommodated on board the French passenger liner *Patria*. The people from the *Pacific* and the *Milos*, who had arrived earlier, were already on board, and our trans-shipment started immediately.

After only a few people had been transferred from the *Atlantic* to the *Patria* by barge, there was an explosion. The *Patria* capsized and sank before our eyes. Over 250 people drowned. As we found out later, the British had no intention of letting us enter Palestine and planned to deport all of us to Mauritius on this ship. The Haganah, after all their

Above: Henry Wellisch, on leave from the Israeli army, at the Tel Aviv seashore, July 1948.

protests to the British against this deportation had been ignored, tried to prevent the ship from leaving the harbour, with unforeseen results. Those who had actually been on board the *Patria* and survived were allowed to remain in Palestine; the rest of us, angry and bitter that we had gone through so much only to be deported to a remote island, were shipped to Mauritius, where the men were accommodated in an old prison, while the women lived in nearby barracks.

One hundred and twenty-eight people died in Mauritius and were buried there in the Jewish Cemetery. We were not mistreated, but the conditions were primitive and the food was insufficient. Eventually, after four long years, the British relented, and in 1945, after the end of the war, the deportees were allowed to return to Palestine.

I joined the Jewish Brigade Group, and as the war was winding down in 1945 I was sent to the Brigade Group stationed in Holland. Our main task was to send as many Holocaust survivors as possible to Palestine – unofficially and illegally, of course.

Below: Volunteers for the Jewish Brigade from the detention camp in Mauritius, late 1945. Henry Wellisch writes, "This picture was taken in Mombassa, Kenya, where we stopped on our way to the Middle East. Note the Zionist flag that we had brought along from the camp. The Australian-style hats are standard dress for the King's African Rifles."

Desperate Times

BY SHMUEL FISH

I was born in 1916 in Bravichea, Bessarabia, and from the age of eight I was part of the "Gordonia" Labour Zionist Youth Movement. For years we studied the principles of Zionism and trained for agricultural work in Palestine in *hachsharot* (model farms).

When I reached Palestine in 1938, I joined Kibbutz Nir–Chaim and was immediately drafted into the Jewish armed forces guarding the northern part of the Galilee near Hanita. In those years we were often attacked by the Arabs, who tried to stop us from building or expanding.

In order to get around the British Mandate restrictions on building new Jewish areas, we would get on a truck in the middle of the night, take barbed wire and construction materials, go to a far spot in the middle of nowhere . . . and in the morning a new settlement would be up. Many kibbutzim and villages owe their existence to me and my friends.

As a Haganah member I helped get illegal Jewish refugees off the ships which the British planned to send back, returning its passengers to the horrors taking place in Europe. In 1940 the *Patria* was bombed and it capsized in Haifa Harbour. There were many Holocaust survivors aboard who were able to save themselves by jumping into the water. But

over 250 people could not be saved. My friends and I took advantage of the tumult and confusion created by the explosion of the ship and mingled with the refugees. We made them seem to be a part of our crowd. We carried out the same plan each time there was a ship carrying survivors into the port. In many cases we would have dry clothes for them, and once they changed their wet, torn garments into khaki ones, they looked just like us and the British soldiers could do nothing!

On November 29, 1947, I was on guard duty. The voting in the UN on Israel's statehood was broadcast on the radio. When we heard the final results we left our posts and rushed home. Everybody was outside; people in pyjamas were dancing and cheering. The whole country was dancing! Then, on May 14, 1948, when the Jewish state was proclaimed, we again cheered and danced, but the Arabs attacked us right away and the War of Independence began.

Above: Shmuel Fish at the northern border, defending Israel in 1948. "An Iraqi plane dropped a bomb on my truck. Miraculously, only the front was hit, and I was not injured."

Willie Zimmerman, third from right in front row, on his first visit to Palestine. He served with the Canadian airforce and was part of the Allied forces stationed in the Middle East. Servicemen from all different branches of the military are lined up on the crest of Mount Scopus overlooking Jerusalem, 1943.

Throw the Baby!

BY MOSHE HAMMER

It was the end of 1946, and the British were patrolling the eastern Mediterranean, on the lookout for illegal boats carrying Jews trying to get to Palestine. I was aboard one of those ships as a six-month-old baby, with my mother, who had survived Auschwitz, and my father.

Near Rhodes, our captain spotted a British patrol and decided to hide in a secluded bay. But the ship was smashed onto rocks by the stormy sea and began to sink. Many of the passengers were injured or killed trying to jump ashore.

My father stood on the deck with me in his hand, almost like a quarterback with a football. Some of his friends who had made it to shore were standing with a blanket spread out like a net, shouting, "Throw him!" My father closed his eyes and tossed me twenty feet through the air. He opened his eyes only when he heard someone yell, "We caught him!" Then he and my mother scrambled to shore. Years later, he told me that if I had not survived, he and my mother would have jumped into the water to drown themselves.

A few days later, after dropping us food and medicine, the British transported us all to a camp in Cyprus, where we spent the next year. We were released in November 1947.

Postscript: Today, Moshe Hammer is a well known concert violinist in Toronto.

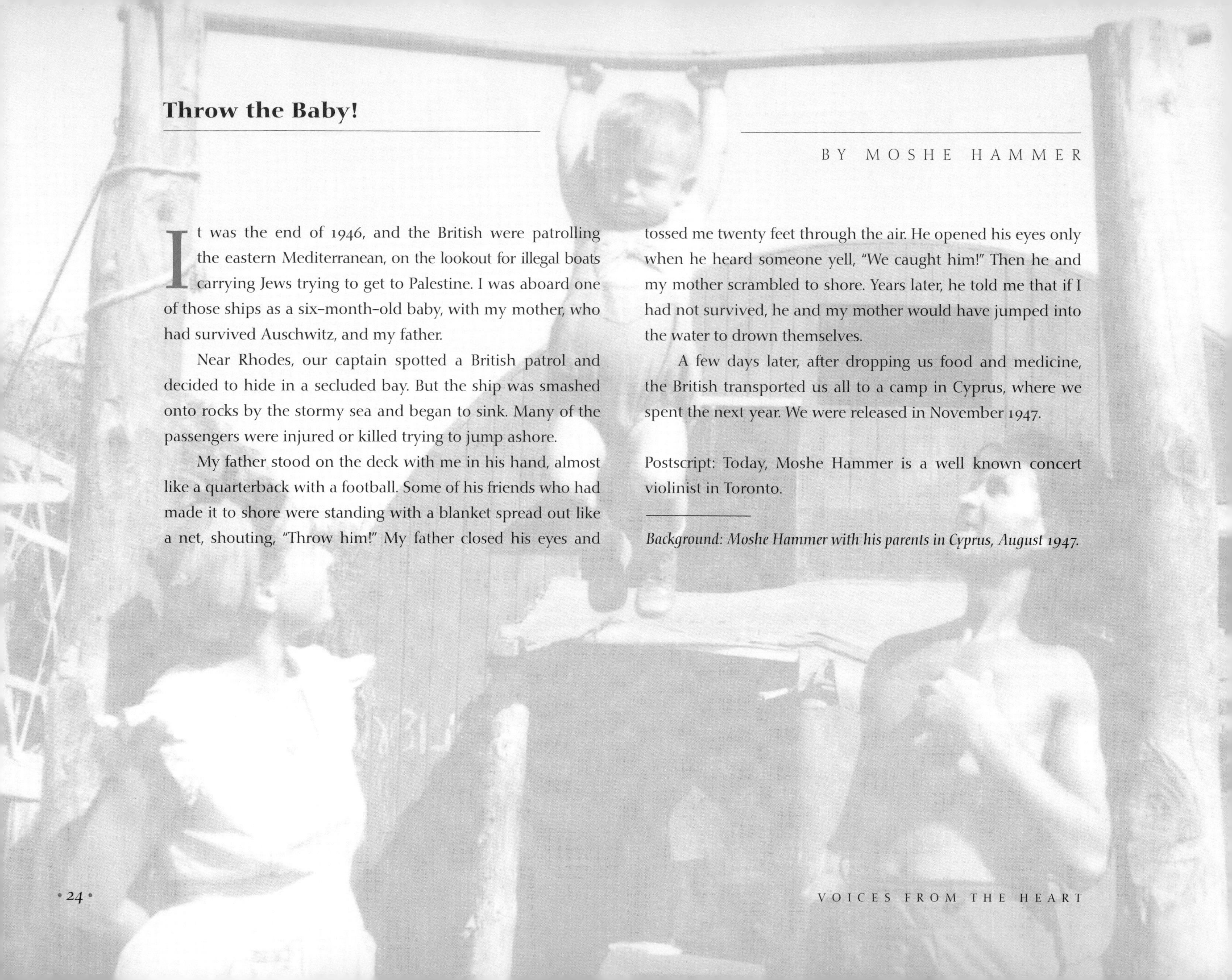

Background: Moshe Hammer with his parents in Cyprus, August 1947.

A Jew in a British Uniform

BY VICTOR SEFTON

I was a British soldier – a captain in the Royal Engineers – who served in Palestine from February to November of 1945. A few weeks after my arrival, I went to seek out my wife's aunt, whom neither of us had ever met, in Kiriat Chaim, a few miles north of Haifa. I had no idea which house to go to, but some children pointed me in the right direction.

I knocked on the door, it opened, someone looked out and immediately shut the door in my face. I waited, and heard some muttering behind the door. It opened again, this time about an inch, and four or five faces appeared at various heights along the crack. In my best grade-school Hebrew I explained that I was a member of their family. They looked at me in my uniform in complete disbelief. I gave them my wife's name in the anglicized version, but they did not recognize it. Then through the door I saw a picture of my wife's grandmother on the wall, and identified her. Eventually, I was allowed in, and as we spoke Yiddish they warmed to me.

One day I went to get my hair cut in a two-chair establishment. While an assistant dealt with me in English, the owner of the shop was lathering up a friend and chatting to him in Yiddish. I listened and realized they were discussing me, the English officer, in unflattering terms. I suppose my amusement must have shown, because the conversation stopped and the owner took a few steps toward me. "*Ihr rett Yeedish?*" ("You speak Yiddish?") he said, in absolute disbelief. "*Avadda,*" ("Of course") I replied. He told me he had not known there were Jews in England, and then went back to his conversation with his friend, this time in Hebrew. When it became obvious that I understood that, too, they just stopped talking.

Above: Victor Sefton, serving with the British army in Palestine in 1945.

A Tragic Result

BY GAD G. HOFMANN

At the age of fifteen I became a sworn member of the Haganah. Two years later I was stationed at Kibbutz Kfar HaMacabi, officially as a member of the Jewish Settlement Police, who were armed and paid by the British. In truth, however, we were all members of the Haganah (to whose commanders we turned over all our pay cheques). During the summer we secretly trained high-school-aged Jewish boys and girls in weaponry and face-to-face combat. At the end of their stay we took them into the forests and mountains to learn survival techniques.

On July 22, 1946, I received a telegram from my brother that read: "There was a huge explosion at the King David Hotel in Jerusalem, and there is concern for the life of our father." My father had been at the

hotel to install the British Army Command's communication system, and planned to rig it, as he had rigged other systems, so that he could listen in and report valuable information to Jewish authorities. If he heard, for example, that an illegal immigrant ship had been spotted offshore, he could get word to the Haganah so that they could redirect the vessel. As we soon learned, Siegfried (Shlomo) Hofmann, who had survived five years of slave labour in Dachau, had indeed been killed, along with ninety other people, sixteen of them Jews.

Above: In an armoured vehicle in 1948, Gad is using his wireless headset; perhaps it is one of those shipped secretly from Toronto (see page 102).

Left: Gad Hofmann, centre, with his brother, Karl, and father, Shlomo.

Facing page: The King David Hotel in Jerusalem, before the 1946 bombing that destroyed the British Headquarters housed in it.

The King David Hotel Bombing

On July 22, 1946, a section of the King David Hotel in Jerusalem, housing the headquarters of the British Army command in Palestine, was destroyed by bombs planted by members of a militant wing of the underground Irgun movement. The movement's commander, Menachem Begin, declared that the bombing – which killed a total of ninety-one British, Arabs, and Jews, and wounded forty-five others – was in retaliation for Britain's pro-Arab policy in Palestine. While most Jews in Palestine shared Begin's frustration over British policy, many disagreed with the Irgun's strategy of directly attacking British targets. The bombing of the King David Hotel was officially condemned by the Jewish Agency in Palestine, and laid bare the differences between the competing Zionist factions led by Menachem Begin and David Ben-Gurion.

Comings and Goings

FROM A CONVERSATION WITH MICHAEL RUDBERG

I was born in Bucharest in 1929 and lived there until 1944. In April of that year, our family left Romania on a little boat along with the Jewish children from camps in Transnistria, in the Ukraine. We sailed to Istanbul and then went by train to Palestine, arriving around the beginning of May 1944.

Years later, when I visited the Holocaust Museum in Washington, I found in the Romania section that they referred to that trip we took. I got in touch with the American Joint Distribution Committee in New York and learned that the ship was called the SS *Bellacitta*. They had a passenger list, and my name and those of my brother and my parents were on it.

The Committee also sent me information about the trip. The *Bellacitta* was chartered by ten wealthy families with enough money to carry, free of charge, 130 children who had been released through the War Refugee Board in Transnistria. The ship arrived in Istanbul on April 24, and was sunk by the Germans on its way back to Romania.

My friends and I used to go to the YMCA in Jerusalem across the street from the King David Hotel after school, because they had a great library for our English studies. We were there

when the bombing of the hotel took place. In a panic, we tried to run home, but we were caught in a road block. We were taken to the police station and detained for a few frightening hours. I had a school identity card, which verified that I was a student, and that's why they let me go. I was only sixteen years old at the time.

My father had a brother in Canada and had been making applications for immigration since 1938. Finally, in August 1946, we obtained the necessary papers. We left Palestine for France, but we had quite a few difficulties with the Canadian embassy in Paris. They kept giving us thirty-day visas to enter Canada, and since we had trouble arranging passage, as did everyone at the time, the visas would expire. Each time we would have to pay for a new medical examination to renew the visa. It was the winter of 1947 before we finally sailed. My father felt our troubles at the Canadian embassy were caused by their lack of desire to have refugees from Eastern Europe coming into Canada.

Above: The Rudberg family in Jerusalem, September 1944. Michael is in the foreground, with his father, Louis, his mother, Coca, and his brother, Dan.

Enroute to Palestine in 1944, aboard the SS Bellacita: Louis Rudberg, Michael's father, is on the lower left, wearing dark glasses, beside Reuben Resnik of the Joint Distribution Committee. Children released through the War Refugee Board are also on board.

xodus 1947 was an "illegal immigration" ship that became the symbol of the struggle for the right to free Jewish immigration into Palestine. In November 1946, the Mosad Le-Aliyah Bet, the main Aliyah Bet (illegal immigration) agency, acquired an American ship, the *President Warfield*, which had been used to transport troops during World War II. They planned to use this ship for an illegal immigration operation of unprecedented size, drawing the attention of world media as well as the members of the United Nations Special Committee on Palestine (UNSCOP), then in Palestine on a fact-finding mission.

In early July 1947, 4,500 Jewish refugees who had been gathered from camps in Germany boarded the *President Warfield* in the port of Sète, near Marseilles, France. Once it was on the high seas, the ship changed its name to *Exodus 1947*.

Even before the ship had entered Palestine's waters, British destroyers closed in and ordered it to proceed to the port of Haifa. There, the British forced the passengers from the ship, with the refugees offering strong resistance. Three Jews were killed and many were wounded in the clash. On July 20, the *Exodus 1947* refugees were put on three British deportation vessels and shipped back to France – not to Cyprus, as earlier "illegal" Jewish immigrants had been.

A member of the UNSCOP who witnessed British soldiers dragging refugees on board the deportation ships said that the scene was the most convincing evidence yet brought before the committee of the need for a Jewish national home. The committee's report to the UN in September 1947, recommending that the British Mandate be terminated and a Jewish state established, did, indeed, reflect the impact of the *Exodus* affair.

Meanwhile, French authorities refused to accede to British demands that the refugees be forcibly landed in France. For an entire month, the three deportation boats lay at anchor off the Mediterranean port of Port-du-Bouc, while the refugees suffered from heat, overcrowding, and poor sanitary arrangements. Almost all the passengers refused a French offer of asylum to those who wanted to stay in France. Instead, they went on a hunger strike, drawing world attention to their plight.

Finally, the British decided to ship the refugees back to Germany. In Hamburg, each refugee was dragged off the ship by steel-helmeted soldiers in full view of the world's press. Most of the refugees stayed in displaced persons' camps in Germany for over a year, only reaching Israel after the state was proclaimed.

Nr. *873*

Certificate

873

Holder of this No. *873* is a Maapil of „Exodus 1947"; he/she was brought by force to Germany from Haifa, and is in exile on his way back to Eretz-Israel.

Date *25.1) 1947.*

Sign.

Camp C

מספר *873*

ת ע ו ד ה

873

בעל התעודה מס.
הנו מעפיל מיציאת אירופה תש"ז שהוחזר בכח לגרמניה
מנמל חיפה ונמצא בגירוש בדרך חזרה לארץ-ישראל.

ש"ז שהוחזר בכח לגרמניה

דרך חזרה לארץ-ישראל.

ניתן במחנה הגירוש בפפנד

התאריך *1947*

החת

מוכירות

ת ע ו ד ה

628

מל מעפיל מיציאת אירופה תש"ז שהוחזר בכח לגרמניה
חיפה ונמצא בגירוש בדרך חזרה לארץ-ישראל.

ת ע ו ד ה

1479

הנו מעפיל מיציאת אירופה תש"ז שהוחזר בכח
לגרמניה מנמל חיפה ונמצא בגירוש בדרך
חזרה לארץ-ישראל.

ניתן במחנה הגירוש בפפ

התאריך *1947*

ת ע ו ד ה

872

בעל התעודה מס.
הנו מעפיל מיציאת אירופה תש"ז שהוחזר בכח לגרמניה
מנמל חיפה ונמצא בגירוש בדרך חזרה לארץ-ישראל.

ניתן במחנה הגירוש בפפנדו

התאריך *1947*

התופת
מוכירות המחנה

The Exodus Children

FROM A CONVERSATION WITH ERIKA BURGER,
MAGDA REINER, LEA KOHUT, ROBERT KOHUT, AND
OTTO BLUMBERGER

Today all five reside in Toronto, but over fifty years ago they were a group of children from Budapest, their families torn apart by the Holocaust.

Erika recalls, "Before the war we never knew anything about Zionism or the Jewish youth movement. We first met leaders from Hashomer Hatzair (the Zionist youth movement) in the ghetto, and they helped us hide and moved us from one place to the other."

Lea remembers, "My brother had left our family home to live with his friends from the youth movement, and, at age nine, I went to join him. My father had already perished in the Holocaust. Our group leaders told us to look for Jewish homeless children on the streets. I saw two boys jumping off a streetcar and asked if they were Jewish. When they said they were, I told them they would get free food and clothes if they came and joined the movement." The two boys, both orphans, were Otto Blumberger and his brother Yacov.

"After World War II ended," Magda recalls, "the Zionist leaders began to get us ready to go to Palestine. We travelled by train to a camp in Leipheim, where we started to learn Hebrew at a school and rehabilitation centre for children who had been sent back to Germany. I had been separated from my mother, Lea Reiner, in Hungary. We were finally reunited at this camp. Mother was later a counsellor on the *Exodus*, looking after the younger children. We were at the camp for about two or three months. It became very filthy, because so many people from all over Europe were crowded in together."

Later, after a stint in much better surroundings in Bavaria, the children were issued with false identity papers and taken to the south of France in overloaded trucks, where they were put on board *Exodus 1947*.

Erika takes up the story: "There were thousands of people, endless rows of refugees – we were packed in like sardines. Even to go to the washroom, we had to join long lines." Robert, from his vantage point as a veteran of the Israeli navy, now thinks "it was completely irresponsible to put so many people on board. I remember that, if another boat appeared, we would all run to one side and the ship would almost sink. The Haganah leaders would call on the loudspeakers for us to move back and distribute the load evenly. Luckily the sea was calm; if there had been the slightest storm, we would all have drowned." Robert's only act of rebellion was to throw potatoes at the British soldiers who came to take them off the *Exodus*.

When the children, along with all the other *Exodus* refugees, were returned to France, Erika recalls that "we were given food, and we even went to school, but we also had hunger strikes where we kept shouting the slogan, WE WANT TO GO TO PALESTINE!"

Facing page: Official certificates from Exodus 1947: *left to right, Morris Bitterman, Hana Zimnowitz, Avraham Rabinovitz, and Malka Rabinovitz.*

The children from the *Exodus* stayed together even when they were finally taken off the ship in Hamburg and put into a former Nazi camp by the name of Pipendorff, which was now being used as a displaced-persons' camp. However, the British guards had machine guns, and the camp was surrounded by barbed wire and lights.

All five friends eventually made their way to Palestine. Robert and Otto participated in the Sinai campaign and in the Six Day War. Lea, who married Robert, was an officer in the army and served in the Sinai campaign. Magda stayed in Tel Aviv with Lea until she was sixteen, eventually moving to Toronto. She worked at the Baycrest Geriatric Centre for fifteen years. Erika founded Kibbutz Nahal–Oz near the Gaza Strip. She has the addresses of two hundred children who were with them on the *Exodus*, and in 1985 they held a reunion in Israel.

———————

Below: Children of the Exodus *now residing in Toronto.*
Above, left to right: Robert Kohut, Otto Blumberger.
Below, left to right: Erika Burger, Magda Reiner, Lea Kohut.

The Birth Certificate

FROM A CONVERSATION WITH BEN SHEDLETSKY

In 1937 I was conscripted into the Polish army. Later, I was captured by the Germans and sent to a POW camp in Germany, which was housed in some stables. Then they sent me to a work camp in Czechoslovakia, but I escaped. I travelled during the nights, hiding in hayfields during the daytime. Finally I made it back to Poland, where I married my childhood sweetheart, Eva. In 1942 we managed to escape from the Ghetto and Nazi liquidation. We were on the run for three years, hiding like animals. Eventually we were liberated by the Russian army. The Irgun helped us travel to a displaced-persons' camp in Germany, and from there we hoped to have the chance to go to Palestine. We heard that a ship was departing for Palestine – the famous boat that would later be named *Exodus 1947*. But by then our son Henry had been born, and he was only one and a half years old. We were told that no babies under two would be allowed on the ship. We went to a Jewish doctor in the camp and paid him a hundred dollars to alter our son's Polish birth certificate so it appeared that Henry was two and a half, and that is how we succeeded in boarding the ship.

Above: Eva Shedletsky holding infant son Henry on board the ship, with the port of Haifa in background.
Left: Ben Shedletsky, in Polish army uniform, c. 1937.
Background: In the hold of one of the deportation ships, 1947.

Singing Hatikvah under a Blue-and-White Flag

BY LESLIE (LASZLO) MEZEI

I boarded the *Exodus 1947* on my sixteenth birthday, along with my brother Louis, who was one year older, and my sister Klari, a concentration camp survivor. On board, Louis and I immediately volunteered to carry and distribute the food. There was always plenty left for us, because so many people were too seasick to eat. And moving around the ship was much better than lying on the many-tiered bunks that were not only our beds, but our entire personal space.

One of the most memorable moments of my life came when we sailed into Haifa harbour with the blue-and-white Jewish flag above us, singing *Hatikvah*. Less than a year later, this became the flag and anthem of Israel, in part because of the world's sympathy with the way we of the *Exodus* were treated.

We ended up back in the children's camp in Germany, and a few months later we were brought to Canada. I am grateful for my good life in Canada, but we have always stayed in close touch with Israel, where the women of my family settled, producing three generations of children, grandchildren, and great-grandchildren.

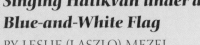

PHOTOGRAPH AND SIGNATURE OF BEARER

Signature

Issued: **30.X.47.** Valid until: **30.XI.47.**

Morale Was Very High

BY HANA STEINITZ ZIMNOWITZ

I was twenty-four years old when my husband, Mayer Zimnowitz, and I went aboard the *Exodus*. Morale was very high on the voyage; we were real Zionists, and we sang songs as if we were on a kibbutz. The Haganah taught us Hebrew. Mayer and I had only been married a year, and it was almost like a honeymoon after being cooped up so long in camps.

I didn't feel the danger – not even when the British attacked us. I just thought, I'll jump into the ocean and swim for it. But there was nowhere to jump. The British didn't even allow us on the soil of Israel; they put us on three destroyers and took us back to Europe.

Above: Hana Zimnowitz and her husband, Mayer, in front of their hairdressing and barber shop in Jaffa, 1949.

Left: ORT vocational school work card issued to Leslie Mezei.

Our Only Ammunition Was Potatoes

FROM A CONVERSATION WITH
MORRIS (MOSHE) BITTERMAN

I was in my early twenties when I first tried to reach Palestine, aboard *Exodus 1947*. When the British boarded the ship in Haifa, we did not have guns of any sort. Our ammunition was potatoes and tin cans of food. One girl was shot and killed by a British soldier because she picked up a British gas bomb and threw it back at them.

The first camp we were in after we were taken back to Germany had barbed wire, watchtowers, and searchlights, like a concentration camp. Two weeks later, however, we were moved to a more comfortable camp, where we had greater freedom to have our prayers and observe all our rituals. We even had kosher food. I was still in a German camp on May 14, 1948, when David Ben-Gurion proclaimed the establishment of the State of Israel, and I heard the exciting news on a radio.

I finally reached Israel in the fall of 1948, and went straight into the army for training. Within weeks I was in the Palmach (the elite strike force of the Haganah) on the front lines near Kibbutz Negbah. I was part of a group of thirty young men who snuck behind enemy lines to get a view of and report on the five thousand Egyptians just across the valley. We had only three machine guns with us. We dug in and managed to stay alive until reinforcements came.

Because of our information sent from this highly dangerous mission, the Israelis conquered the Egyptian position. The Israelis then forced the Egyptians to teach us how to use their captured equipment and ammunition, which was considerably more advanced than the kind we had used on board the *Exodus*!

Above: Morris Bitterman, 1947.
Background: Waiting to hear their fate aboard the Exodus.

A Jew in the German Army

FROM A CONVERSATION WITH AVRAHAM RABINOVITZ

As a young man in Romania, my Zionist activities brought me to the attention of the Fascist Iron Guard. Barely escaping their clutches, I adopted a new identity – Andrei Micheleskiew – and under this name, I was later pressed into service by the German army. From 1941 to 1944, as Private Micheleskiew, I was a cook in the German army. My most haunting memory is of sixteen Jewish slave labourers who passed by the kitchen in their striped uniforms. I persuaded their guards to let me slip them some food. As the prisoners marched away, I heard one say to another, "See, not all the Germans are bad. Some feel sorry for us."

I managed to keep my true identity secret, although I had some close calls. I narrowly avoided being recruited by the SS when my commanding officer, who treated me like a son, pulled strings to keep me out. Finally my unit was captured by the Allies. By speaking Yiddish I was able to convince them I was a Jew.

I met my wife, Malka, a Holocaust survivor, in a displaced-persons' camp, and together we boarded the *Exodus 1947*. When the British accosted the ship, the women were sent below decks. The men fought with potatoes and chains, and I was injured in the battle. Finally, in 1948, we were able to enter Israel legally, and I fought in the War of Independence.

Many years later, my heart still skips a beat when I think of those Jewish prisoners in Germany. God helped me – and I believe I'm alive because I helped those people. But I wish I could have helped more.

– Based on an article in The Canadian Jewish News *by Paul Lungen, June 9, 1988.*

Above: Avraham Rabinovitz in Israel, 1950

Just Happy To Be Alive

BY CILA DRUCKER

In 1948 I was living with my father in Karlovy Vary, Czechoslovakia. I was twenty years old and the political winds were changing; they were turning towards communism. My father and I decided to emigrate to Israel.

I volunteered to join the Israeli army, and was sent to the Czech village of Strelna for training. Strelna was an army training centre, and because the Czech government was then still on friendly terms with Israel, they let us use it. They also sold Israel small arms and lent us their officers as instructors.

We were divided into different training programs, and as I spoke a few languages, I was assigned to be the censor of the outgoing mail.

After two or three months, we were ready to leave. We were allowed to ship our belongings and take our parents with us, free of charge. We took the train to Vienna en route to Naples, where we were to board a ship to take us to Haifa.

In Vienna, the Jewish organization put a few illegal passengers on board our train. We were told to move about the train and lend our papers to others to confuse the authorities. We were kept for hours whilst officials tried to figure out what was going on, but in the end they gave up and let us leave.

I think it took us four days to get from Prague to Naples.

We slept sitting up, and were unable to wash, but we young people had a great time. It was harder on the older people, like my father.

In Naples we boarded the Caserta, an Italian freighter converted for civilian use by installing hundreds of bunk-beds. The crossing was a nightmare for me; the Mediterranean was very stormy and I was very sick. But it was worth it.

When we sighted the shores of Haifa the emotional high was unbelievable. We cried, we laughed, we sang *Hatikvah*.

After disembarking, we were taken directly to Sarafand, the military camp. For the first few days we had to be retrained, as all commands had until then been given in Czech and we did not understand Hebrew. Each one of us was assigned a job, and I was sent to Teletwinski, to the army hospital, as a nurse's aide.

It was a heartbreaking job looking after and helping the young soldiers, some of whom had lost an arm or a leg, or had been otherwise seriously injured. What was amazing about them was that they still could laugh, sing and tell jokes. They were probably just happy to be alive.

Above: Cila Drucker in Israel, 1948.

The Siege of Jerusalem

BY RAMY DISHY

My mother, older brother, and I reached Haifa illegally in the spring of 1947, when I was not yet fifteen years old. By the end of that summer, I was living with my mother and brother in Jerusalem, in the last row of houses where Jews lived before the Arab section began. With the resolution of the UN on the partition of Palestine, a tense situation developed between Arabs and Jews. There was daily violence, sniper attacks, and a struggle for control of territory.

By the winter of 1948, Jerusalem was isolated from the rest of the country. The flow of water was cut by the Arabs controlling the route to Jerusalem. However, most houses were built with reservoirs in the basement to catch rainwater from the roofs. We screened out the bugs and dirt with a handkerchief, and drank it. Severe food rationing was imposed, and I remember collecting *koubeize* (a wild weed) that my mother cooked like spinach or made into salads.

We heard constant sniper fire and developed tricks to dodge the bullets. But soon we had to flee our home, which now stood in the front line, and move into a refugee centre housed in a school. Many schools were used for this purpose, because they had heavy walls that could withstand shelling. I saw history being made around me, and was willing to take

any risk. Although at fifteen I was underage, I volunteered to help out in the army wherever I could. I was assigned to carry messages from headquarters to the northern front where we used to live. Soon headquarters became my "residence."

From a few hundred metres away, I witnessed the massacre of seventy-eight doctors and nurses who had to drive past the Arab section of Sheik-Jarrah to get to the Hadassah hospital at Mount Scopus. Their trucks were covered with such light armour that bullets could pierce it. British troops who stood by did nothing to stop the carnage.

During the bombardment of Jerusalem, anyone who stayed outdoors risked being killed. Shells fell, on average, every two or three minutes. Mortars were the most dangerous, because their flight allowed them to fall in very narrow spaces. We at headquarters lost several people, including one of our commanders and a nurse, when they were hit by a shell while going to get a meal in the next building.

The biggest setback to our confidence was the fall of the Jewish Quarter in the Old City. At headquarters we discussed

Above: Ramy Dishy, his rifle in hand, during the Siege of Jerusalem, 1948.

in secret what we would do If the Arab Legion, which was now occupying the police fortress north of the city, succeeded in entering to the south. Would we fight from street to street? But such thoughts were not in our minds all the time, because we had basic day-to-day survival to contend with. We had only 120 grams of bread a day to eat, plus whatever else was available. Often this was chocolate powder, and for many years after the war, I could not bear the taste of chocolate. Since events occurred around the clock, I used to have a chair in the corner so I could rest my head against the wall if I had to sleep.

I always had confidence in our ultimate victory, and so did the people around me. Looking back, it seems hard to explain, considering the seemingly hopeless situation the Jewish state was in. Yet, even when outnumbered by our enemies, by arms and resources, we felt a very powerful elation. *Hatikvah* ("The Hope") was not only the new Israeli national anthem, but a fundamental strength of the Jewish people.

Let's Do the Horah for Them

BY ANNE BROWN

My husband, Max, and I were married in Toronto on March 7, 1948. After a very short honeymoon, Max had to leave for Israel with Ben Dunkelman to volunteer in the War of Independence.

I followed a little later, on a converted troop ship called the *Marine Carp*. When we stopped at Beirut, Lebanon, I stood on deck with a group of young people destined to become kibbutzniks. There were many small fishing boats in the harbour, and suddenly I said to my friends, "You see that little boat, there? That's an Israeli spy boat. Quick, let's do the horah for them." My friends thought I was crazy, but we danced the horah anyway.

When I arrived in Haifa, I told my husband what I had done. He couldn't understand how I had singled out one little fishing vessel as a spy boat, but I replied, "I just had a feeling!"

About a month later, we were having lunch in a hotel dining room when two young men, dressed in the Israeli navy uniform, entered and spotted me. They came over to our table. "Were you on the *Marine Carp* in Beirut last month?" one of them asked in halting English. I said yes. They smiled broadly. "You made us feel so good when you danced the horah!"

Above: Max and Anne Brown near Netanya, Israel, 1948 – great legs for the horah!

I Was Bought from the Germans

FROM A CONVERSATION WITH AMRI SUSMAN

My life was bought from the Germans. In March 1944, I and about 1,600 other Jews were transported from Bergen-Belsen concentration camp, where we had spent six months on an interim basis, and then were sent on to freedom in Switzerland.

I was part of the "Kasztner Transport." In 1944, "Rezso" Rudolf Kasztner carried on negotiations with Adolf Eichmann – who had come to Hungary to effect a "final solution" to the Jewish problem. An agreement was reached to save Jewish lives by permitting Jews to emigrate to Palestine and other countries in exchange for trucks and large quantities of war materials to be purchased in neutral countries by Jewish organizations and delivered to the Germans.

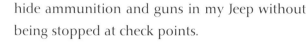

By September 1945 I had legally entered Palestine, where I served with the British. During the day I worked with the Jewish Settlement Police Division, but at night I served in the Palmach. Because I was in British uniform, I was able to hide ammunition and guns in my Jeep without being stopped at check points.

In November 1947 I was stationed at the Iraqi settlement of Kfar Uria, which is situated in the Judean hills on the way to Jerusalem. As a member of the Haganah, I was teaching the locals how to fortify their walls and use their guns. Everyone was in a different uniform. They just grabbed a uniform if they had one, and any weapons at hand – so we were all dressed and armed differently.

The Jordanian Legion organized bands of infiltrators in this region and so at night we were regularly attacked and we successfully beat them back.

We were so cut off from everything and everyone that it wasn't until much later that we learned that on November 29, 1949, the United Nations had voted for an independent Israel. We just kept on fighting.

Above: Amri Susman, having graduated from the British Jewish Settlement Police School, takes his place in a special commando unit, Israel 1946.

Left: Amri, standing far left, helping the people of Kfar Uria to reinforce their walls for battle, November 1947.

Insert: Amri and his Division, raising the Israeli flag in victory on the beaches of Eilat.

Below: Amri, standing far right, with men from his platoon, in front of their truck armoured with thin plates of sheet metal. Chulda, Israel, 1948.

Lily **Barr**, in Jerusalem, 1948. Early in the war, uniforms for women officers in the Israel Defence Forces (IDF) were unavailable, and she is actually wearing a Polish scout's uniform. "Luckily, I was very slim and could fit into this uniform! I was privileged to be in Israel when the state was born, and when I look at this picture, that time is still very much alive for me."

This Year in Jerusalem

I was born in 1925 in Upper Silesia, and survived three years in a concentration camp. Except for my mother and sister, my entire family perished in the Holocaust. After four years in a displaced-persons' camp, I arrived in Israel in 1949.

The first observance of Yom Ha'atzmaut (Independence Day) in 1949 was a memorable occasion. We waited for hours for the parade to start. When the soldiers marched into Tel Aviv, airplanes flew above in formation, creating a Star of David. These were our boys, many of them camp survivors, now wearing Israeli uniforms and protecting our own country.

I visited Jerusalem for the first time in 1950. Although the city was then divided and part of it occupied by Jordan, I knew that from then on, and forever, we would be saying, "This year in Jerusalem."

In 1953, I emigrated to Canada and dedicated myself to Holocaust education, supporting the State of Israel, and serving the Jewish community.

I came back to Jerusalem for a gathering of thousands of Holocaust survivors in 1981. Once, we had sung *Hatikvah* in a whisper, after lights out in a concentration camp barracks, as an act of defiance. Now, we raised our voices proudly. In 1997 I returned to Israel on a hiking trip. We began in Haifa, and when we finally reached Mount Scopus and saw Jerusalem at our feet, I remembered those whose dream, "Next year in Jerusalem," died with them in the gas chambers. As Elie Wiesel said, "You don't visit Israel; you come home to it."

Above: Gerda Steinitz Frieberg milking a cow in the Land of Milk and Honey.
Left: Gerda with her sewing machine in Jaffa, 1949.

We Were There for a Purpose

FROM A CONVERSATION WITH IRVING BUCHBINDER

I arrived in Palestine on the *Latrun* in the summer of 1946, but since our boat was not legal, the British boarded it. We were taken first to Haifa, then on to a detention camp in Cyprus. While I was interned in the camp, the Haganah trained me in self-defence.

In the summer of 1947, I was allowed to travel to Palestine and was taken to a kibbutz in Evan Yehuda called Lahat. In September I attended a Haganah officer-training course and was drafted into the regular Israeli army in May 1948. They trained us as commandos, teaching us to climb ropes in order to cross rivers. It was very dangerous. In fact, two of our people drowned. I was good with a machine gun – an MG, we called it. It was a German machine gun.

We were there for an important purpose: to fight for our existence. But what I recall is that every fight was difficult, and we didn't have a lot of ammunition. I remember a time when we only had three rifles with five bullets in each, as well as sticks and knives. We made a lot of noise to show that we were there. One night we went out to see where the Arabs were, and somehow I lost my knife, so I went back out into the darkness to look for it. The captain said I was crazy, but I needed that knife for fighting – I didn't have a rifle.

When I completed my service and came to Toronto in 1952, I started fund-raising for the Association for the Welfare of Soldiers. I am very proud to have helped make life a little easier for them.

Background: Yoseph Klein (Yupe) and Irving Buchbinder in the Galilee near Nazareth, 1948.

The First Jump of the Paratrooper Unit

FROM A CONVERSATION WITH DOV DUVDEVANI

I was born in Israel in 1925 with the name Kirschenbaum ("cherry tree"), which was later translated to Hebrew: Duvdevani. As a teenager, I was in the Haganah, and after the announcement of the partition of Palestine, my Haganah comrades and I officially enlisted in the Israel Defence Forces. My serial number had only four digits; today you cannot find one with fewer than seven. Our unit was involved in patrolling areas on the way to Jerusalem; also we fought in the famous battle of Latrun.

Starting from nothing, the army began to build up specialized units. Headquarters appointed Yoel Palgi, who had parachuted into Europe during World War II, to command a paratrooper unit, and I volunteered to join it. At first we had no one to train us. We found some old British parachutes from World War II and some training books. Then we got a few airplanes. I believe that I participated in the first jump of the paratrooper unit of the Israeli army, in September 1948.

When I first volunteered, some of the guys in my unit had kidded me and asked if I was really going to jump out of

planes. I replied jokingly, "No, I'm not going to jump; I'm going to be the guy who stands inside and tells everyone, 'One, two, three – JUMP!'" But later on I was the one who jumped, and they didn't say one, two, three; they said, GO, GO, GO! The first time I jumped, I was looking forward to it, but after a few times, I started to be scared. We did have some casualties. One jumper's parachute caught in the tail of the airplane and he fell to the ground.

One by one, people joined who had once been in paratrooper units in Europe, and as we became more experienced, we started to train other soldiers. Later, of course, the unit became one of the most respected units in the Israel Defence Forces. In those early days, although we may not have been the best, we did the best we could.

Above: Paratroopers before the jump, 1948. The parachutes were old even at that time. Dov Duvdevani is fifth from left.

Henry Cowen writes, "I am a sixth-generation sabra [Israeli-born], born in Haifa. My family came to Palestine, then under the Ottomans, from England in 1820. Prior to 1948, I served in the Jewish Agency's special unit sent to safeguard the port of Haifa and its workers from local Arab attacks. I was eighteen when I celebrated Israel's Declaration of Independence; immediately afterward, I joined the airforce and was among the crew who received the much-needed arms sent from Czechoslovakia in 1948." Henry Cowen is pictured here with an Israeli airforce plane, 1948.

Nurit Teitelbaum Barr writes, "My uncle **Jacob Levy** [pictured left, 1948] joined the Israeli army as a medic when he was only fifteen years old. Caught in an ambush, unarmed, he was killed as he ran to help a wounded soldier. His whole platoon died that day. They are buried in the Judean Hills near Jerusalem, where there is also a small museum in their honour. While my parents, with my infant sister, were sitting shiva [mourning] for Jacob at my grandparents' house, my parents' apartment was totally destroyed by a bomb. If they had been home, they would surely have perished."

Uri Sommerfeld served in an Irgun platoon in the spring of 1948. "I was in a trench with my friend Joseph, armed with two old rifles and a single Bren light machine gun. Joseph did not know how to operate a Bren, so I took it apart to show him. A small, vital part flew off into the sand. If an enemy patrol had come by as we searched frantically, it would have meant the end of us. Fortunately, Joseph found the little piece, and we reassembled the gun." Uri Sommerfeld, far right, is pictured with friends while training at a military camp in Beit Jurbrin, 1949.

During the War of Independence, **Abraham Feifel**'s brigade was assigned the mission of capturing Lod airport. "Before dawn we attacked, and in a few hours we captured and held the airport. When we entered the airport barracks, to our amazement, we found hot pita which the enemy soldiers had prepared for breakfast. Being able to fill our stomachs really raised our morale. Shortly thereafter, we received orders to capture a nearby village. The fighting went on until dark, when we finally took the village at the cost of many lives. As I was lying exhausted after the battle, I heard a group of people speaking Romanian – the language of my birthplace. They were young boys just arrived in the country, assigned to help with engineering fortifications. I was delighted to discover they were from my own city in Romania." Abraham Feifel is pictured second from the right, front row.

Chaim Schneider was an "illegal" immigrant sent to Cyprus by the British. After the UN vote on partition, boatloads of children were allowed to leave Cyprus for Palestine. "The Haganah changed my age from seventeen to fourteen so that I could be included. We were sent to Gan-Ephraim to guard the orange groves, while the Palmach trained us with guns. Later I was on a kibbutz in the Negev, cut off from supplies. An enemy bomb hit our cow shed, and then we had meat for a few days!" This photo was taken when Chaim Schneider (front row, right) was an assistant in the "pharmacy" in Cyprus.

Top Secret

BY SHIMON SHER

In the 1940s, the port of Haifa, where I lived with my family, had a very large Arab population. The Jewish residents, particularly those who came from Middle Eastern or Arabic-speaking countries, were quite integrated with them. My father was a very committed patriot, and for many years worked for the British agency, smuggling in "illegal" immigrants and placing them on kibbutzim. I was only four years old when he was killed, unloading heavy carts of ammunition from a boat in the port of Haifa.

Left alone with four children, and with the War of Independence breaking out, my mother decided to move all of us to Kibbutz Mishmar Hashron. Security problems on the kibbutz became more and more serious. Two men there were part of a special unit within the Israeli army – the "101 Unit." Their actions – which included retaliation for casualties suffered by the kibbutz – were not discussed, even among friends. We, the young boys in the kibbutz, looked up to these

fighters, and our dream was to be just like them. I volunteered for the paratroopers' unit, which was considered to be the best route into the 101 Unit. Many of us succeeded and our dream came true.

Later, I joined the Chief of Staff Patrol Unit. Our actions are still not to be revealed, but one thing I *can* say: I was of great use to the unit because of my command of Arabic. One of my comrades was Ehud Barak, later to become Israel's chief-of-staff. His special talent was disguising himself as an old Arab woman or a beautiful European tourist, an ability put to good use in military actions on the other side of the border. He is now the leader of the Labour Party in Israel and is a possible candidate for prime minister in the next election.

Above: Shimon Sher, on the right, with his old army friend,
Ehud Barak, present leader of the Labour Party in Israel.

We Fought Almost with Our Bare Hands

FROM A CONVERSATION WITH JACK SCHWARTZ

In April 1948, I was among 150 young men and women who left Hungary, heading to Palestine via Yugoslavia. We sailed from the small port of Bakar on an Italian cargo ship.

Near the island of Crete, we were met by British destroyers. The Haganah commanders ordered us to hide in the hold, and they covered us with some heavy cloth. We remained there for a few hours, hardly able to breathe, until we heard the engines start up again.

When we arrived in Haifa, the War of Independence was already underway, so the buses that carried us to a camp for new arrivals did not turn on their lights. I remember we were given oranges and grapes, fruits we could only have dreamed about in Europe.

At that time they were looking for young married couples to go to Safed, on the northern border, to be guards. My girlfriend, Sosana, and I got married right away so that we could be accepted.

We found Safed completely deserted. The Israeli army had fired on it with a "Davidka" cannon, which made a terrible noise, but didn't do much harm. The fifteen thousand Arabs who had lived there had fled their houses and scattered to neighbouring villages.

We were trained by an old Orthodox man with a long, white beard and a young boy about twelve years old. In an old, run-down house, using matches for light, they showed us how to operate our rifles, which came from Czechoslovakia and had been originally intended for Germany during the war. Five men shared one gun and five grenades.

When we first arrived in Safed, we fought almost with our bare hands, although later we fought with the regular army. With us were some Holocaust survivors who would arrive in Haifa in the morning and be killed in the war that same night.

Above: Jack Schwartz, soldier in the War of Independence.

So He Could Look Into His Children's Eyes

BY RUTH, BRUCE, AND LISA WATERS

Our father, Philip Waters (originally known as Efraim Wakswasser), survived the Holocaust, and after the war became an active leader in his displaced-persons' camp, working to smuggle people into Palestine. His own effort to get there by sea was thwarted by the British, who placed him in an internment camp in Cyprus, where he continued his underground work. When he finally made his way to Israel, he became a commando in the Palmach's Hariel (Mountain) Division, Platoon 3, fighting in the War of Independence.

He was one of the first commandos to arrive in Eilat, placing a flagpole in the ground that allowed the Israeli emblem to fly in the hot desert winds. He risked his life many times, going out into the desert in search of the weapons his platoon desperately needed, and he was almost killed by a sniper's bullet that just missed his heart.

Philip's captain, nicknamed "Gingy," was a tough commander who still showed his love for his troops. If one of the men saluted him, he would show his dissatisfaction by swearing, because he felt that no man was greater than another. The captain led from the front, not from the rear. On the day before he was to go on leave to get married, Gingy was cut down by a grenade as he directed his troops to safety.

After all he had suffered in Europe, Philip could have avoided the risk and heartbreak of the War of Independence; he had an uncle who would have sponsored Philip to live with him in Brazil. But when people asked our father about his choice, he always answered, "When I marry and have

Above: Philip Waters in uniform, proudly displaying his Palmach pin.
Left: On this Italian freighter, repainted and with one mast removed to disguise its identity, Philip tried to reach Palestine in early 1948. On its port side is the British frigate that later boarded the ship and took Philip and the other refugees to a Cyprus internment camp.

children, and they ask me, 'Daddy, where were you when the Jewish people were willing to give their lives to create a homeland?' I can look into their eyes and say in truth and moral certainty, 'I fought to create the State of Israel, so that the Jewish people would have a place in this world that they can call home.'"

He believed that as long as Israel thrived, the atrocities the Jewish people had experienced would not occur again.

Left: Philip, fourth from the front, with his platoon, led by his beloved captain, "Gingy," far right.

Below: Philip, third from the right, and his platoon, after the capture of Eilat, 1948.

The Mahal

Who Were the Mahal?

Mahal" is the abbreviation for the Hebrew words *mitnadvei hutz la'aretz*, meaning "volunteers from abroad." It refers to the three thousand young people – most of them newly demobilized veterans of World War II – who came to Israel to serve in the Israel Defence Forces (IDF) during the State of Israel's bitter 1948 war of survival, the War of Independence.

The largest contingent, an estimated fifteen hundred, came from South Africa. Canada provided the second-largest group, probably about four hundred men. Other volunteers came from the United States, Britain, and Western Europe. About forty of the Mahal were non-Jews, including fifteen Canadians, the most famous of whom was World War II fighter ace George "Buzz" Beurling. He was among thirteen Canadian Mahalniks who lost their lives in the War of Independence.

The Canadians' contribution to the military effort was crucial, because they had skills, talent, experience, strong motivation, and familiarity with modern ammunition. The navy, the artillery, and especially the recently established Israeli air force – which at first was 95 per cent Mahal – benefited from these attributes.

Ben Dunkelman, who later commanded the 7th Brigade of the IDF, was a key figure in organizing the Canadian contingent. After Dunkelman went to Israel in March 1948, D. Lou Harris took over the recruiting.

Many of the volunteers broke the laws of their native countries by making this commitment. They could not be officially recognized by the State of Israel; neither could their families be acknowledged in public for the brave deeds of their loved ones. As Ben Ocopnik, who served in the Mahal, put it many years later, "For me, and I'm sure for most of us who were there, it was our day of glory. We fought for the re-establishment, after nearly two thousand years, of a Jewish state. I'm sure that, when I die, the last thing that will pass through my mind will be what I and others did in Israel then."

Facing page: A group of volunteers from Canada serving with the Israel Defence Forces during the War of Independence, Israel, July 1948.

Remembering Ben (1913–1997)

I Felt Obliged to Volunteer

BY BEN DUNKELMAN

I don't want to dwell on my experiences during World War II; they are well summarized in my autobiography, *Dual Allegiance*. I rose from rifleman to major, commanded a rifle company, and won the Distinguished Service Order. Another far-off war beckoned in 1948, and I felt obliged to volunteer. The newborn State of Israel seemed doomed to die before it could even crawl. Its raw, untrained army was hopelessly out-numbered by the joint forces of a half-dozen Arab countries.

Even before the British pulled their troops out of Palestine, I had been serving as Canadian chairman of the Haganah, the underground Jewish organization that recruited Canadian volunteers to join Jewish fighters in Palestine. I became the first member of the Mahal to sneak through the blockade imposed by my erstwhile British comrades-in-arms. To get around British immigration restrictions on Jews, I sailed from Marseilles to Haifa with a forged passport, and tried – mainly in vain – to affect the British accent of its bearer, a "Mr. Fox" from Twickenham.

My immediate superior upon my arrival was a tall, hand-some lad with a fair complexion and blue eyes. At twenty-six, he was the youngest brigade commander in the Israeli forces. He was Yitzhak Rabin, later to serve two terms as prime minister and be felled by an assassin's bullet for his daring peace initiatives. "We Jews have a secret weapon in our struggle with the Arabs," Rabin once told me. "We have no place to go."

I started as his assistant planning officer. Rabin's orders were to reopen the road from the coastal plain and relieve the Arab siege of Jerusalem. Soon he handed me the authority to open the road, using the knowledge I had picked up in the Queen's Own Rifles. Employing mortar over impossible terrain and repulsing counterattacks, we retook the entire thirty-mile strip, bypassing the Arab garrison at Latrun that had prevented supplies from reaching Jerusalem.

I will never forget my first meeting with the fledgling state's top commander and first prime minister. David Ben-Gurion expressed a keen personal interest in me, firing one question after another at me about my background. In time he came to trust me – a trust likely based on the practical mili-tary know-how I had acquired during World War II.

At the time, the Jews of Palestine were making their own six-inch mor-tars. These were very primitive weapons,

Right: Ben Dunkelman in Israel, 1948.

and in fact the Ordnance Corps refused to approve them. Ben-Gurion gave me the unprecedented authority to give orders to anyone in civilian production or in the army to see if we could successfully put them into production. I quickly proved these mortars could be handled safely and effectively, and they were soon put to use.

I had hoped to return to Jerusalem on the very road we had just freed, but instead Ben-Gurion appointed me head of the Armoured 7th Brigade.

When the war was over, Ben-Gurion offered me a supreme military honour: the peacetime job of commanding the entire Israeli armoured corps, with the very real chance of becoming chief-of-staff. I suggested I could be of more service by joining his efforts to provide food and housing for the stream of immigrants who had entered the country and who continued to arrive in enormous numbers.

– excerpted from Growing Up Jewish: Canadians Tell Their Own Stories, edited by Rosalie Sharp, et al. (Toronto: McClelland & Stewart, 1997).

Above: Ben and Yael Dunkelman on the Lebanese border road, 1953. The sign reads "Gesher Ben" ("Ben's Bridge"), named in his honour. On the right is Hoter Ishai, 7th Brigade's DAQMG.
Background: In Northern Israel after the Yom Kippur War, Ben Dunkelman, centre, with Avigdor Kahalani, commander of the 7th Brigade, right, and another officer, visit a memorial for the fallen soldiers of the 7th Brigade in the battle of 1973.

A Son, Husband, and Father

A CONVERSATION WITH BEN'S WIFE, YAEL DUNKELMAN, AND HIS DAUGHTER, DEENAH DUNKELMAN MOLLIN

Yael: My mother-in-law, Rose Dunkelman, and her husband, David, entertained a lot of dignitaries, but only people who had to do with the welfare of Israel, at that time Palestine. Anyone who came from Palestine was a guest in their home in Toronto, which was nicknamed "Kibbutz Dunkelman." My mother-in-law was also one of the founders of the Hadassah Bazaar, whose prime focus was raising money for children's homes in Israel. She lived and breathed and worked primarily for Israel. As a result, my husband, Ben, as a young man used to travel with her to many cities in Canada, mainly at a time when Hadassah–WIZO was trying to save children from Hitler's regime.

Deenah: At one time, Hitler would accept five hundred dollars per child, and you could bring a child out of Germany. [Youth Aliyah of Hadassah–WIZO brought these children to Palestine, where they were lodged in kibbutzim and boarding schools.] My grandmother's role was to wine and dine and tea party anyone who could help, and then my dad would come and speak. She was an incredibly hardworking and dedicated woman. In 1930, Rose sent her son Ben to Palestine.

Yael: She didn't send him. He wanted to go. Having been associated with his mother, he had a calling to go to Israel. Israel was her dream, and later, when Ben married me, she was so thrilled because I was an Israeli.

In 1948, I was secretary to the divisional commander of Northern Operations, and I typed most of the operational orders, including the order of battle for the capture of the Northern Galilee: Operation Hiram. I was supposed to find someone who would be eligible to deliver the order to the four brigade commanders under our jurisdiction. I was a mere corporal at the time, but since I typed the order and they couldn't find anyone to deliver it, I suggested that if they let me have a driver I'd be happy to go myself.

One of the brigade commanders was Ben. When I came to his brigade, which was the 7th, he wasn't available. I hung around with friends I knew in the brigade until he showed up. He happened to come down and in a very gruff manner asked me what I wanted. I told him I had an operational order to deliver; that I could only hand it to him; and that he needed to sign for it.

The four brigade commanders were supposed to meet later in our divisional headquarters in Nazareth. We were stationed in the McTaggert Police Station, which was like a fortress. I bumped into Ben with his adjutant in the corridor.

_____

Above: A portrait of Rose Dunkelman, Ben's mother, painted by Francis J. Hoxby in 1938.
Facing page: Wedding ceremony of Ben and Yael Dunkelman at Mt. Carmel, November 10, 1948.

He recognized me and apologized because he had been so gruff. In Israel in those days, nobody ever did things like that, so it gave me a good feeling.

After the meeting, Ben came by and invited me to join him and the adjutant, who happened to have been a class-mate of my brother's. We went to a little coffee shop, and while we were having dinner, Ben asked me if I'd join him at a New Year's party that was being held at his brigade's head-quarters in Naharia. I said I'd love to, but I wouldn't have any means of getting there. He said he'd send a car for me.

We had a very nice New Year's celebration. Soon after, Ben phoned me. He said that his friend Meir Weisgall was vis-iting from the States and that he would like me to meet him and have dinner with them. Meir, at the time, was the fund-raiser for the Weizmann Institute.

I joined them at the hotel. Meir grabbed me by the hand, pulled me over to a standing light, and looked me up and down. Luckily I had known him before this, so nothing he did shocked me. Then we sat down to dinner, and Meir started asking Ben, "Where are you going to live?" and other very forward questions.

At that point, Ben looked at me, and I just nodded. Meir was making the *shidduch* (matchmaking), and I had only gone out with Ben three times! Not long thereafter, we were married.

When Ben met my father to ask for my hand, my father already knew that an important battle was looming. My father asked him, "When do you want to get married?" Ben replied, "Right away." My father said, "I don't think you'll be able to do it."

The following weekend, Ben commanded the troops in the battle that captured the Northern Galilee. I was sitting at the switchboard at headquarters in Nazareth. There was a designated person who would call us and tell us the progress of the Israeli troops. It was my job to go to the map room and give the commanders that information, which they then marked on the map. Fortunately, it was not a long battle. Shortly after the fight, we were married.

My parents made all the preparations, and we had lots of people from the army as guests. The only people who were upset were the Druze, because they didn't get a formal invita-tion. In those days people didn't invite the way we do today. You just put an ad in the paper and you wrote, "All friends and relatives are invited." You never knew how many people would show up. Well, the Druze decided to repeat the wed-ding festival for us. They knew my husband because they had helped him during the fighting.

Deenah: My father believed he had a guardian angel. He had instance after instance when he just should never have made it. But he did. He believed he made it because that was his mission. There was an aspect of him that made everyone whose path he crossed want to respect him. He'd walk into the mountains and say to the Druze leaders, "Look, you can work with me and I'll defend you and take care of you." He wanted to co-exist. He was a real humanitarian. He was driven in his cause to give Jews a place to live, a homeland.

Impressions of a Remarkable Man

BY DOUG GIBSON

Ben Dunkelman entered my life as a halting voice on the telephone, wondering if I might be interested in publishing his life story. I was polite, of course, agreeing to take a look at his manuscript and, by way of conversation, asking if he was associated with the Dunkelman Art Gallery. Yes, he admitted, that was part of his life, but I would see that he had been involved with other things.

This proved to be a typical understatement. If Ben Dunkelman had been born in the United States, the "other things" in his life would have made him a household word, and ensured that Hollywood made a movie of his life story. All the ingredients were there, as I learned when I read the shyly proffered manuscript with mounting astonishment.

Before I published *Dual Allegiance*, I wanted to be sure it was accurate. Could we find someone in Israel to speak to the accuracy of his 1948 war role? Ben raised his leonine head and looked at me seriously. Would Prime Minister Rabin do? Within a month, a foreword from Yitzhak Rabin, his old comrade-in-arms, arrived, attesting to the major role played by Ben in Israel's first war, and noting that "Ben's Bridge" on the Lebanese border was named in his honour.

A few months ago, we spoke of Yitzhak Rabin's assassination. "He was my dearest friend," said Ben, and his eyes filled with tears. Anyone who had come in touch with Ben Dunkelman in his dazzlingly varied and accomplished life must have greeted the news of his death with that same stinging sense of loss.

———————

Above: Prime Minister Yitzhak Rabin greeting Ben Dunkelman in Jerusalem, 1976.

We Felt It Was a Sacred Mission

BY ROBERT B. EISEN

During the 1947–48 school year, I was enrolled as a second-year political science and economics student at the University of Toronto. With the historic vote at the United Nations on November 29, 1947, to establish a Jewish state, the life of the Jewish people, including my own, was thrown into a frenzy of activity. An armed struggle appeared to be inevitable, and I was determined to participate in what was to be a glorious chapter in the history of our people.

How could I concentrate on such mundane subjects as statistics and political theory when the real thing was bursting upon us? I and others immediately responded to the call of the Haganah underground army, which was recruiting volunteers in Toronto. We began to make the necessary arrangements for our departure – medical and dental check-ups and so forth – for what we felt to be a sacred mission.

As soon as I completed my school examinations in May 1948, I threw my books aside and with other university friends, among them Irving Matlow and the late Albert Rosenberg, sailed from New York to Le Havre, France. From there, we were spirited away to a remote campsite in the south of France, where we received initial training in the use of rifles and grenades. In early July, under cover of darkness, we set sail for

Israel in an old battered ship. Some of the passengers were volunteers like ourselves, but most were Holocaust survivors who carried with them a new hope and vision.

As we approached the port of Haifa, we emerged en masse onto the deck from the hold of the ship, filled with excitement to be nearing the newly founded State of Israel. We spontaneously started to sing *Hatikvah*, many with tears in our eyes. On landing, my friends and I were transported to a military base near Tel Aviv, and we were formally inducted into the recently organized Israel Defence Forces.

During those first weeks, we were sometimes allowed to leave the base in the evenings. On our first visit to Tel Aviv, we walked through the streets with pride, taking in all the sights. Suddenly we heard the wailing of air-raid sirens. The first person we met was a young woman, whom I asked in my Canadian-accented Hebrew, "Could you please tell me where there is an air-raid shelter?" To which she replied in her native Hebrew, "Why don't you stop putting on those English airs!" And she briskly walked away in a huff. Apparently,

Above: Robert Eisen in the Israel Defence Forces, 1948.

she had taken me for an Israeli who was showing off by imitating an Englishman.

After a few weeks at the induction camp, we were sent to a base in the north, and it soon became clear that the Galilee would be our field of operations. We were to become part of a reconstituted battalion that had suffered severe losses in the battle for Latrun, a fiercely defended Arab stronghold overlooking the road from Tel Aviv to Jerusalem. In time, the 7th Brigade, of which my battalion formed a part, came under the command of Major Ben Dunkelman of Toronto.

Our first weeks were spent in basic military training under the watchful eyes of officers recruited from a number of countries, including Canada, the United States, and South Africa. Since Irving Matlow and I were proficient in Hebrew, we were assigned to the communications section, where we learned the mysteries of wireless operations and the use of codes.

A wireless operator served two functions. In column formation, he marched immediately behind the commanding officer, who headed the column. In addition to translating and relaying orders from English to Hebrew and vice versa by means of a 34-pound wireless set strapped to his back, he was expected to use his rifle as the demands of battle required.

In larger actions involving the battalion or brigade, he might find himself operating a more sophisticated and powerful wireless set mounted on the back of a Jeep. These sets had been manufactured in Canada for use on the Russian front in World War II, but the war had ended before they could be shipped to our then-ally. In Israel in 1948, every piece of available equipment had to be pressed into

immediate service, and so the Cyrillic lettering beneath the dials and switches had not been replaced with the Hebrew equivalent.

I participated in several actions, including the campaign that saw the liberation of the central Galilee. The thrill of military victories was tempered by the sight of comrades who fell or were wounded in battle. After eleven months of service, and when all the cease-fire agreements had been signed with the enemy forces, I applied for and was granted a discharge from the army.

I am forever grateful for the privilege of having been able to serve in the war to defend the State of Israel. The hopes and sense of mission that accompanied me through that crucial period continue to shine brightly and inspire me to this day.

Below: A military base in the central Galilee, spring 1949. Robert Eisen is on the extreme left.

A British destroyer firing tear gas at Ben Ocopnik's boat as it approaches Haifa. The photo was given to Ben by a British soldier.

We Did the Job

I came out of the Canadian Armed Forces at the end of the war and decided I wanted to go to Palestine, which was very difficult to do at the time. I was told that the only way to get there was on ships being outfitted in the United States, so I went to New York, and then to Baltimore, where we were given an old banana boat and three weeks to make it ready to sail. We were going to pick up refugees from Europe and take them to Palestine.

I had been in the Canadian air force and the Canadian army, so I had knowledge of guns and other equipment, but I had not yet seen combat. When we were approaching Palestine and could see Haifa, British anti-boarding parties began ramming our boat and firing tear gas at us. We managed to run the ship right up onto the beach, but it was a British army camp. We were dragged off the ship, taken prisoner, and deported to Cyprus.

The Haganah arranged our escape from Cyprus, and we made our way back to Haifa, where I received naval training. I came back to Canada in late 1947 to recruit more men, then returned to Palestine with the first group of Canadian volunteers. I went into the navy first, because I could steer a ship, then later joined the air force and became a flight controller. I spent the rest of the war in Beersheba until the final cease-fire, when we were demobilized. We went back to Canada, and that was the end of a two-and-a-half-year adventure! We felt we had done the job and that it had been very important for us to be there at the time.

Left: Ben Ocopnik's unit, after fighting in the hills outside of Jerusalem for three days and nights without sleep, May 15, 1948. Front row, left to right: Moe Dankeley, Murray Ginsberg, Al Spiegel, Joe Abramson. Back row, left to right: Murray Cappel, Jack Berger, Joe Gerstl, Al Siegel, Ben Ocopnik, Irving Kaplansky.

Send Reinforcements!

BY IRVING MATLOW

About seventy-five young men from the Toronto area responded to the call to join in the battle for Jewish statehood. The majority had served in the Canadian Armed Forces during World War II, and their military experience and technical training were most needed. Some, like myself, had no previous military service. But every able body was welcome.

My friend Robert Eisen and I were attached to the communications unit of the 72nd Battalion, 7th Brigade, under the command of Major Ben Dunkelman. In November 1948 we took part in Operation Hiram, which freed the central Galilee from the control of Arab irregulars, who were assisted by units of Sudanese soldiers.

As the company signalman, I was attached to the commanding officer of Company B of the 72nd, Captain Norman Shutzman, a U.S. Army veteran. Our second-in-command was Lieutenant Feldman, a sabra from Haifa. The men had come from various countries of the Jewish Diaspora, but all spoke English.

Company B, after securing the Arab village of Sasa, on the northern border, was ordered to take up a position on a mountain ridge further east. A counterattack by Sudanese

troops from Lebanese territory was expected at this point.

Once the company had taken up its position, the two commanding officers went to survey the area from which the enemy attack was liable to come. After they disappeared from sight, we received a radio message from our headquarters, requesting a report. I asked the runner, who was attached to the company commander, to find out from the captain what was happening. The runner returned quickly, saying that he had not managed to get near the captain. Now the voice on the radio was asking in a more urgent tone, "What is going on up there? *Mah korah?*" I left the radio to clarify the situation.

As I neared the edge of the ridge above the mountain slope where the officers had gone, I heard a voice yelling, "Send reinforcements! Send the machine gun!" I rushed to where the company was stretched out, and told the machine-gun unit to get to the edge and start firing. For several minutes the machine gun spewed bullets, and the counterattack was repulsed. But there had been a terrible cost: Lieutenant

---

Above: Irving Matlow at an army camp, January 1949.

Feldman, only twenty-two years old, a handsome and bright young man, had been shot and killed. Captain Shutzman had seen it happen.

Some fifteen years later, while on a summer visit to Israel, I noticed an ad in *The Jerusalem Post*. It read: "Anyone who served in Company B of the 72nd Battalion is invited to meet with Captain Norman Shutzman, at the Accadia Hotel in Herzlia." My wife, Esther, and I drove to the Accadia Hotel to meet Norman. This was his first trip back to Israel since he had left in 1949. We recalled the events on the mountain that day when Lieutenant Feldman was killed. Only then did he learn who had heard his cry for reinforcements. "When I was pinned down by the shooting, with Lieutenant Feldman lying dead beside me," he recalled, "I was only thinking, 'What will my mother say when she hears that I have been killed?'"

Thankfully, Captain Shutzman's mother – and my mother and father – never had to hear such words. But unfortunately, from that time until now, fifty years after the victorious War of Independence, many parents *have* heard such words, and many more parents live in dread of hearing them. The sacrifices of their sons and daughters have ensured that Israel has remained the national homeland of the Jewish People.

The Altalena Incident

On May 29, 1948, the *Altalena*, a cargo ship that had been converted into a warship, set sail from the French port of Marseilles. On board were 900 immigrants as well as Irgun members, a cargo of 5,000 rifles, 450 machine guns, and thousands of rounds of ammunition. The *Altalena* and its military cargo had been purchased by European supporters of the Irgun, the paramilitary wing of the Revisionist Zionist movement. (The ship had been named for the literary pseudonym used by the founder of the Revisionist movement, Vladimir Ze'ev Jabotinsky.) The Irgun, led by Menachem Begin, had resisted becoming part of the Israel Defence Forces, even after independence.

The ship reached Tel Aviv on June 20, 1948. The Irgun demanded that 20 per cent of its military cargo be allocated to its still-independent fighting units on the Jerusalem front, but Prime Minister David Ben-Gurion ordered that the *Altalena* and its contents be transferred to the central authority of the Israeli government. When this order was not complied with, a confrontation broke out between Irgun activists and the regular forces of the Israeli army, in the course of which the *Altalena* burst into flames, leaving several of its crew and passengers dead and others wounded. Soon after this incident, the Irgun agreed to disband and have its military units integrated into Israel's army.

Harold Kates snapped this shot of the
Altalena on fire in Tel Aviv Harbour.

With the Israeli Air Force

BY HAROLD KATES

I returned to Canada after five years of World War II service in the Royal Canadian Air Force, and joined the Governor General's Horse Guards, where I trained as a driver-mechanic on a Sherman tank.

When the trouble started in Palestine in 1948, I volunteered and was sent to Haifa. Because the British knew they were soon to leave, it seemed to me they looked the other way as a group of able-bodied men arrived, ready to serve in the Israeli army.

Even though I had been recruited because of my expertise with tanks, there were none there when I arrived. So, in May of 1948, I was transferred to the air force. I was first sent to an air-force repair depot in Sarona, but I wanted to see action. I requested a transfer and was sent to 101 Fighter Squadron near Herzliyya.

Messerschmitt aircraft in cargo planes were flown in from Czechoslovakia, and I helped to assemble them. The Western powers had imposed an arms embargo on Israel, and the only country prepared to give aid was Czechoslovakia. My greatest thrill was to see the Magen David on the fuselage of a Messerschmitt, an aircraft that in Nazi hands had done

so much damage to the Allies. Now the Jews were using them in the fight for a Jewish state.

The pilots in 101 Fighter Squadron were mostly from South Africa and England; Canadians and a few Israelis also served. They did much to push back the Egyptians who were advancing on Tel Aviv. Then in September 1948, I was sent to a kibbutz south of Haifa to prepare landing strips for Flying Fortress bombers.

When the *Altalena* sailed into Tel Aviv with a load of arms, I was at the Siegal Hotel on Frischman Street. When she tried to land on the beach, a lot of firing went on between the Irgun and the Haganah. Because the ship was expected to blow up, endangering the whole area, my hotel was evacuated. Fortunately, the explosives on the ship did not ignite, and I managed to get a picture of the *Altalena* on the beach. The Irgun people were very angry. They wandered around with their red berets, ready to shoot anyone that night.

Above: Harold Kates, serving in the 101 Fighter Squadron near Herzliyya. He writes, "It made me very happy doing for Israel what I had done for five years in the RCAF."

A Professional Volunteer

BY JERRY ROSENBERG

I guess I was a professional volunteer! During World War II, I lied about my age to get into the Canadian navy, where I served as a marine code decipherer. Afterward, the idea of Jewish Holocaust survivors fighting to get into their homeland, and being thwarted by British soldiers who not long before had fought shoulder-to-shoulder with Jewish soldiers against the Nazis, was too much for me. I volunteered to go to Palestine as a Mahalnik.

We were about nine hundred people on the ship when we sailed to Palestine, and none of us had a document with his real name. The Zionist leaders did not want to get in trouble with the American or Canadian government by "officially" accepting their citizens as soldiers for a country not yet born. The Haganah photographed us and issued me a passport for a "Morris Boriz" with my own picture attached. I was to pose as a Palestinian Jew of Dutch descent.

On the ship that brought us to Haifa, we had to pass a whole line of British majors and colonels who checked our papers very carefully but could find nothing incriminating. At the end of the line we met a tiny Jew with a small beard who asked me in Yiddish, *"Un vos iz dein richtiger nomen?"* ("And what is your real name?"). He belonged to the Jewish Agency but

worked for the British Mandate. He looked very harmless, so the British trusted him.

When we were taken to the army, they asked us what our preferences were. Ben Dunkelman, who was to be our commander, wanted us to join the forces escorting the food convoys to Jerusalem, which was then under siege. We refused because we wanted to join the infantry. (And as we later found out, this saved our lives, because the convoy we would have joined was ambushed and most of its people were killed.)

Finally, we were taken to the 52nd Battalion in Kfar-Bilu, near Rehovot. Our first operation was in Bashit, under the command of an Israeli whose nickname was Aldubi. He was a hero. With three bullets in his body he would not let stretcher-bearers take him away, because he wanted to stay and make sure his men were safe.

I witnessed the destruction of the *Altalena*, which was a terrible sight. I could never have imagined that two committed Jewish fighting groups would be shooting guns at each other – and over what? We all wanted the same thing: an independent Israel where every Jew could be accepted.

Above: Today, Jerry Rosenberg carries on the volunteer tradition by participating in the Sar-El army program, along with his wife, Rita.

The Lesson of the Altalena

BY MOSHE RONEN

My father, Mordechai (Motke) Ronen, is a survivor of Auschwitz. In 1945, after his liberation, he briefly returned to his hometown of Des (then in Hungary), to find that only his two brothers had survived, out of an extended family of two hundred. He then went to Italy, where he joined the Irgun, led by Menachem Begin. Motke, together with others who had enlisted in the movement, sailed for Palestine on the

Altalena. Their first taste of Israel, sadly, was the internecine Jewish struggle in Palestine between the mainstream Haganah and the more militant underground movements. As they disembarked off the Tel Aviv coast, the *Altalena* Irgunists, many of them Holocaust survivors, were shot at by other Jews, on orders from the Haganah leadership.

Motke subsequently served in the Israel Defence Forces for eighteen years, retiring as a senior officer. He married Ilana, a Holocaust survivor from Poland. His *Altalena* experience committed him to striving for the unity of the Jewish people. He imparted this determination to me, his first-born son. I was born in Ramat Gan on December 6, 1958, and named Moshe after my father's father, who had perished in the Holocaust.

My family came to Canada in 1966, when I was seven. Raised as I was in a family shaped in the crucible of Auschwitz and Israel's struggle for statehood, I become a vigorous Jewish student activist. When I assumed the leadership of Network, the political arm of the North American Jewish university student movement, it was not surprising that I steered the movement in a very Zionist direction.

Menachem Begin, for over two decades, was outside the mainstream of Israeli political life. But this internal exile ended in 1977, when he became the first prime minister of Israel not to come from the Labour-led alignment. He had finally reclaimed the heart of the Israeli people.

Above: Moshe Ronen writes of this picture, "Menachem Begin, then prime minister of Israel, and I, then chair of Network, were photographed by my father, Motke Ronen, in the prime minister's office in Jerusalem, in August 1982. For me, this picture captures the principal strands of twentieth-century Jewish history, through the experiences of one Jewish father, one Jewish son, and one Jewish leader. It speaks to the survival, the continuity, the eternality, and the unity of the Jewish People." Moshe Ronen is currently national president of the Canadian Jewish Congress.

How I Became Israel's First Bomb Disposal Commander

BY ERNEST DRUCKER

Where was I on May 14, 1948? I was dancing with my wife and daughter – and most of the Jews in the area – in Hadar HaCarmel in Haifa, after David Ben-Gurion's statement on the radio, declaring the establishment of the State of Israel.

Early the next morning, two men from the new Israeli police came knocking at our door. They handed me a summons to present myself at the temporary headquarters of the Israeli Army at 9:00 AM on May 17. I was not the only one to be summoned. Most of the Jewish officers who had attended the British officer's-training course at Djebel Miriam, in Egypt, were there.

We all stood in line, and Ben-Gurion, accompanied by Yigael Yadin, the new chief-of-staff, started to hand out the duties: "You, Reuven, shall command the artillery. . . . You, Simon, shall command the communications. . . . You, David, shall be in charge of all the supplies," and so on – until it came to me.

I was addressed as "Mr. Drucker," not by my first name, as the others were. Ben-Gurion said to me, "Mr. Drucker, I cannot order you to take command of the Bomb Disposal Squadron, since it is only a volunteer's position. However, you, Mr. Drucker, are the only one here who managed to pass the

bomb-disposal course at Djebel Miriam. So what is it going to be? Are you volunteering?"

I did not reply. A minute passed – it seemed like a long, long hour! Ben-Gurion looked at his watch. "A person who does not say anything is saying yes," he concluded, quoting King Louis the Fourteenth of France.

"Congratulations," said Yigael Yadin. "So you are Israel's first bomb disposal commander!"

Later, I approached Ben-Gurion and asked, "Where do I get the equipment for the job, and who will serve in this outfit?" He looked at me, nonplussed. "Listen, listen – the commander of the Bomb Disposal Squadron is asking a politician where to obtain supplies? As if I would know!" But Ben-Gurion went on to say that I had full authority to get or construct anything I needed.

I managed to round up an initial eleven "volunteers" for my unit, with great assistance from Yigael Yadin, most of them from the Engineers. I spent every moment explaining the basics of modern bomb disposal to them. We could not use any regular equipment, since anything metal – such as

---

Above: Ernest Drucker, an officer in the British army, 1943.
It was during this service that he received bomb-disposal training.

shovels, picks, hammers, and pliers – might automatically detonate the bombs. We had to design and construct shovels out of bamboo sticks, hammers of rubber from the Vulcan factory, and very crude picks made from eucalyptus trees. We could approach bombs only in swimsuits and rubber sandals – anything else might set them off.

By the middle of July 1948, I had reached my quota of thirty volunteers, and we were working day and night. It turned out we were relatively lucky; only three of my men, or 10 per cent, were killed in the line of duty, far below the World War II bomb–disposal unit average of over 40 per cent.

_____

Below: Commander Drucker, standing second from left, with the eleven volunteers of the First Bomb Disposal Squadron of the Israel Defence Forces, June 14, 1948.

Homecoming

BY VIVIAN RAKOFF

I have been here before," said Pityu, a young man with an Auschwitz tattoo on his forearm. Below us was a slightly choppy sea, and quite close by were the shore lights of Tel Aviv. He had been on the refugee ship *Exodus 1947* when it had approached Palestine and been turned back by the British to return to Germany. He had then travelled through Europe to a transit camp in Marseilles, where I had met him. And here we were on the deck of the SS *Negba*, waiting to go ashore in small boats, which bobbed against the side of the ship.

It should have been a moment of deep emotion, a historic homecoming. But for me, aged nineteen, a South African travelling from England, it was still something of a lark. I had been diverted from my comfortable student life by an impulsive decision to follow some friends who had gone to the war in Palestine. But for Pityu it was a redemptive moment. He had survived the camps; he had, in the end, outsmarted the British blockade; and here he was again, and this time he was going ashore. There should have been music, an oration, a singing of *Hatikvah*, at least. But the truth was, many of us were in the grip of undignified gastroenteritis, and our historical glory was muted by vomiting and barely controlled diarrhea!

On shore, we were quickly processed by United Nations people. We were all designated "tourists." We were given charcoal pills for our nausea and put on a darkened bus for a long drive through the rain. We were taken to Netanya, an army camp recently vacated by the British, and spent our first night sleeping in cots on the stage of the recreation hall.

I knew that fellow South African members of the youth movement Hashomer Hatzair were supposed to be in Natanya. One of the guards at the rickety gate of the camp told me that they weren't too far away. Although I had thought it might be quite difficult for me to leave this camp, with its wire perimeter fence and gates, the guard was quite happy for me to go and find my friends. Dressed in the clothes I had worn when I left England for what was supposed to have been a two-week holiday

in France – a blazer, fedora, white shirt, grey flannels, and shoes – I took the dusty little track close to the edge of the cliffs above Netanya's empty rock-strewn beach.

Presently, I came to a small vegetable garden, where a young woman was weeding. As she looked up, I saw that it was my friend Ora. We embraced, and then she looked at me and started to laugh: "You can't walk around dressed like that!" Soon she had provided me with a *chultzah russit* (a Russian-style shirt very popular back then), khaki shorts, and sandals. Then she returned with me to the army base to retrieve the rest of my things. Again, I was surprised at how

easy this was, but as Ora explained, "They're only too happy to get rid of people to any place that will have them."

As we passed through the camp, an elderly woman I had come to know in Marseilles saw me and marvelled at my transformation. "O Chaim, Chaim," she said in Yiddish, "You have so quickly become a *chalutz* [pioneer settler]." And she kissed me on the cheek.

———— ————

Opposite: Vivian Rakoff, right, at Crusader Arch on Mt. Tabor, 1948.

Samuel Cohen is remembered as a soldier and friend to be depended upon. Born in Poland, he joined the Israeli army in 1948, after serving in the Canadian army in World War II. In this picture, he is wearing an Israeli army badge on his beret.

I Guess I Must Have Become a Zionist

BY LESLIE READ

Like most Jews in England, I found it difficult to watch Britain dealing unfairly with the Jews in Palestine so soon after World War II. I guess I must have become a Zionist; or why else would a twenty-year-old lad from Manchester want to help found the new Jewish state?

I travelled from London to Marseilles, and was put in a large camp with Jews who had no place else to go. To pass the time, we were given some training with wooden rifles and learned a few words of Hebrew. I was there for about two or three weeks, and then one morning was told I would move out that very night. Later that evening we were taken by truck to the Marseilles airport. This was my first airplane flight. Just before dawn, we landed in Israel, and I was inducted into the 7th Brigade, mostly formed of English-speaking volunteers and commanded by Ben Dunkelman. I was in Company B of the 72nd Battalion. My sergeant-major was Canadian; my officer was South African; and the captain was American. All were Christians.

The war itself was very strange, being fought by Israel on three fronts. The United Nations would negotiate a truce, and we used those interludes for training; when the shooting started again, we went from training to fighting. I remember we had only two tanks, and these were moved frequently to different battlefronts, to give the impression of more armour than we had. We also had a homemade mortar, which fired dynamite sticks.

One day I was sitting on a hilltop in Northern Israel, shooting my machine gun. The next minute I woke up in a hospital bed – only it was six weeks later. I'd been shot in the head.

After the war, I returned to England, and in 1961 I emigrated to Toronto. Years later Ben Dunkelman and I met again. This time we had coffee together in Toronto.

Above: Photo from medical card issued to Leslie Read, 1950.

Meeting a Legend

When I arrived in Haifa in March 1948, Ben Dunkelman wanted me to meet the legendary Colonel David "Mickey" Marcus from the United States. During our meeting, at a hotel on the Tel Aviv seashore, I mentioned that my suitcase had not yet arrived. Marcus asked with concern whether I had a change of clothes. When I said I had only what I was wearing, he quickly gave me one of his U.S. army shirts. I said, "Thanks, I'll return it to you as soon as my suitcase arrives." Mickey replied, "No, you keep it." Needless to say, I treasured that shirt very much!

I will never forget our exciting conversation and exchange of helpful information. Mickey was truly a hero and a remarkable historic figure.

Background: Max Brown and his wife, Anne, far left, near the Lebanese border, 1948.

Ensuring This Would Never Happen Again

FROM A CONVERSATION WITH ABE LEVINE

I was born in Whitby, Ontario, in 1922 and raised on a farm. I tried on two occasions to sign up for overseas duties during World War II. The first time, my father dragged me back to work on the farm, but the second time, I was sworn in before he got there, so he had to accept the situation. My unit was stationed in Germany and arrived at Bergen–Belsen two days after the liberation. We knew of the camp's existence, but nothing could have prepared us for what we saw there. At that moment, I knew that if I could do anything to ensure this would never happen again, I would!

After I returned to Canada in 1947, I was approached to enlist in the Israeli War of Independence. This time my parents encouraged me to go. A few of my friends and I were smuggled through Buffalo, then to Marseilles, and finally onto a displaced–persons' ship bound for Palestine. The ship was outfitted for 250 people, but 1,300 people were crowded aboard. My friend and I got jobs in the galley, where I cut beef for the stew. A benefit was that we always had a lit–tle extra to eat. We arrived safely, in the middle of the night, and anchored offshore by Caesarea. We held onto a rope and waded through the water to make it ashore.

I ended up in Northern Israel in an armoured car. My troop included men from South Africa, the United States, Canada, Romania – even one fifteen–year–old boy from Hungary who had survived the Holocaust. At twenty–three, I was one of the oldest in my unit. I think my greatest contribution to the war effort was snatching some of those younger boys out of the line of fire. Some of them had no training at all, and were constantly popping their heads out from behind their protection at the sound of the bullets whizzing by. My deep friendships with the men of my unit have lasted down through the years.

Above: Abe Levine and his tank unit prepare for a victory parade to be inspected by Prime Minister Ben-Gurion, 1948.

The difficult conditions on the displaced-persons' ship that brought Abe Levine from Marseilles to Caesarea as a Mahal, 1948.

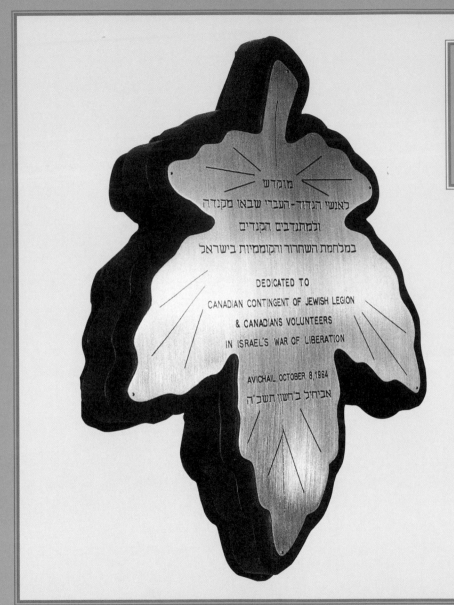

War Volunteers from Canada Who Were Killed or Proclaimed Missing in Action in Israel's War of Independence, 1948–1949

George "Buzz" Beurling

Wilfred (Ze'ev) Canter

Harvey Cohen

Len Fine

William Fisher

Leonard Fitchett

Syd Leisure

Ed Lugech

Ralph Moster

Sidney Rubinoff

Reuben Schiff

Fred Stevenson

Marjory Ziff

This plaque is dedicated to the Canadian contingent of the Jewish Legion and to the Canadian volunteers in Israel's War of Independence.
It was dedicated at Avichail, 1964.

War Volunteers from Toronto Who Fought in Israel's War of Independence

Harold "Hess" Abells
Joe Abrams
Stanley Anger
Harry Bugelman
Bill Baltman
Jacob Benn
Jack Berger
Sid Beube
Sam Binder
Jack Blank
Allan Brown
Max Brown
Rod "Tiny" Cameron
Wilf Canter
Murray Cappel
Harvey Cohen
Sam Cohen
Morry Cooper

Perry Covent
Moe Dankevy
Harry Dinkin
Dave Drutz
Ben Dunkelman
Bernard "Bob" Eisen
Alex Epstein
Morris Epstein
Len Fine
Leonard Fox
Lionel Freeman
Saul Freeman
Ansel Garfin
Joe Gerstl
David Gerztbein
Murray Ginsburg
Phillip Good
Irving Hambourg

D. Lou Harris (recruiter)
Sol Jacobs
Harold Kates
Percy Katz
Albert Langer
Art Lashinsky
Norman "Alter" Leff
Syd Leisure
Philip Leventhal
Ernest Levin
Julius Lewis
Edward Lipschitz
Ed Lugech
Irving Matlow
Jim McGunigal
Frank Newfeld
Morris Nezinsky
Ben Ocopnik
Norman Perry
Gordon Quitt
Wally Reiter
Jerry Rosenberg
Benjamin A. "Barry" Ross

Sid Rubinoff
Reuben Schiff
Avrom Siegel
Albert Spiegel
Joe Sussman
Morris Swartz
Joseph Talsky

Daniel Tate
Al Troube
Joseph Warner
Sam Wasser
Philip Waters
Herky Weiner
Izzie Weinzweig

Above: Colour-guard member Jerry Rosenberg recalls those Jewish servicemen who fell in battle during World War II, at the Royal Canadian Legion – General Wingate Branch parade and service. The ceremony is held annually at Rosh Hashanah.

SECTION III

The Homefront–Toronto

How Zionism Got Its Start in Toronto

BY STEPHEN SPEISMAN

At the First Zionist Congress, held in Basel, Switzerland, in 1897, Theodor Herzl expressed the goal of political Zionism: "To create for the Jewish people a home in Palestine secured by public law." Within months of the Congress, Zionist organizations had begun to emerge in Toronto. Their members, as was the case elsewhere in North America, were mainly Eastern European Jewish immigrants. The first society in the city, Agudath Zion, was founded in 1898 by Samuel and Abe Lewis.

In 1899, Ida Siegel, Abe Lewis's sister, founded the first women's Zionist organization in Canada, the Toronto Daughters of Zion (now a chapter of Hadassah-WIZO). Ida soon had teenage girls selling shares of the Jewish Colonial Trust door-to-door, collecting funds for Jewish colonists in Palestine. For younger girls, she established the Herzl Girls in 1906, who raised money for the Jewish National Fund by selling *shekalim* (certificates of contribution) for the purchase of land. For boys, there was the Zion Cadets, founded in 1905 by Abe Lewis and Barney Stone. Barney would later head the Zionists of Toronto.

By 1906, Toronto had such a strong image as a Zionist city that the Federation of Zionist Societies of Canada held their convention there. Zionism continued to cut across ethnic and religious lines, and by this time was prospering financially. The Local Central Council (now the Toronto Zionist Council) was able to acquire a building on Simcoe Street housing a library of Hebrew and Zionist literature.

The Balfour Declaration of 1917, committing Britain to the concept of a Jewish national homeland in Palestine, assured the legitimacy of the Zionist movement. But for large numbers of Toronto Jews, no such assurance was necessary. Zionist youth groups proliferated; indeed, the Simcoe Street building could no longer accommodate them all, and a house was purchased at Beverley and Cecil streets.

Above: Dr. Stephen Speisman, centre, director of the Ontario Jewish Archives, with Howard Markus, left, assistant archivist, and Brooky Robins, right, chair, archives committee, ensuring that we will always remember our early Toronto days.

Facing page: A Pioneer Women convention in Toronto in the 1940s.

Efforts to purchase land in Israel continued through the Jewish National Fund, and their little blue money box became a fixture in many Toronto Jewish homes. Attempts to support Jewish colonists proceeded through efforts such as the Hadassah Bazaar, first held at Varsity Arena in the 1920s.

In line with the Zionist principle of encouraging the training of Jewish youth, efforts in the agricultural sphere were intensified in the late 1930s and 1940s as life in Europe became more precarious for Jews. *Hachsharot*, Jewish model farms, were established – for instance, in Smithville by Habonim (Labour Zionists) and in Guelph by Hashomer Hadati (Religious Zionists) – to train those who hoped to settle in Israel.

On November 29, 1947, the Jews of Toronto, along with Jewish communities all over the world, sat by their radios to hear the results of a historic United Nations vote. In just three minutes, the vote in favour of the partition of Palestine into separate Arab and Jewish states cleared the way for the creation of a Jewish state in Palestine that would have legitimacy in the eyes of the world. The final step toward independence came on May 14, 1948, when David Ben-Gurion proclaimed the creation of the State of Israel. Jews everywhere took to the streets in joyous celebration.

Above: Jewish National Fund Women gather, 1941.

UNITED JEWISH COMMITTEE
for
...ALIYAH

...office

...DINA

...O

...Ingsd

MR. SAMUEL KRONICK, CHAIRMAN
ONT. ZION REGION, Y.A. COMMIT...

MRS. D. DUNKELMAN, TREASURER

MRS. CHARLES ROTENBERG, CHAIR...
ONTARIO YOUTH ALIYAH FUND

MRS. M. JOHNSON AND MRS. H. J...

MRS. M. A. LEVY, CHAIRMAN
TORONTO YOUTH ALIYAH CAMPA...

MR. J. J. GLASS, VICE-CHAIRMAN

1940 UNITED JEWISH APPEAL OF TORONTO

$1,800,277 MINIMUM

UNITED JEWISH WELFARE FUND — COMBINED PALESTINE APPEAL

Room 219
KING EDWARD HOTEL
ELgin 0181

April 23, 1948.

Dear Doctor Pivnick:

We are writing this letter to you at the beginning of Passover, to urge you to redouble your efforts during Passover week on behalf of the United Jewish Appeal. Traditionally, this is a holiday of great rejoicing. But this year, we must dedicate Passover to our brothers in Palestine and in Europe -- to our brothers who will spend this week continuing their heroic struggle for us and for themselves. Their fight, our fight, cannot wait for holidays -- our work must go on with even greater intensity.

This year our age-old prayer of "Next Year in Jerusalem" can be given meaning, if you will make this Passover a week of dedication -- if you will use this week to complete all of your UJA cards, and to obtain maximum contributions on all cards.

Europe and the Yishuv will be spending Passover in toil and in battle. Yours is an easier task -- working completely and wholeheartedly for the UJA.

Sincerely yours,

Abraham Kelman   *Abraham Price*   *Reuben Slonim*

Rabbi A. Kelman   Rabbi Abraham Price   Rabbi Reuben Slonim

Maurice L. Perlzweig   *Abraham Feinberg*

Rabbi Maurice L. Perlzweig   Rabbi Abraham L. Feinberg

Dr. David Ochs.   *Judah Washer*

Rabbi Dr. David Ochs   Rabbi Judah Washer

— *Hurry! They Stand Alone* —

COMBINED PALESTINE APPEAL, Robert H. Soren, President, Toronto Zionist Council

Keren Hayesod
(Palestine Foundation Fund) ... Mifal Bitzaron ... Youth Aliyah (Emergency) ... Keren Mizrachi ... Keren Kayemeth (Jewish Nat...)

UNITED JEWISH WELFARE FUND, Samuel J. Granatstein, President

United Jewish Relief Agencies in conjunction with Joint Distribution Committee
Canadian Jewish Congress
Jewish Immigrant Aid Society
Associated Hebrew Schools
Bals Yehuda Talmud Torah
Borochov School and Kindergarten
Euclid Avenue Hebrew Free School
Jewish National Workers' Alliance Folk Schools
Jewish Public Library
Keren Hatarbut

Morris Winchevsky School
Talmud Torah Eitz Chaim
Workmen's Circle Schools
Yeshivah Torath Chaim
American Fund for Palestinian Institutions
Bitzaron
Canadian Friends of the Hebrew University
Chaim Weizmann Research Institute
Council of Jewish Federations and Welfare Funds
Dropsie College

Hebrew Institute of Technolo...
Hebrew Theological College
Hebrew Union College (Cin...)
Histadruth Ivrith
Jewish Institute of Religion
Jewish Teachers Seminary (
Jewish Theological Seminar...
Menorah Association
National Council of Beth J...
Yeshiva University
Yiddish Scientific Institute...

✡ AID TO ISRAEL — *Toronto Division*

FOR MEDICAL, CLOTHING, AND FOOD SUPPLIES

August 13, 1948.

PRESS RELEASE FOR IMMEDIATE RELEASE

An Aid to Israel train, composed of fleets of trucks, will cover the entire city to gather contributions for Israel under the sponsorship of all Jewish organizations in Toronto. A meeting to discuss plans for the project will be held on Monday evening, August 23rd, in the Library of the Royal York Hotel.

A steady flow of material has been going forward from Toronto to the national warehouse in Montreal. Included in the shipments are food, clothing and medical supplies. Hundreds of dresses have been contributed by the dress manufacturers who are cotinuing their efforts under the co-chairmanship of Nat Laurie and I. Fram. A strong committee under the co-chairmanship of A. Matlow, B. Silverstein, Al Pattenick, A. Savlov and J. Steinberg have contacted the wholesale dry goods firms and have received generous contributions.

Plans are being made to place containers in all Jewish retail grocery establishments, L. Weinstein and Irving Fields, co-chairmen report. Gifts of much needed food are being received daily at the Central Depot, 317 College St. A collection in Belle Ewart over the week-end resulted in 800 cans of food being contributed.

In the men's clothing division arrangements are now being completed for a collection of men's clothing from the various manufacturers and final arrangements will be made with the representatives of employees to participate in an arrangement whereby they

November 29, 1947

BY RABBI W. GUNTHER PLAUT

I was a rabbi in Chicago, married, with two children, and had served in the U.S. army and been present when we opened the concentration camp of Dora/Nordhausen on April 11, 1945.

On November 29, 1947, it was Shabbat, but many of us in Chicago forsook the habitual *menucha* (rest) on that afternoon and made our way to the Civic Opera House. More than a thousand Jews had assembled there, not to see a show, but to be present when the result of a historic vote would be announced. For the United Nations was in session, and its members were casting ballots on the Palestine–partition plan. If approved, the land would be divided between an Arab and a Jewish entity, and for the first time in nearly two thousand years we would be accorded international recognition in our own land. A "yes" vote would in effect mean the future establishment of a Jewish state.

Many doubted that our side had a chance, but we could not at that moment afford to be pessimistic. The *gevirim* (leaders) of American Jewry, led by the legendary Rabbi Stephen S. Wise, were to talk to us. My wife and I needed to be there.

My imagination fails me when I try to recreate the sentiment of that afternoon. While the UN argued and began the process of voting, we sang, we listened to the worthies

who addressed us, and many of us – with the Holocaust still fresh in our memories – prayed that we might at last determine our own future as a people.

Rabbi Wise had already addressed us and was sitting on the stage with the other speakers. It was getting late. The vote should happen at any moment. Suddenly a young man ran across the stage and handed the rabbi a piece of paper. Rabbi Wise looked at it and broke into tears. I knew the worst had happened. I still see him struggling to get to his feet and then walking to the lectern as if in a dream. In the dead quiet of the magnificent theatre he raised the paper like a flag.

"Fellow Jews," he proclaimed hoarsely, "we have a Jewish state!"

The effect was one I remember as clearly as anything in my life. We jumped to our feet in uncontrolled joy, and then burst into the street, dancing, chanting, celebrating. I cannot recall where I was a few months later when David Ben-Gurion proclaimed the Jewish state. For me, Yom Ha'atzmaut (Independence Day) started on November 29, 1947.

Above: Rabbi W. Gunther Plaut, presently Senior Scholar at Holy Blossom Temple, Toronto.

Left: Twenty thousand people attended the rally at Maple Leaf Gardens celebrating the independence of Israel after thirty years of British rule. The rally called for Canada's immediate recognition of the new country of Israel.

Right: At a special service of Religious School children celebrating Israel's independence, Holy Blossom Temple. Greta Title and Bernard Davis, right, hold the British and Israeli flags. On the left is Rabbi Abraham Feinberg.

The Globe and Mail

Page 17

TORONTO, MONDAY, MAY 17, 1948.

Second Section

...ionist and Red Cross Flags Hoisted as Union Jack Lowered

On May 16, 1948, **Herb Lastman** was visiting his cousin in his apartment on College Street. "We were discussing the exciting news of the declaration of Israeli independence when we heard a commotion outside. We looked out the window and saw a parade, not overly organized, but very enthusiastic. It was moving east along College Street toward Spadina Avenue, the heart of the Jewish community at that time. We took two snapshots with an old camera. I put the photos in my photo album, which I bring out now and then to remind me of that glorious time."

Mass **RALLY**

MAPLE LEAF GARDENS

SUN., MAY 16th - 8.15 p.m.

● Come and proclaim your solidarity with the Provisional Jewish Government in Palestine!

We have waited for this day for 2,000 years

● *Come early and participate in this event of historical importance!*

Noted Speakers Will Address The Meeting

Doors open at **7.15 p.m.**   No solicitation for funds

Sponsored by the
United Zionist Council of Toronto

7

In the spring of 1948, **Mira Koschitzky** was twelve years old and had recently immigrated to Canada with her family. "I remember marching along College Street as a proud member of the Jewish community, celebrating the establishment of the new State of Israel. After the horrors of the Holocaust, which my family was lucky to survive in Slovakia, to be able to march into Maple Leaf Gardens with thousands of fellow Jews, not because we had to, but because we wanted to, was an unbelievable experience! I'll never forget the wonder, excitement, and goodwill of that evening." Mira is shown here about a year later, in front of her family's first Canadian residence, a house on Major Street.

412 Spadina

M y father, Ben Zion, had just graduated as an electrical engineer when he left Russia with his mother and sister in 1914. My grandfather, Menachem Mendel, had preceded them to Canada the year before and wound up in Guelph as a *shoichet* (ritual slaughterer) and teacher. They joined him in Guelph and then came to Toronto a few years later.

My grandfather and my father both started teaching Hebrew, and at the same time my father taught himself English. My father then went to the University of Toronto and once again graduated as an electrical engineer. General Electric offered him a job, working underneath railway cars for eighteen dollars a week, but Father said, "Keep your job," and continued working as a Hebrew teacher. He organized the new Talmud Torah (Jewish religious school) and hired the teachers for it.

Eventually, my father tired of teaching and decided to go into business. He was living in J. B. Salsberg's home on Cecil Street at the time, and from that house he began selling books that he had collected. Then he decided he would open a store, and eventually rented space on the west side of Spadina. That's the one everybody remembers – 412 Spadina.

The store had several names, but the name that was on the glass shield hanging in the window was "Hyman's Book and Art Shop." Later, it became "Hyman & Son Booksellers." By that time, I was in business with my father, in between working at a pharmacy. Most of the books were Judaica, but some weren't. We sold things like mezuzahs and menorahs – everything for the Jewish home – but we also had a complete line of office supplies. My father was the first one to start a bar mitzvah registry, to make sure that a boy wasn't loaded up with six of the same book, although I must say that my mother, Fanny, was the businessperson. It was with my dad that someone would have a long discussion on literature.

People from every political persuasion would come into the store, and they would argue politics for hours. The only people my parents would not allow in the store were the communists. Everyone else, and their political viewpoints from the right to the left, including the religious, was welcome

Above: Gurion Hyman in front of the family store at 412 Spadina Avenue, 1948.

there. They discussed Israeli politics and Canadian, too, but mostly whatever affected the Jewish community. It was a place where people of varying opinions could come and exchange ideas.

My mother organized the Golda Meir chapter of Pioneer Women of Canada. They swept out streetcars, and the money that the TTC paid them was donated to the Jewish National Fund. They were raising funds to purchase trees even before the establishment of the State of Israel. There was a tremendous Zionist feeling in that bookstore.

Above: A birthday celebration in the 1940s for Gurion's father, Ben Zion Hyman, founder of the Jewish Public Library on College Street. At the head of the table stands Menachem Mendel Hyman, wearing his hat, and to the left is his wife, Bayla, his son, Ben Zion, and his grandson Gurion. To the right is Fanny Hyman.

Land Uncultivated for Thousands of Years

BY MIRIAM DASHKIN BECKERMAN

When the Hechalutz movement, committed to preparing young people for life as *chalutzim* (pioneers) in Palestine, sprang up in Canada and the United States, I joined to fulfil my dream of making aliyah (immigrating to the Land of Israel).

I travelled from my home in Toronto to Creamridge, New Jersey, where there was a *hachsharah* (a model communal farm) for members of the Hechalutz. Some of the young people at the *hachsharah* attended a nearby agricultural college, while others looked after the cows, worked in the fields, and took turns at kitchen and laundry duty. We also had daily private Hebrew lessons.

After I had been at Creamridge for about a year, a *hachsharah* opened in Smithville, Ontario, and I moved there. Smithville is in the Niagara fruit belt, not far from Toronto, and on the weekends our house was always crowded with visitors. In time, two *shlichim* (emissaries) from kibbutzim in Palestine arrived at the *hachsharah*. They told us that, because we were British subjects, we could enter Palestine as tourists, and that once there, we would be able to remain.

I set out from New York in December 1946 aboard a converted World War II troop ship, the *Marine Carp*, and arrived in Haifa about two weeks later. I still remember the

overpowering fragrance of citrus blossoms that greeted us there. Representatives of the Jewish Agency came aboard the ship, asked us for our passports, and in their place gave us wallet-sized identity cards, which the British required everyone to carry at all times. Anyone without a card was considered an "illegal," and could be shipped out of the country. As soon as we got ashore, we were told we must have our photographs taken and placed in the allotted space on the card.

As all this was happening, I heard someone call my name. It was a uniformed British soldier with a gun, and I was frightened that he might have come to arrest me. The soldier told me, however, that we had mutual friends, who had asked him to come aboard and assist me. That was when I learned there were Jews from Britain serving in the British army in Palestine, and he was one of them.

With the other Canadians from the Smithville *hachsharah*, I was taken to the newly established Kibbutz Kfar Blum in the Upper Galilee. It had a wooden dining hall, but both shower

---

Above: Miriam Dashkin Beckerman and her son Nonny, in Tel Aviv, September 1949.

stalls and toilets were outdoors. As the newest arrivals, we slept in any bed left vacant when kibbutzniks were absent on business.

It was now January, the rainy season. There was plenty of mud, and we had no sidewalks. Outside the dining hall was a hose we could use to wash off our rubber boots before we entered. The dining-hall floor was covered with sawdust to soak up the water we tracked in.

Kfar Blum's land lay on both sides of the Jordan River, and we crossed by canoe to plant fruit trees. What a feeling it was to work on land that hadn't been cultivated for thousands of years!

Since there was really no space for us at Kfar Blum, however, I later transferred to Ramat-Yochanan, near Haifa. Here, I had a tent to myself, and it felt like a palace!

Many times I asked the secretary of the kibbutz when I would get back the passport I had surrendered. Each time I asked, I was told not to worry about it. When it was finally returned to me, months later, I realized what had caused the delay. My photo had been removed, and as I flipped through its pages, I saw that there was a fresh stamp from Italy. It had-been used to help a desperate person enter Palestine from a displaced-persons' camp in Europe.

Background: Miriam Dashkin Beckerman, far left, Hechalutz Hachsharah in Smithville, July 1946.

The Camp Boys

BY PAULA J. DRAPER

During the panic that followed the Allied retreat in 1940 from Dunkirk, the British pressed the Canadian government to accept prisoners of war and "dangerous enemy aliens" who had been living in Britain. In June and July 1940, three ships brought 2,284 Austrian, German, and Italian Jewish refugees, aged sixteen to sixty, to Canada. Upon arrival, these men were incarcerated in prisoner-of-war camps. But Ottawa soon learned that, rather than dangerous aliens, they had been sent innocent refugees, and the Canadian government was flooded with petitions for their release.

In the years leading up to World War II, Canada had resisted all pressure to permit entry to Jewish refugees, and so the government was not about to let them enter through the back door of internment. It was more than three years before all the refugees interned in Canada regained their freedom.

Those who chose not to risk the dangerous wartime Atlantic crossing and return to England in order to regain their liberty languished in camps located in New Brunswick, Quebec, and Ontario. They called themselves the "camp boys." Most wanted to join the Allies in the war effort, yet were incarcerated by those with whom they had sought refuge.

The irony of their situation led to constant tensions.

What is most remarkable about the story of these interned refugees is the life they created for themselves. The camps were like little male cities, replete with cafés, sporting areas, schools, workshops, and places of worship. Everyone learned English, and struggled to maintain a sense of humour. They even managed to save their paltry pay for doing war work and made donations to Jewish charities. Among the most politically active were the Zionists. They watched the situation in Palestine as carefully as they could. Refugees in the Sherbrooke camp mounted a large campaign for the Canadian Zionist Organization, using the slogan, "One Day's Pay for Palestine." Above all, however, they wanted release, to help their families trapped in Europe and to fight in the war against fascism.

By the end of 1943 the camps were all closed, after a long struggle by the Canadian Jewish Congress, other refugee advocates, and the internees themselves. In October 1945,

---

Above: European Jewish refugees with their Canadian guards, at the Ile aux Noix Internment Camp in Quebec, early 1940s.

former internees were formally permitted to apply for citizenship. The "camp boys" had become Canadians. Five years in limbo were over.

Among those interned in these camps were Torontonians Kurt Rothschild, Eric Exton, Rabbi Albert Papenheim, Rabbi Erwin Schild, Walter Homberger, Jack Hahn, Heinz Warschauer, and Emil Fackenheim.

_____

Background: "Camp boys" studying university-level science in a school they organized at Ile aux Noix.

Clandestine

Undercover
BY DIANNA ROBERTS ZAUDERER

THE FACTORY

It was after the war, and all over North America munitions factories were putting their surplus up for sale. Norman Grant, who had been chief engineer of York Arsenal in Toronto during the war, was visiting New York with his wife. A member of the Haganah who was living in New York asked him to set up and run a secret machine shop in Toronto. It was to be a small-scale version of York Arsenal, producing tool-and-die parts for guns to be shipped to Israel.

The location Grant found was National Motors, on Bay Street in downtown Toronto. The garage was owned by Ben Sadowski, a prominent member of the Jewish community. The tenant who rented the second floor told the landlord he was doing scientific research for Palestine. It was necessary to be discreet, because only one staircase led to the second floor, and anyone who used it could be observed.

At first the work was divided up and subcontracted to machine-tool shops in Toronto. Ben Ocopnik picked up and delivered blueprints to the various shops, none of which knew what they were producing.

"Within a matter of months I was bored to death," recalls Ocopnik. "One day, I was the chauffeur for a Palestinian Jew. We were sitting in the car, waiting for someone at Yonge and Queen. It was a warm fall day, and I said, 'I'm giving up this job. It's too boring.'

"He said to me, 'You're needed.'

"'I'm not staying,' I repeated. 'Anyway, who are you?'

"'I'm the general of the Haganah,' he told me. He was Yaacov Dostrovsky, the commander-in-chief of the Haganah."

Ocopnik left Toronto with the first group of Canadian volunteers (Mahal) to fight for the new Jewish state. D. Lou Harris, the owner of Atlas Radio, collected the money to send the group to Palestine.

That left Grant with one less man, and he set out to look for someone to run the operation. Max Brown was a university student who had served in the Canadian air force. When Grant and Dostrovsky approached him, Brown at first thought they were recruiting him to fly planes for Palestine.

Left: Max Brown in Toronto in 1948, while he was working for the Haganah, manufacturing tools and dies for guns to be shipped to Israel. Right: Ben Ocopnik in Toronto.

THE GUN

There were now six men working on the second floor of National Motors: Grant, Brown, a Swedish-American cabinet-maker from Rhode Island, and three others. Carl Ekdahl, the Swede, had worked for twenty-six years in the small-arms industry in New England, and in 1942 he had helped design the Johnson light machine gun. In 1945 he had been contacted by the Haganah in New York and asked to design another machine gun to be used by the Jews of Palestine in a battle against their enemies. Ekdahl had agreed, because he believed that all people had a right to a homeland.

They produced the first six samples of the gun in early 1947. There were production setbacks. Ekdahl had produced blueprints for a gun that required American bullets, but Dostrovsky said they must make the conversion to British army ammunition, because Israel already had three big caches of British bullets. Unfortunately, when the war started, spies exposed all three caches and the bullets were gone.

Finally, the gun was ready to be tested. It had a name, the Dror, which means "freedom" in Hebrew. Grant suggested testing the gun in some remote part of Northern Ontario, but Dostrovsky was in New York and didn't want to take the chance of getting caught crossing the border. They decided instead to go to Ekdahl's farm in Vermont.

Left: Norman Grant, left, and Akiva "Kiev" Skidell in New York,
c. 1948, doing undercover work for the Haganah.

NIAGARA FALLS

That wintry morning in February, Grant, Ekdahl, and Brown left Toronto in Ekdahl's 1942 Mercury, with two prototype machine guns disassembled in the trunk. They picked up a second car with a driver in Hamilton.

"We're driving along, and parts of the gun are loaded under the front seat," recalls Max Brown. "Noseworthy, the driver of the second car, is going so fast to keep up with the other car that the stuff starts creeping forward, and with my feet I'm trying to kick it back under the seat."

They were stopped at the border, and when their stories didn't match, they were taken into the customs building. "Everything was all laid out on the counter," Brown remembers.

"'What's this?' they ask me.

"'I don't know.'

"'A gun?'

"'I don't know. I was a *pilot* in the air force.'

"'Looks like a machine gun.'

"'I'm a machinist. I just produce the parts.'

"For three days the Mounties and the FBI questioned me. I'm sure they knew damn well, but all I could do was keep acting dumb. I spent three days and three nights in jail on the American side of Niagara Falls. They transferred me to the real jug with all the criminals."

Brown refused to call anybody, but someone called Senator David Croll in Ottawa and a lawyer showed up. Brown and Noseworthy were each freed on four thousand dollars' bail. Brown was met by Dostrovsky, who kept asking him if he'd mentioned his name. Why would he have done that? asked Brown. However, the authorities traced Brown back to the operation on Bay Street. Grant was arrested as soon as he returned to Canada, and the tools, dies, and jigs from the Bay Street operation were confiscated. Grant was fined, but the machinery was returned a few months later, possibly thanks to Senator Croll as well.

What upset Brown more than his three-day detention and interrogation was the news that someone called his parents to tell them that their son was in trouble and all his personal papers must be burned. "All my books, all my materials from the air force," says Brown, "were burnt in the furnace. I could never forgive that."

THE TRIAL

Max Brown's trial was to be held in Buffalo, but the two lawyers handling the case, Max Fleishmann and David Diamond, had the case transferred to Rochester, New York. It was postponed until May, because the lawyers were waiting for an Irish judge to hear the case.

Brown's lawyer told him, "I'll ask the judge, 'Did you see *The Informer*? It's a film about the Irish revolt against the British.'"

On the day of his trial, Brown sat nervously in the courtroom. "Finally, my case came up," he recalls. "My lawyer said

---

Above: David Croll, pictured here in 1953, provided help for Israel on the home front.

to the judge, 'Your Honour, I'd like to speak with you privately before the case starts. Did you see *The Informer?* This man is a character in the film.' So the judge says, 'A case of smuggling. One hundred dollars.' I was barred from entering the States for one year."

NEW YORK

Gradually, all the tools and dies were shipped out of Toronto and sent to New York. Haganah headquarters was a five-room apartment at 512 West 112th Street. It was the apartment of Mr. and Mrs. Pines and their son.

One blustery day in January 1948, on Pier F in Jersey City, a couple of longshoremen were loading wooden crates marked "Used Industrial Machinery" onto the cargo deck of the SS *Executor*, destined for Palestine. As one crate was being hoisted up, it broke open and out rolled tins labelled "TNT." The police and the coastguard were alerted, and they pried open all the boxes destined for Palestine. Twenty-six crates contained TNT, and the others had machinery that looked as if it could be used to manufacture ammunition.

Headquarters received the news, and people started emptying out anything they could stuff into their cars. Max Brown, who was in the apartment, told Mrs. Pines that no matter who knocked on the door, she should tell them she was alone and couldn't open the door.

"We were on the eighth floor, and the secretary of the Labour Zionist movement was on the fifth floor," says Brown. "I started loading up the blueprints as quickly as I could and taking them down to the fifth floor. We saw cars pulling up out front. They were knocking on the door."

While Mrs. Pines told the visitors that no one was home, I started rolling up the rest of the blueprints," continues Brown. "The building next door was five storeys high, and I threw the blueprints out the window of the eighth floor onto the roof of the building next door.

"We waited several days to get the blueprints off the roof. There were two guys standing outside the main entrance of our building. I didn't think it was the FBI, because they'd be sitting in a car. A couple of our friends started asking them questions and found out that they were Jews. The Jewish FBI, our new Mossad."

EPILOGUE

As a participant who prefers to remain anonymous recalls, "The work gave purpose and meaning to our relationship with Israel. We had all come out of Zionist youth groups. We had an emotional involvement with Palestine, and we always hoped it would become Israel. I don't think anyone thought they were doing anything heroic or special. People just pitched in and did what they did because everyone regarded it as a personal responsibility."

– this story is based on interviews, as well as on certain chapters of The Pledge *by Leonard Slater (New York: Simon and Schuster, 1970).*

Bullies and Gunrunners: Early Memories of Israel

BY IRVING ABELLA

My first memories of Israel are not pleasant. When I was six years old, my parents had just moved to Queen and Spadina in Toronto from the heart of the Jewish community near Harbord. Besides losing my close friends, I was also forced to go to a school where almost no one was Jewish. At the time I probably spoke Yiddish better than I did English. It was the fall of 1947, and like everybody else in the community, my father was caught up in the excitement of the pending UN decision to partition Palestine into Jewish and Arab sections. And what better way to show his support than to give his son a Jewish flag to take to his new school.

I did not get far. Two older boys jumped me, broke my flag, and began to pummel me, until a nearby shopkeeper ran out, chased them away, and carried me back to my father's restaurant. My father took one look at me, understood what had happened, and for the first time in his life hailed a cab. We drove directly to the Talmud Torah on Brunswick Avenue. Though he could barely afford it, he enrolled me in the day school to continue my education amongst Jews. It is to those two bullies that I owe my Hebrew education.

But it was not in school that our generation learned to love Israel. It was in our Zionist summer camps. And mine, I think, was the very best, perhaps because it possessed the very least.

Located near Dunnville on Lake Erie, Camp Kvutza had nothing but spirit. There were no cabins, no boats, and no facilities of any sort. But we loved it. It was also a hotbed of Zionism. Everything revolved around Israel – the songs, the stories, the activities – and in reality the camp served as a recruitment centre for aliyah.

At Kvutza I met my first Israeli, learned my first Hebrew folk songs, and danced my first horah. But I also came face to face with the life-and-death struggle of the new Jewish state.

On the first day of camp in the summer of 1947, all of us were gathered around the flagpole to hear the camp director. He told us we would see strange things over the course of the summer and a lot of people we didn't know wandering about. But under no circumstances were we to tell anyone, including our parents.

And sure enough, over the next few weeks we saw trucks arrive full of boxes, which were carried off and buried. Small boats landed on our beach regularly to offload packages and pick up the buried boxes. But most exciting was the weekly arrival of the Mounties, resplendent in their uniforms. They would talk to the staff, snoop around our tents, tramp through the fields, and dig holes in the beach. Clearly, they

---

Above: Irving "Itche" Abella, age six, just before his meeting with the bullies!

were looking for something, but they always left empty-handed. We campers felt as if we were part of a great mystery.

And of course, as I learned later, we were. Camp Kvutza was the centre of a gun-smuggling operation, collecting and sending arms to the Jewish population of Palestine. It was then illegal to ship arms to the fledgling Jewish army, so everything had to be done with utmost secrecy. The location of our camp made it a convenient transit point for shipments to and from Cleveland, Ohio, just across the lake.

Whether the Mounties were tipped off or whether they actually knew what was going on and preferred to turn a blind eye, I never discovered. Nor did I tell my parents about the gunrunning. I suspect my father knew, but we never talked about it. It was our secret.

————————

Below: Renee Rosenberg Topper and friends cleaning their tent at Camp Kvutza, 1945. Pictured, left to right, are: Shoshana Disenhouse, Beryl Atkins, Norma Blitzstein, Renee Rosenberg, and Anne Glassman.

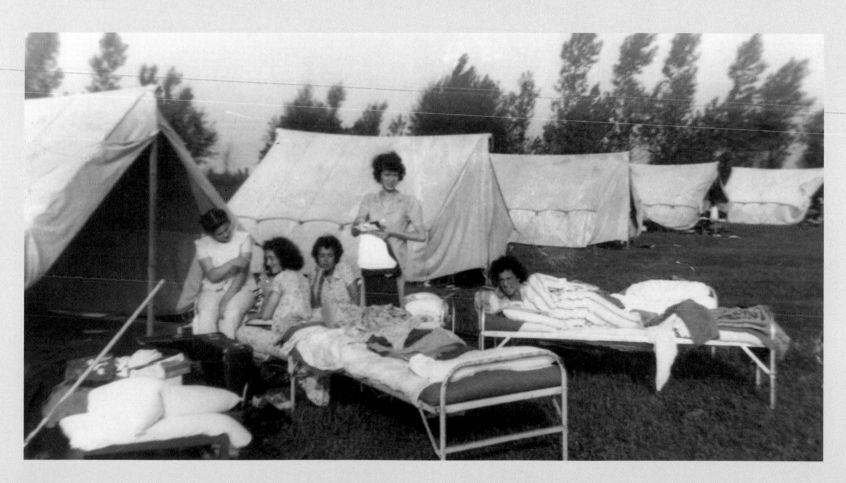

Harry Mitz, standing in front of a train stacked with goods going to Haifa, Israel, in 1948. Harry recalls, "The items on the train were hydraulic shell presses that had been used for the manufacturing of 155-mm shells. They were bought from the Canadian War Assets Corporation as surplus."

"It was my greatest pleasure to help Israel by supplying three hundred wireless radio sets," says Harry Mitz. "They needed the sets for tanks and Jeeps. They had been bought as war surplus and were shipped from the Montreal government warehouse by train, eventually landing in Israel via the United States. These sets were so large that one boxcar held only twenty of them."

A Circle Completed

BY ELI RUBINSTEIN

My grandfather, Elias Schwartz, did not like what was happening in Hungary in the late thirties. The government was introducing ever more restrictive anti-Jewish legislation, and he concluded that there was no future for Jews in Hungary. In his capacity as secretary of the Jewish community of Szerencs, he arranged safe passage out of the country for many people. He hoped eventually to take his own family to Palestine, but his strong sense of communal responsibility dictated that he first help others. The noose kept tightening, and in time it was impossible for any Jew to leave Hungary. In April 1944, Elias Schwartz and his family, along with all the remaining Jews of Szerencs, were transported to Auschwitz. My mother, Judith, and one of her brothers were the sole survivors of the family.

After the war, Judith met Bela Rubinstein, a fellow survivor who had suffered grievous losses. They wandered through Europe, finally arriving at a camp for displaced Jews in Grugliasco, Italy, where they married. The camp was a hotbed of Zionist activity. At a time when the nations of the world showed no enthusiasm for taking in Jewish refugees,

Eretz Yisrael was an alluring destination, despite British determination to keep Jews out. Judith and Bela patiently awaited their turn. In March I was born, and they named me Eli, after my grandfather, the tragic visionary. Two months later, the State of Israel was proclaimed and was immediately attacked by its Arab neighbours. It was impossible for the new state to take in people with small children.

My parents were anxious to begin a normal life. When the opportunity arose to emigrate to Canada, they jumped at it, arriving in Toronto in October 1948. Slowly, order emerged from chaos. My sister, Rochelle, was born; Bela (anglicized to "Bill") became a successful real-estate developer; Judith became a popular speaker to young people about her experiences and the evils of racism; and now Bill and Judith have seven grandchildren. The oldest, my daughter Tamar, recently moved to Israel with her husband, Jonathan Koschitzky, and their son. I am certain Elias Schwartz would be deeply gratified.

Above: Judith and Bill's wedding, Grugliasco, Italy, June 9, 1946.

A Jewish Standard

BY JULIUS HAYMAN

My interest in publishing grew out of my experience with various publications of the University of Manitoba, from which I graduated with a law degree. My dedication to Jewish survival, to a Jewish state, and to a comprehensive Zionism, I derived from my Russian-born father, who had experienced anti-Semitism. From my mother, I learned that non-Jewish cultures also had their contributions to make.

My early childhood was spent in a small town in Saskatchewan. I remember that the most inspiring conversations in our home, in back of our store, were about the State of Israel, which would undoubtedly be established some day. My father always believed it. From my earliest days, I was told about the return to Israel.

I believe that the future of Zionism depends on the extent to which world Jewry helps ensure Israel's survival, helps resolve her religious, cultural, and ethnic tensions, helps Israel achieve economic stability, and develops, with Israel, a Jewish peoplehood in the Diaspora.

– Since 1937, ninety-year-old Julius Hayman has published the Jewish Standard, *a privately owned Zionist periodical in Canada.*

Above: Julius Hayman, left, with Samuel Chait, middle, first president of the Canadian Zionist Federation, and Lawrence Freiman, former national president of the Zionist Organization of Canada, 1960s.

A Living Language

BY ORAH BUCK

After my father died, I was rearranging some papers that had sat untouched for years. I picked up an album and an envelope fell out. Inside were twenty-five letters in Hebrew, written to my brother and me during the 1940s. They were written by Shlomo Hillels, who was called the Poet of Bessarabia, and sent to us so we would practice our Hebrew. He was the administrator of Bialik House, home of one of Israel's foremost poets.

Shlomo's letters are a combination of charm, warmth, and humour, against a backdrop of the stark realities of the time. He was one of the visionaries who helped transform Hebrew into the living language of the State of Israel.

Our family had formed a friendship with Shlomo Hillels when he lived in America for some years. After he returned to Israel, his letters were full of vivid descriptions of his life there: "I sit at my table that stands next to a window open to the garden, while in it grow figs, grapefruit, oranges, bananas. . . .

The sun shines brightly on them and gladdens my eyes." However, he bemoans the lack of apples, pears, and plums and says, "If you could send me only one of these by airmail, I would bless you and send you kisses in the air!" In a letter he wrote to my father, he expresses his belief in the importance of Hebrew to the unity of our people, and in particular for the rebuilding of Israel and its culture. He also expresses the wish that Hebrew be brought to schools everywhere in the Diaspora so that Jewish youth could understand that "Hebrew is really the language of our land and the language of everyday life in Israel."

I believe that his wish has come true.

Above: Orah Buck has recently published her correspondence with writer and educator Shlomo Hillels in a book entitled Love, S.H. and the Mrs.

Surrounded by beaming Israeli soldiers, Betty Zweig, in chevron stripes, along with Toronto friends, salutes Israel, 1959.

PART THREE

BUILDING

BRIDGES

Making Plans

D. Lou Harris

FROM A CONVERSATION WITH HIS DAUGHTERS, CHARLOTTE BAKER AND MOLLY SHAPIRO, AND HIS BROTHER, FRED HARRIS

David Louis Harris and his wife, Eva, visited Israel for the first time in 1948, but were sent out of the country before the war broke out. Because of his international business connections, and his military experience in World War II, D. Lou was able to assist in Israel's defence. He was one of the first Canadians to make an on–the–spot survey of the new state's needs, and upon his return to Canada, D. Lou organized a campaign to send over necessities to the Canadian, American, and Commonwealth volunteers fighting in Israel.

D. Lou's brother, Fred Harris, was then working with him at the Atlas Radio Corporation on King Street in Toronto and recalls: "Canadian flyers would come through our office on their way to Israel. They would stay at his house for a few days, and were only introduced to the family by their first names. It was all done very secretly. Very few of them were Jewish. My brother arranged the payments for them. I myself took about twenty thousand dollars in cash from Toronto to Montreal to pay the flyers with money that was raised through donations. My brother was great at giving, and also at asking others to give. He was not only a worker; he was one who inspired others."

In a letter to D. Lou in 1972, on the occasion of the ORT (Organization for Educational Resources and Technological Training) dinner honouring both his commitment to Israel and his seventy–fifth birthday, Golda Meir wrote: "We well remember your timely and precious help during Israel's War of Liberation in obtaining vitally needed supplies under hazardous conditions."

"My dad was in Israel almost every single year after 1948," recalls his daughter Charlotte Baker, "and each time he visited, he strengthened his ties with the country, not only through liaisons with government, Jewish agencies, religious, military,

---

Above: Mayor Teddy Kollek, left, and D. Lou Harris, 1971.
Facing page: D. Lou Harris, left, chatting with Prime Minister David Ben-Gurion in his Jerusalem office, 1953.

and industrial leaders, but also by the very practical business of investing capital in the country." While in Israel in 1953, D. Lou was asked by the Zionist leaders in Toronto to run Toronto's first Israel Bond Campaign. "He was the one who started speaking at the High Holiday synagogue service to sell bonds."

In 1971, D. Lou attended a ground–breaking ceremony in Israel for the building of a dormitory for married students. Unfortunately, he didn't live to see it completed. "He was supposed to go to Chicago to speak for Israel," recalls daughter Molly Shapiro. "His doctor wanted to put him in the hospital for a few weeks because of his heart, but Dad said, 'Oh, I can't do that.' And he died in Chicago, on October 22, 1972. He died with his boots on." The D. Lou Harris Dormitories in Canada Village at Technion City, Mount Carmel, Haifa, was dedicated in his honour in 1978.

"The Jews' love for Israel does not spring only from a deep religious conviction," D. Lou Harris once said. "It is a practical prompting to go to a place that they can really call home."

Left: D. Lou Harris and his wife, Eva, arriving in Israel.

A Friend of Israel

FROM A CONVERSATION WITH JOHN BASSETT

I first went to Israel in 1958, the tenth anniversary of the state, as a guest of the Israeli government. The Israeli ambassador to Canada, David Lurie, was a pal of mine. I paid my own way to get there – but once there, I was in their hands. Israel was just a little place; Jerusalem was split and you couldn't go to East Jerusalem. Israel reminded me so much of what it had been like in England during the war. No selfish desires or agendas were a part of Israel then. Everything was subjugated to the good of the country, and I found the spirit to be absolutely uplifting.

Because I was the publisher of the *Toronto Telegram* at the time, I met all the leaders. I had long talks with Prime Minister David Ben-Gurion. He was very short, and I'm very tall, and the first time I was in his office he made me sit down. He said jokingly, "I'm not going to stand up next to *you*."

But my favourite of them all was Golda Meir, who was then the foreign minister. I don't know why, but we just hit it off particularly well together. The foreign ministry of the Israeli government had a very nice house in Jerusalem, built around an open courtyard, and my wife and I dined privately with Golda there. I was horrified to learn that Canada did not have an ambassador in Israel, only a chargé d'affaires. We

had an ambassador to Greece *and* Israel at the time, a fellow named Darcy McGee, but he remained mostly in Greece.

I remember saying in a boastful manner to Golda, "I'll get you an ambassador."

She said, "How will you get me an ambassador?"

I said, "Never mind, trust me."

You see, in 1958 John Diefenbaker had just been elected prime minister. The *Telegram* was the strongest supporter he had amongst the media, and he and I were very close. When I got back to Canada, I informed him of the fact that Israel had no ambassador of its own. He hadn't been aware of this, and he said, "Yes, we absolutely should have an ambassador to Israel." He appointed Margaret Meagher immediately.

At that time, the *Telegram*, like other papers across the country, published a magazine supplement every weekend. I got in touch with Golda, and when Margaret Meagher presented her credentials, we had a wonderful front page. The whole front page of the weekend magazine showed Golda

Above: John Bassett with his favourite prime minister, Golda Meir, 1950s.

Meir leading Margaret Meagher through the guard of honour – all women from the Israeli army!

In 1971 I was the honouree of the Negev Dinner in Toronto, the first non-Jew to be so recognized. With the money raised, we built the John Bassett Sports Centre, serving three kibbutzim about twenty miles north of Eilat, in Yotvata. It supplied them with two Olympic-sized swimming pools, tennis courts, and an auditorium for meetings, theatre, concerts, and so on. About forty of us went over from Toronto for the opening. I cut the ribbon, and it was *very* emotional.

A little boy, not more than eight years old, came running out of the crowd, jumped up into my arms, and said, "You're a wonderful man."

I said, "How do you know I'm a wonderful man? You've never met me."

"Ah," he said, "You've brought us water – swimming pools."

Of course, I started to cry, as this little guy hugged me.

I wanted to get a television licence for Israel. I saw David Ben-Gurion and asked him, but the Israeli government wouldn't give it to me, though I tried hard to persuade them. Instead, I went into partnership with Margot Klausner, an Israeli who owned a motion-picture company in Israel, to start up the government-owned Israeli television station. Of course, they never would have gotten to air without us. They wouldn't have had any programs.

Because of all this, I became great friends with Shmuel Tamir, who was Margot Klausner's lawyer, and perhaps the leading lawyer in Israel at the time. Then he left and formed his own political party. When Menachem Begin was elected as prime minister, Shmuel had three or four members of his party who allied themselves with Begin, and he became minister of justice. I saw him in Israel every time I visited.

The Israeli people were dejected after the Yom Kippur War. I made a speech in Tel Aviv along with the president of Israel, Chaim Herzog, and I said, "You've no right to be downcast. You had an early setback. But you won the bloody war!" I said, among other things I always believed, "Israel is not just for the Jews. Israel stands also for all of us who believe in freedom and democratic principles." It's the only country in the Middle East that has those principles.

You know, Ben-Gurion said he didn't like the term "Zionist." He always said, "The only Zionists are those who live in Israel. Those who don't are 'friends of Israel.' We welcome them, we want them, we love them. But they're not Zionists." That was his view.

I never call myself a Zionist; I just call myself a friend of Israel. I'm as big a friend today at eighty-two as I was then.

– *John Bassett passed away in April 1998.*

Left: John Bassett cutting the ribbon at the John Bassett Cultural and Sports Centre in Yotvata, c. 1970.

Prime Minister John Diefenbaker and Prime Minister Golda Meir, possibly congratulating each other on the appointment of Margaret Meagher as Canada's first ambassador to Israel thanks in part to John Bassett's efforts.

Tuxedos in the Ma'abara!

BY KURT E. WEINBERG

It was September 1952, and Israel was just over four years old. From everywhere, and especially from the liberated camps of Europe, hundreds of thousands of homeless refugees streamed to the new nation. Almost all of them came with only the clothes on their backs, depending on others for housing, food, and dress. Toronto industrialist and ardent Zionist Louis L. Lockshin conducted a city-wide campaign for used clothes, known as "Materials for Israel," over a six-month period. I was engaged by the Zionist Organization of Canada to help the drive reach success.

Our headquarters was the Toronto Zionist Centre at 651 Spadina Avenue, now demolished. Two big rooms were set aside for storage; telephones were installed; and racks for pick-up slips were built. We launched a massive advertising blitz in the newspapers and on the radio, calling on the community to open their wardrobes and empty them of everything that could be spared. Soon the phones were ringing off the hook with offers of all kinds of wear, from furs to jeans. Nothing was refused.

We mobilized a large corps of drivers to work three-hour shifts, picking up used clothing throughout the city along

predetermined routes. Clothing tumbled in by the ton and was stacked from the floor to the ceiling. After a couple of months, we were close to exhaustion from the effort, but we formed many close friendships in the excitement of the moment.

Shippers kept busy packing the materials into crates for transfer to Israel. Transport trucks were parked outside 651 Spadina Avenue every day to move the crates to warehouses.

Messages soon arrived from Jerusalem, gratefully acknowledging receipt of the shipments and urging us to do even more, since there were still thousands of *olim* (immigrants) waiting for a suit, jacket, or dress. We approached local manufacturers for their current stock and discontinued lines from previous seasons. Those who had nothing to contribute were enrolled as route drivers. And so it went on, for six glorious months, until finally word came that we had sent enough and could end the campaign. Toronto had clothed a large part of Israel's new population.

Above: Team consultation at the "Materials for Israel" campaign, Zionist Organization of Canada headquarters, September 1952. From left to right: Kurt Weinberg, Aaron Sokolsky, Louis Lockshin, Mr. Weinreb, Sonee Cohen.

The quality of the goods we received was good, and most of the clothing contributed was clean and appropriate. But once in a while, from the more affluent sections of the community, we received tuxedos, frock coats, and evening gowns! We shipped these anyway, with a whimsical smile, imagining how they would look on an immigrant in a government established *ma'abara* (temporary camp for new immigrants) in the middle of nowhere.

Shula Jacobi as a young child, in her red coat.
"It was 1956, and we were in the middle of a bomb attack on Mahne Israel, a *ma'abara* [immigrants' camp] at an old British military base near Tel Aviv. I was only three years old, but as we ran for cover, I remember screaming, 'Mom, I want my red coat, why can't I get my red coat?' I can't remember much about that time, but I do recall that coat, maybe because it kept my body and soul warm and secure. I later found out that the coat had been donated by the Jewish community in Toronto."

The People Came to See Itche Meyer

BY ROCHELLE DIAMOND

In June of 1950, my grandparents, Itche Meyer Korolnek and his wife, Alta Toba Korolnek, boarded the *Queen Mary* en route to the new State of Israel. This journey was the lifetime dream of two people who had begun life in Poland in 1884. My grandparents took with them, their eldest grandson, Howard Karoll, thirty pieces of luggage stuffed with clothing to be left behind in Israel, and a new black Pontiac four-door sedan. At the time, there were few cars in Israel, and they planned to present this one to one of their nieces, Raisel, a Holocaust survivor.

Their return trip was somewhat easier, with only Howard, four suitcases, and, unfortunately, the Pontiac, which the new government had not allowed them to leave.

By their later trips to Israel – in 1957 (accompanied by their son, Herb Karoll) and 1968 (accompanied by their daughter, Anne Wolff, and granddaughter, Beverley Ogus) – my grandparents had perfected the art of *tzedakah* (charity). They no longer brought suitcases of clothes, but instead a purse full of thousands of American dollars.

Beverley recalls how, following the long flight to Israel in 1968, they all went to their rooms for a rest. When they re-assembled, Zayde was missing. Bubbie urged them not to be

angry, but she had to tell them that Zayde had gone to the newspaper office to place a notice: "Itche Meyer Korolnek is here from Toronto, Canada, and anyone who wishes to see him should come to the hotel in Tel Aviv." By the time the family had finished dinner that same evening, the small hotel lobby was crowded with people who had come to see Itche Meyer. He and his family were in Tel Aviv for one month, and on every evening except Shabbat, Itche Meyer distributed *tzedakah* to those who came.

But a deeper reason for this trip, undertaken when Itche Meyer and his wife were eighty-three years old, was that he wanted to visit and touch the Kotel (the Western Wall), which had just been recaptured in 1967. Itche Meyer and his driver had an understanding: whenever they were in the vicinity of Jerusalem in the afternoon, they would go to the Kotel so that Zayde could pray.

As they travelled the countryside, visiting schools, yeshivahs (religious schools), and orphanages, Itche Meyer was always asked to sing for the students. As a nine-year-old in Poland, he had daily recited prayers with a blind

Above: Itche Meyer Korolnek at the Western Wall, 1968.

neighbour, and this man had blessed him and told him that, because of his good deed, he would have his beautiful voice until the end of his life. And so it came to pass that my grandfather was able to go to the Kotel to raise his voice in chanted prayers, praising G–d for the miracle of the Jewish state.

Background: A "Melave Malka" – a festive party held at the end of Shabbat so that the spirit of Shabbat will linger on – given in Itche Meyer's honour by the eminent Rabbi Shlomo Kahaneman, the Ponevez Rav, Israel, 1957. From left: Rabbi Kahaneman, Itche Meyer Korolnek, and an unidentified guest.

My Father, Meyer Gasner

BY LEON GASNER

Meyer Gasner was one of the driving forces that helped build Toronto Jewry into the organized community it is today. He and others set up the standards for *kashrut* (Jewish dietary laws) in Canada, helped organize and develop such noteworthy organizations as the Mount Sinai Hospital, Baycrest Home for the Aged, and various other charitable institutions and foundations. MW (as my father was known) had a deep love for and devotion to Israel. One day, when someone expressed to him their great concern about the number of Jews serving time in Israel's jail system, he remarked almost proudly, "Yes, but they're our people and our jail system, and we've finally arrived."

By the early 1950s, my father was already participating in Israel's burgeoning manufacturing sector by importing Israeli goods into Canada. The establishment of Carmel Wines in Canada was one of his successes. Not satisfied with promoting Israeli exports, he became involved with associates to develop industry within Israel itself, helping to build the Four Seasons

Hotel in Netanya and entering retailing with the Supersol chain of supermarkets, among many other ventures in such varied fields as agriculture, education, banking, and tourism. In 1956, MW was one of the early honourees at a Jewish National Fund Negev tribute dinner. A *nachla* (border settlement) in the Negev was established in his name, but he could never find it during his many trips to Israel, so he renamed it the "Stealth" Nachla.

In 1974 my father passed away prematurely at the age of sixty-eight, but his effective age was 680, because in his lifetime he accomplished the deeds of ten normal people. The driving force which he imparted to this community continues to influence people today.

Above: A toast, l'chaim, with Carmel wine. Meyer Gasner is in the foreground. In the middle row, from left to right: Paul Martin Sr. and Prime Minister David Ben-Gurion.

At the airport in 1957, before flying off on the United Jewish Appeal's first Canadian study mission to Israel are, from left to right: **Dr. I Sackin**, **Leon Weinstein**, **Anne Weinstein**, **Arlene Weinstein**, **Morley Pape**, **Bill Weinstein**, and **Gus Weinstein**. Also on that pioneering mission were Sam Shopsowitz, Sam Sable, Murray Koffler, and Alex Fisher.

"J. Irving Oelbaum," writes his daughters, **Helen Simpson** and **Dorothy Koven**, "lived with 'Chai' ['Life,' symbolized by the number 18], always recognizing the joy in life and giving gifts in multiples of eighteen. He was actively involved in many charitable causes and helped to found the Canadian Council for Christians and Jews. He was the best kind of Jewish leader – involved with all kinds of institutions and at home with all kinds of people.

"J. Irving Oelbaum led two missions to Israel, once bringing back a crate of oranges from his own nachla [border settlement] to share with family and friends in Toronto. Though he proudly explained they were his very own oranges, overzealous customs officials would not allow them into Canada!"

This Was Their Home

As chairman of the United Jewish Appeal Campaign, I first visited Israel with my wife, Jean, during the Suez Canal Crisis in October 1956, along with more than seventy people from various countries.

You've heard the expression "kissing the ground of Israel" – well, it was a very emotional time, and we did literally kiss the ground when we arrived. My wife and I were the only Canadians on this international mission, and we had an opportunity to meet with David Ben-Gurion. What I recall clearly is that he had three rooms with high ceilings, and each room was packed solid with books from every country of the world, and in different languages. Mr. Ben-Gurion spoke to us off-the-cuff and told us what the situation was in Israel at the time. He said, "I regret to tell you this, but in several days we will be at war."

Later, we visited the partitioned city of Jerusalem. They said it would be better to travel by daylight, but it didn't strike

us as serious. By the time we left, it was dusk, and before we knew it the taxi driver had pulled onto the shoulder and shut off his lights. They were shooting from atop the Judean Hills. Then we began to understand how it was for these people, who constantly lived with the threat of war. There is a beautiful quotation in *Pirkei Avot*: "Don't judge your friend until you sit in his place."

Yet even under these tense conditions, there was a common thread among the immigrants we met on this trip. They were happy and grateful to be in the land of Israel. They realized that this was their home and that they had a country and would no longer be "Wandering Jews."

Above: Moishe Dayan, left, and Sam Sable, late 1960s.

Gun Bolts and Diplomacy

BY EDWIN GOODMAN

Because I grew up in a Zionist home, my personal connection with Palestine and Israel goes back to my early youth. But my first trip to Israel came in 1963. After a boat trip in the Aegean with friends, Ann Dubin, my late wife Suzanne, and I flew on to Israel. The day we arrived and checked in to the King David Hotel, Ann and I went for an evening stroll. We were not more than two hundred yards from the hotel when we heard a guttural shout and the noise of a gun bolt being drawn back. We looked up quickly and saw a huge pile of sandbags and a shouting Arab sentry. We beat a hasty retreat.

Another vivid memory also dates from the 1960s, and is one of many examples I could give of Canadian politicians helping Israel. I received a telephone call from the late Yaacov Herzog, Israel's ambassador to Canada at that time. He asked whether I could persuade Prime Minister John Diefenbaker to invite David Ben-Gurion to Canada. He explained that President Kennedy was in the midst of discussions with the Arabs, and would not allow Ben-Gurion to come to the United States. However, Yaacov Herzog went on, if Ben-Gurion were in Canada, the Americans could not very well stop him from continuing across the border. I approached Mr. Diefenbaker and he agreed. The Americans raised hell, but Dief told them he was the prime minister of Canada and made the decisions, not them, and Ben-Gurion did indeed come. Our prime minister entertained him – and then he went on to the United States.

Above: Eddie Goodman in Israel, October 1995.

Left: Eddie Goodman with two Bedouin friends.

The 1959 UJA Mission

BY BEN SCHNEIDER

I want to share an experience that indicates the devotion and the commitment of the Jewish community in Toronto. In 1959, I went on one of the first UJA (United Jewish Appeal) study missions to Israel. I was the campaign director of the UJA at the time. The mission was made up of a group of young people plus three elder statesmen: the late J. Irving Oelbaum, Mac Lewis, and Willy Wagman. The mission was led by Alvin Rosenberg, then chairman of the UJA campaign.

At that time, Toronto study missions were kept small – fewer than twenty members if possible – so that everyone could ask as many questions as they liked, and experts they met could speak to each person individually. They became a highly successful means of strengthening the Jewish community's awareness of Israel's needs, even when there was no emergency or calamity to respond to. On the 1959 mission, for instance, Moshe Kol, director of Youth Aliyah, told them, "Go and see the slums. You are not tourists here, but partners. We must be alert to use this quiet period in immigration and the military situation to improve the conditions of those already here. This is the best preparation for additional mass immigration which will inevitably take place."

Once home, our group related their experiences in a photo and slide presentation before an audience of over five hundred people at Beth Tzedec Synagogue. The response of the community was overwhelming and generated a great deal of support for Israel and its needs. This was part of the long string of study missions to Israel that continue to the present time.

We were visiting Eilat toward the end of our trip when we heard that Roland Michener, then the speaker of the house in Canada's parliament, was to arrive shortly. When Mr. Michener walked down the steps from the airplane, there were fourteen men – all Canadian – lined up in front of him, singing "O Canada." This was a very thrilling experience for us, visiting the soil of Israel and coming face to face with this symbol of Canada. It showed that the ties between the Canadian Jewish community and Israel are very strong.

Above: Speaking to the visiting UJA mission from Toronto at a luncheon in Jerusalem in 1959 is the then-speaker of the Canadian House of Commons, Mr. Roland Michener. From left: Albert Latner, Ralph Fisher, Mrs. Michener, Alvin Rosenberg (mission leader), and Roland Michener.

On the airfield in Eilat, the 1960 UJA Campaign Mission from Toronto.
Included are: Ben Schneider, far right, with Mike Barzalay, Norman Simpson,
Dave Romberg, Lou Stulberg, Willie Wagman, Al Latner, Alvin Rosenberg,
Sam Torno, Laurie Shankman, Ralph Fisher, Henry Sussman, Bert Fine,
Irwin Lightman. Also present were Ted Richmond, J. Irving Oelbaum,
Mac Lewis, Nat Hennick, and Harry Sherkin.

Hadassa Agassi Rosenberg

BY HER DAUGHTERS, RACHELLE TAQQU, RONNI ROSENBERG, AND ELISSA ROSENBERG

Our late mother, Hadassa Agassi Rosenberg, native of Jerusalem and long-time Toronto writer, lecturer, and therapist, was widely known and loved here for her ability to open doors to Israeli culture.

At the University of Toronto School of Continuing Studies, at her own very popular series of public lectures, and in gatherings organized in private homes, she attracted a large following who came to hear about Israeli literature, the Bible, archaeology, and art. Most of what she taught grew directly from her Israeli roots.

She met our father, Stuart Rosenberg, while both were students in New York. He was a fervent Zionist, and they hoped to settle in the new State of Israel. However, this was

not to be. Eventually, in 1956, our father became the senior rabbi of the newly merged Beth Tzedec Congregation in Toronto.

Over the years our mother led many archaeological tours in Israel and the Middle East. She also joined a number of archaeological digs. In Ashdod, during the summer of 1970, she unearthed an early sculpture depicting a group of musicians; it is now part of the permanent collection of the Israel Museum.

Above: Hadassa Rosenberg, studying the model of King Herod's Temple in Jerusalem, c. 1973.

Rabbi Stuart Rosenberg Remembers David Ben-Gurion

BY HIS DAUGHTERS, RACHELLE TAQQU,
RONNI ROSENBERG, AND ELISSA ROSENBERG

Rabbi Stuart Rosenberg, who died in 1990, was the senior rabbi of Beth Tzedec Congregation from 1956 to 1972. He worked tirelessly for the Jewish community in Toronto. Among his accomplishments was the founding of the United Synagogue Day School. He was also instrumental in bringing Camp Ramah to Canada; and his 1961 trip to the Soviet Union and subsequent activism invigorated the burgeoning effort of North American Jews to rescue Soviet Jewry. He was a prolific writer and journal-keeper, and in March 1967, while he was chairman of the UJA of Toronto, he made an entry in his diary describing David Ben-Gurion's visit to Toronto on behalf of the UJA:

"On [Ben-Gurion's and his wife, Paula's] arrival at the airport in Toronto, there were about four hundred children from various Jewish schools, waving Canadian and Israeli flags. Limousines took us to the Royal York Hotel, where the vice-regal suite was waiting for the Ben-Gurions.

"At four o'clock in the afternoon, after a very short rest in the hotel, the Ben-Gurions arrived at Beth Tzedec. The sanctuary and other halls were overflowing with about four thousand children. Ben-Gurion insisted . . . that his first speech in Toronto – he hadn't been here since the days of the First World War, recruiting for the "Jewish Legion" – must be to children, *and it must be in Hebrew.* All the day schools cooperated, madly. Their Hebrew-speaking kids were given passes. Suddenly, all the Jews in town passed themselves off as Hebrew speakers – they wanted tickets of admission. But they couldn't pass as school children, though some of them did sneak in.

"At night, Paul Martin, as acting prime minister, came from Ottawa and spent time visiting with the Ben-Gurions in their suite; then we marched into the great fund-raising banquet in the Canadian Room of the Royal York Hotel.

"The next morning, the newspapers were filled with stories and pictures. A great day had come and passed."

– above diary excerpt is from Stuart E. Rosenberg's The Real Jewish World: A Rabbi's Second Thoughts *(Toronto: Clarke, Irwin, 1984).*

Above: Rabbi Stuart E. Rosenberg, right, with Prime Minister David Ben Gurion at Toronto's Pearson Airport, March 1967.

Betty Zweig, pictured here with a group of soldiers during a trip to Israel in 1959, became involved with Israel Bonds through Hadassah in the late 1940s. She served first as bond chairman of her Hatikvah chapter, then of Hadassah on a city-wide basis. Betty worked diligently for these causes through the fifties and sixties and made numerous trips to Israel. She became national vice-president of the Women's Division of State of Israel Bonds in Canada, and was the first woman ever appointed honorary chairman of the board of governors of the State of Israel Bonds Organization in Toronto. In 1972, Betty was presented with the rarely bestowed Eleanor Roosevelt Humanities Award for her contributions to Israel.

"Stephen Berger," named Man of the Quarter Century in 1974 by the United Jewish Appeal, was involved in community work for more than forty years. He was president of the Toronto Zionist Council, honorary life member of the board of governors of the Technion, and president of the United Jewish Welfare Fund, to name just a few of the positions he held."

Ruth Grossman Godfrey and husband, **Bert**, share a proud moment at the 1966 Negev Dinner held in Bert's honour.

Metro Toronto chairman **Paul Godfrey**, seated, signs document proclaiming Histadrut (Labour Federation) Month. Standing, from left, are: **Max Federman**, president of Trade Union Council for Histadrut Campaign; **Ken Signoretti**, vice-president, Toronto Labour Council; **Stephen Lewis**, regional chairman, Israel Histadrut Campaign; and **Ben A. Himel**, vice-chairman, Israel Histadrut Campaign, and a founder of the labour Zionist Borochov School.

The Promise

BY TOM LIBAN

My late father, George Liban, was born in Czechoslovakia. As a young man he was active in the Zionist movement and earned his doctorate in international law from Prague's highly respected Charles University. He served four years as a sergeant-major in the Czech army, until the Nazi occupation, when he and his family were all deported to Theresienstadt and then to Auschwitz.

Having survived the extermination selection, which took both his parents, he heard a group of his condemned friends, all fellow Zionists, call to him as they were sent to the gas chambers: "Liban, never forget us! *Chalutz*! Never forget Israel. You must work for Israel!" He vowed to survive and devote his life to carrying out their last wish.

As the European war drew to a close, he was sent from Auschwitz to labour in the Schwartzheide concentration camp. He gained freedom only after enduring the infamous "death march" of liberation, during which, to stay alive, he munched one clove of garlic a day from a bud he'd hidden. He weighed less than eighty pounds at war's end. He never ate garlic again.

In 1951 my father emigrated to Canada with my mother, Ann, her mother, and me. He became the executive director of the Zionist Organization of Canada, Central Division, where he served for almost thirty years. One of the first to lead hundreds of prominent members of the Canadian Jewish community on study tours to the newly created State of Israel, he visited Israel twenty-nine times through his career.

He organized the first Canadian Zionist convention in Jerusalem and spoke tirelessly during the fifties, sixties, and seventies to many local groups about his ordeals during the war, warning Canadians to be ever-vigilant against totalitarianism.

He loved life, loved Toronto, loved Israel. And he never forgot his promise.

Above: Ontario Premier Leslie Frost, centre, examines the Ben-Gurion Medal, presented to him by George Liban, executive director, Zionist Organization of Canada, Central Division, right. Allan Grossman, cabinet minister, looks on.

Getting Involved in Israel

BY ROSE WOLFE

My late husband, Ray, had never really been interested in going to Israel, but when we were planning a visit to Italy in the late fifties I suggested we extend our trip and go to Israel. Rather reluctantly, he agreed.

In Rome we visited Titus's Arch, which depicts Jewish slaves being brought back to Rome from the Holy Land. The carvings showed them tied together, bent over and dragging heavy loads. We were both very moved. When we arrived in Israel, among the first things we saw were the viaducts built for the Romans by Jewish slaves. The connection between the scenes on Titus's Arch and the viaducts gave us a real sense of the plight of Jews at the time of the Romans. Ray was overwhelmed by this and other sites we visited, and thus began a life-long connection to the Land.

From that time onward, Ray became intensely involved with Israel. His interests became family interests, and I, of course, became a participant in many of the activities. On the economic side, he was active in founding and running the Supersol chain of food markets and became involved with a number of leading politicians, including Prime Minister Ben-Gurion. In 1968 he served as a member of the economic

advisory council to the then Prime Minister Levi Eshkol and Finance Minister Pinchas Sapir.

We visited Israel many times, and first took along our children, Jonathan and Elizabeth, when they were eleven and nine. That began a deep emotional connection for both of them. Jonathan as a teenager worked in an agricultural moshav near Haifa, and as an adult Elizabeth studied at the Shalom Hartman Institute for a year.

One of my favourite experiences in Israel was a biblical tour put together by a friend in Toronto, Professor Hannah Himsley, a former Israeli doing research at the University of Toronto. I found it inspiring to go with a small group that concentrated on one specific interest. We followed the paths of some of the main characters in the Bible, supplemented by lectures at the Hebrew University. I particularly remember

Above: Rose Wolfe, visiting with her daughter, Liz, in Israel, 1986.
Liz studied at the Shalom Hartman Institute. Also shown is
Zvi Marks, a senior fellow of the Hartman Institute.

one trip to the top of a hill north of Jerusalem where Isaiah was said to have written his psalms. The landscape in that area can be terrifying but magnificent. These times, and those spent in the wilderness of the Sinai, the Negev, and the Golan, are for me among the happiest memories of my many visits.

When I became chancellor of the University of Toronto in 1991, we decided to have a reunion of all U of T graduates living in Israel. This coincided with a conference on Canadian studies at Hebrew University, supported by Roz and Ralph Halbert. Rob Pritchard, the U of T president, and I attended a rather modest gathering of about sixty-five people. As a young man Rob had lived in Israel for three months, and so had a real attachment to the country. In mid-1997 our vice-president, Heather Munroe-Blum, spear-headed the organization of another reunion. To our great surprise and delight, about three hundred people attended. They represented an amazing cross section of Israeli society, coming from every part of the country, from every walk of life, and with different political and religious points of view. It was a wonderful

evening as alumni reconnected with old friends and their alma mater. This has resulted in a further gathering, which took place in late June 1998, when we celebrated the official July 1 opening of the University of Toronto program at the Hebrew University.

The University of Toronto marked Israel's fiftieth anniversary on May 14, 1998, with a special day celebrating its many research and intellectual ties to Israel's institutions of higher learning.

It is my hope that as scholarships become available, many U of T students will have the opportunity to spend time studying in Israel and strengthening their own ties to Israeli culture.

—————————

Facing page: Mike Barzalay, Rose Wolfe, and Ray Wolfe, from the left, in 1962, feeling overwhelmed after hearing about the hangings of men from the Jewish Underground that took place in the mid 1940s at the former military prison in Acco, which the Wolfes were touring.

Israel: Morris Kaufman's Passion

BY HIS CHILDREN, IRA AND SHERRY KAUFMAN,
DEENNA AND MICHAEL SIGEL, LYNN AND SKIP SIGEL

Morris Kaufman involved himself in every facet of the Canadian Jewish community. Beginning with Israel's independence in 1948, he formed, together with the other major fund-raisers of Canadian Jewry, the inner circle of a committed group of leaders who created the blueprint for Israel–Diaspora relations.

He had a passion for Israel, and worked to make the country flourish every day of his adult life, zealously educating all in his reach to do the same. He believed that without Israel, Jews had no security. "MBK," as he was known, conceived the idea of the Endowment Fund as an adjunct to the United Jewish Welfare Fund of Toronto. Its purpose was to ensure that the needs of the Toronto Jewish community would be adequately met in perpetuity, thereby ensuring that Israel would always receive at least 50 per cent of all funds raised by the Jewish community from its United Jewish Appeal (UJA) campaigns.

He understood that the land itself had to be properly protected, and so he worked tirelessly for the Jewish National Fund. He got to know the land while travelling the wadis and deserts by Jeep, often with his children and grandchildren,

guided by the scouts of the Israel Nature Reserves Authority. Together with Golda Meir and key North American leaders, he conceived an external method of financing for the state – through State of Israel Bonds. In 1957 and 1958 he was State of Israel Bonds chairman for the city of Toronto. In 1965 and 1966 he was the UJA chairman for Toronto, and during the Six Day War he was asked to form the Past Chairman's Committee to canvass for major gifts. There were many days when he personally canvassed from 7:00 AM till midnight. His energy never waned.

A strong supporter of education in Israel, he was a founder or co-founder of the Canadian fund-raising arms of many major Israeli educational institutions, from the Technion, Weizmann Institute, and Haifa University, to Tel Aviv University, Ben-Gurion University, and the Arts and Sciences Academy. He believed Israelis could achieve anything, and we, Diaspora Jews, were an extension of that energy.

Above: Morris and Rose Kaufman visit Paula, David Ben-Gurion's wife, centre, at her home, 1958.

We remember his eager anticipation and then joy as he met the plane he'd sponsored when it landed at Ben-Gurion Airport – packed with *olim* (immigrants) arriving from the Soviet Union during Operation Exodus. He continued his involvement with the *olim* by raising the money necessary for their integration into Israeli life. It was his dependable, generous heart and his tireless efforts that stirred the community to understand and act on this need.

Israel was Morris Kaufman's passion, and working for it was his love.

———————

Above: Some of Toronto's prominent fund-raisers meet at the Primrose Club, 1959. From left to right: Sol Saltzman, Mr. Farber, Morris B. Kaufman, Henry Rosenberg, Nicholas Munk, J. Irving Oelbaum, Egmont Frankel.

Canada's Leading Christian Zionist

BY JANE MOWAT MARTIN

My father, Herb Mowat, was a lieutenant in the "Black Devils," the 118th Battalion from Winnipeg, during World War I. In August of 1918, his regiment suffered catastrophic losses at Amiens. Herb was severely wounded by a sniper's bullet, which lodged in his spine, and he lay on the battlefield among the dead, unable to move or speak. First reported dead by two officers, he was later transported to hospital by an ambulance driver who detected a heartbeat. When he was rescued from the jaws of death, my father believed that he had been spared for a reason. For the rest of his life, he took great care of his health, and amazed everyone with his robust energy.

After being invalided to Britain for a lengthy convalescence, Herb was sent home to Galt, Ontario, and in 1919 he married my mother.

My father was a devout Anglican and, as general secretary of the Brotherhood of St. Andrews, he was required to travel across Canada to speak at many cathedrals and churches. However, during the Depression of the 1930s, with jobs hard to come by, Herb had a very difficult time earning a living. He sold encyclopaedias and worked on construction crews to build roads. During World War II, he was general foreman on the construction of the Alaskan highway in the summers, but in the winter he worked as a freelance writer, producing articles for *Saturday Night* and other magazines. His involvement with Zionism began around this time.

Herb was doing research for a biography of Field Marshal Archibald Wavell, the British general who scored the first Allied victory against the German–Italian Axis in World War II by defeating the Italians in North Africa. In the course of his research, his attention focused on issues that already concerned him: the British Mandate in Palestine, and the passionate desire of Jews to have a homeland there. He had also been dismayed by a rising swell of anti–Semitism in Canada in the prewar years.

Instead of finishing the biography, he founded the Canadian Palestine Committee. Later, this would become the Canada–Israel Association, an organization of pro–Zionist non–Jews. Among them were prominent government officials and business and professional people, but most markedly, many were clergy of the Protestant and Roman Catholic faiths, all of them interested in seeing to it that the Jews could

Above: Herb Mowat, 1950.

establish a home in Palestine. Having been a great biblical scholar all of his life, my father used to say he ploughed into the Zionist cause "like a freight train on the run!"

For twenty-eight years, both before and after the founding of Israel, Herb worked tirelessly and passionately for a permanent national home for the Jews. He traversed Canada from St. John's to Victoria, again and again, throughout the forties, fifties, and sixties, also making forays into the United States, speaking dynamically and persuading large audiences to join in his enthusiasm for a Jewish homeland. He spoke in synagogues, churches, cathedrals, and meeting halls, and his speeches were sometimes broadcast on radio on the CBC and CKEY in Toronto.

On March 31, 1944, Prime Minister William Lyon Mackenzie King received a delegation of the Canadian Palestine Committee, which was introduced to the prime minister by Senator Arthur Roebuck. My father presented an oral brief to Mackenzie King. Although King's response at the time was negative, he later softened his position. Some of his appointees – particularly Justice Rand, Canada's representative on the Anglo-American Committee of Inquiry (into the status of Palestine), and Lester B. Pearson, Canada's UN delegate – helped push through the partition plan at the United Nations. Ben Dunkelman, in his autobiography, *Dual Allegiance*, credits the work of the committee headed by my father for this change in government attitude.

Senator Roebuck echoed this view. In recalling my father and his work for the Canadian Palestine Committee

Left: Lieutenant Herb Mowat in the "Black Devil" Battalion, 1918.

and later the Canada–Israel Association, he said, "This was the one organization in Canada that kept the flag flying of peace and goodwill between ourselves and the State of Israel. It had its effect upon the opinions of the people and government of Canada, and without Herb Mowat there would be no such association."

During 1958 and 1959 Herb sent letters of invitation to many prominent people, asking them to become members of the National Advisory Council to the Canada–Israel Association. Almost all accepted with pleasure, including future prime minister Lester B. Pearson. During his many years of work on behalf of Israel, my father arranged several luncheons per year. He would always astound the many guests at these functions with his ability to introduce from 50 to 125 people by name and occupation – often complete with an anecdote about them – all without a single note in his hand.

On February 6, 1968, the Zionist Organization of Canada paid tribute to Herb on his seventy-fifth birthday at a celebration which they held in his honour at the Zionist Centre in Toronto. Sadly, Herb was critically injured in a car accident four years later. After two years and eight months in hospital, he died in 1975 at the age of eighty-two.

I believe that my father would want to be remembered as a man who loved his God and therefore his fellow man, be he Jew or Gentile, and as someone who unified people so they would come to know and therefore have respect and perhaps even love for one another. World peace, he felt, would be the outcome.

_____

Below: At Herb's seventy-fifth-birthday tribute, given by the Jewish community and the Zionist Organization of Canada in 1968, are the Honourable Justice Ivan C. Rand, left, Herb Mowat, centre, and Senator Arthur W. Roebuck, right.

"**M** y father, **Sam Kronick**, was a product of the Jewish renaissance in the late nineteenth century," recalls **Joe Kronick**, "when young Jews were stirred by the new winds of Zionism, liberalism, and socialism. He arrived in Toronto in 1900.

"As J. B. Salsberg wrote in the *Canadian Jewish News* on November 3, 1972, 'He was in the forefront of what we now call fund-raising, but in the era when public services were extremely limited, Sam Kronick personally "took care of things." A Jewish student needing help, a widow requiring capital to open a grocery store, a man in need of assistance to bring his family from overseas, they all came to Sam, who operated a private charity and welfare service out of his business office.'

"Sam and his wife, Gert, later took an active role in more formal charities, such as the Zionist Organization, Hadassah, and Baycrest. They were among the outstanding Jewish community leaders in Canada, and in 1949 Sam was Toronto's first Negev Dinner honouree."

National president of the Jewish National Fund (JNF) **Lou Lockshin** is pictured having a chat with then Prime Minister **Pierre Trudeau** at a Negev Dinner.

Anne Tanenbaum, former chair of the UJA Women's Division, with her late husband, **Max**, far right, a past chair of the UJA. The couple shared a deep commitment to Israel. Here they are on their 1973 trip to Israel, shown with an Israeli ministry official.

Madeleine Epstein, left, and **Lily Oelbaum** chat with **Edward Gelber** in his home in Israel. Madeleine Epstein helped to pave the way for women to hold leadership positions in the community. She is one of the few Toronto women to have been honoured by the Jewish National Fund.

Forging Bonds

The Maccabiah Games

BY MYRNA RIBACK

Maccabi Canada is a national non-profit organization and a member of the Maccabi World Union (MWU). The concept of Maccabiah began in central Europe in the nineteenth century, when German Jews were invited to join Germany's gymnastic movement. In 1927, the Twelfth Zionist Congress in Carlsbad set up a new central sports organization, the Maccabi World Union.

The Maccabiah Games not only encourage physical training and discipline, they gather Jewish athletes from all over the world to compete at four-year intervals, giving them the opportunity to learn about the historical, religious, and cultural traditions of Israel.

The first Maccabiah Games were held in Palestine in 1932 and drew 390 athletes from fourteen countries. They were followed by the 1935 Maccabiah Games, with 1,700 athletes participating. The third Maccabiah, planned for 1938, was postponed due to the threat of war in Europe, and it was 1950 when the next games were held, in the new State of Israel. A Canadian team competed for

the first time that year and won fourteen medals, including one gold.

The Maccabiah movement has evolved into an international tradition that brings pride and the spirit of competition to thousands of young Jewish athletes. The games are recognized by the International Olympic Committee as an international sports federation of Olympic standing.

Above: Ready to compete in the 1961 games are: left to right, Syd Charendoff (weightlifting), Della Freedhoff and David Freedhoff (tennis), Arthur Sanders (track), and Anne Freedhoff (tennis).
Left: Top to bottom, Alex Fisher (team manager), Stan Levinson (track), Walter Unger, Larry Bell and Marv Chapelle (swimming), Roy Fisher (team mascot), and Ben Freedhoff (tennis).
Facing page: Waving their white Stetson hats, the Canadians march into the stadium, 1957.

A Promise Kept

BY RABBI W. GUNTHER PLAUT

In April 1935, I was living in Germany, had graduated from law school, and by dint of Hitler's decrees had become a man without a profession. Though it was the third year of the Nazi regime, the German team that participated in the second Maccabiah Games, of which I was privileged to be a part, was allowed to travel to what was then British-mandated Palestine. I had been a Zionist since my youth, but had promised my parents to return to Berlin. They hoped that things would get better and that our family in Germany would have a livable existence once again.

Thus I was privileged to see the *yishuv* (settlement) in the days of *chalutziyut* (pioneering), when a magnificent sense of idealism, unity, and the willingness to sacrifice prevailed in Eretz Yisrael.

In the 1935 Maccabiah, 1,700 athletes participated from twenty-seven countries. So many of them remained in Palestine that the meet became known as the "Aliyah Maccabiah."

Marching through the streets of Tel Aviv and into the stadium will always be an unforgettable memory. The impact of that first visit made my love for the land forever part of me. I would have stayed, were it not for the promise I had made.

Below: Opening-day ceremonies at the Second Maccabiah Games, April 1935. Gunther Plaut, marching with his German teammates, is the third team-member from the right.

Canada on Parade

FROM A CONVERSATION WITH ALEX FISHER

In 1949, I was asked by the late Fred Oberlander, one of the founders of the Maccabiah movement in Canada, to organize a contingent of athletes and raise the necessary funds to send a Canadian team to participate in the 1950 games.

In 1953, I went with the team as captain. As I boarded the El Al plane, the late Eddie Gelber stuffed a document into my hip pocket and told me to spend it in Israel, and to pay him when I returned. It was my first purchase of a State of Israel Bond – a wonderful way to get started.

During the games, we were housed in tents formerly occupied by British military forces. My tent-mates were Ted Reeve, *Toronto Telegram* correspondent, and the late Phil Givens, former mayor of Toronto. The late Ann Freedhoff, and my wife, Cecille, came away with bronze medals in tennis.

The big thrill of the Games is the opening-day parade. Today, six thousand athletes from some sixty countries march to the roar of sixty thousand spectators and "present arms" to the president of Israel. The Canadians are outfitted in

distinctive white Stetson hats and red blazers. There is not a dry eye in the stadium. Never are you more proud of being both a Canadian and a Jew in your own land.

Above: Alex Fisher, left, receiving a prized Maccabiah team uniform at a dinner given in his honour, from Joe Frieberg, chairman of the evening. The dinner was held in support of the Maccabiah Games, September 1985.
Below: Canadian fans will give you the shirt off their backs to show support for their hockey team at the Maccabiah Games!

Medals and Memories

BY SYD CHARENDOFF

Little did I know, when I accepted Uncle Bill Gryfe's invitation to the Y on my sixteenth birthday, that it would lead me to an adventure I would cherish all my life. For, after watching in awe the performances of Maurice Strauss, the Belgian champion weight lifter, I knew that weight lifting was what I wanted to do.

I trained in earnest, entered and won several competitions, then in September 1957 found myself in Israel as a contestant in the fifth Maccabiah Games. Never in my life had I felt so proud to be a Jew. The Maccabiah Village was located in a large national park next to the Ramat Gan Municipal Stadium. We slept in tents, and used bed-sheets we had brought with us, because there was a textile-workers' strike at the time. The washroom facilities consisted of outhouses; the fact that toilet paper was at such a premium presented us with new challenges. Air-conditioning, of course, was non-existent, and the weather was unbearably hot. But the joyful camaraderie, the excitement of being in Israel, surrounded by Jewish athletes from around the world, and the pride of being part of such an event, made the living conditions a mere inconvenience.

Waving our white cowboy hats to the crowd, the Canadian team did outstandingly

well in our events, winning many medals. I won a bronze in these games, and four years later, at the sixth Maccabiah Games, I won the gold – this, of course, after a torturous nine-day fast (just water and lemonade) to reach my weight requirement!

Not only was I rewarded with medals, but also with memories of Israel to last a lifetime.

Above: A proud moment. Syd Charendoff wins a gold medal in weightlifting for Canada in 1961. Israel wins silver and Switzerland, bronze.

Left: Syd Charendoff, flexing his muscles, 1961.

Field of Dreams

BY LARRY GREEN

What a magical moment in Israel in the summer of 1997 when I watched my three sons, Ricky, Bobby, and Mark, play baseball for Canada at the Maccabiah Games and win the gold medal. It was the first time in Maccabiah history that three brothers were on the field together.

When my youngest son, Ricky, pitched the gold-medal game against Mexico, the thrill I experienced was the greatest in all my years of playing and watching sports.

My only sadness was that my beautiful wife, Judi, couldn't be with me on the field in Kibbutz Gazer. In some ways, though, I could feel her there when our baby came through for us and drove in the winning run.

Above: Three brothers strike gold! From left to right: Bobby, Mark, and Ricky Green, members of the winning Canadian baseball team, 1997.

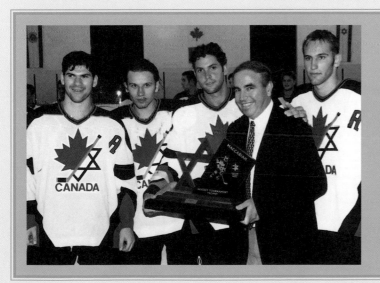

They shoot, they score the gold! Canadians, left to right: **Aaron Brand** (Toronto), **Mikhail Nemrofsky** (Toronto), **Harold Hersh** (Montreal), and **David Nemrofsky** (Toronto) receiving their trophy from **Yossi Goldberg**, mayor of Metulla.

Robert Palter, right, sailed to a silver medal in the 1989 Maccabiah Games.

A Journey with My Mother

BY HESH TROPER

My first glimpse of Israel was in the late spring of 1951. A year or so earlier, my older brother had made aliyah. He wrote home that he had fallen in love and planned to marry. He wanted family from Toronto with him at his wedding. My mother quickly arranged to go, and while my father stayed home, I went with her. I was only nine years old.

Getting to Israel from Toronto in 1951 was no simple matter. It took more than two weeks, mostly by ship. For a working-class family like mine, this trip also represented more than a huge financial outlay; in retrospect, I now understand that for my mother the trip was a daunting undertaking. She was an immigrant to Canada, but her integration into Canadian society was uneven at best. Her proximate world was almost completely and insularly Jewish. She was more or less comfortable speaking English but could barely read and write it. Yiddish was spoken at home. She was hesitant about encounters with the non-Jewish world, not so much out of fear as discomfort. It was just not her place. And travel? We didn't have a car, and the drive to Pontypool in the summer was a big trip for her. So a two-week journey halfway around the world must

have seemed an intimidating prospect and only undertaken out of the deepest love for her son now in Israel.

My childhood memories of the trip have blurred, but some things stand out. I recall the train to Montreal, then the seemingly endless hours until we boarded another train to Quebec City and the waiting ship. I remember it was dark when we boarded the SS *Atlantic*, an Italian liner. I don't recall much about the week-long Atlantic crossing to La Havre in France except that the ship was grand and breakfast my favourite meal. I think my mother was lonesome on the Atlantic crossing. I don't recall her making friends.

Once in La Havre, we took a train for Paris. I don't recall where we stayed in Paris or how my mother negotiated her way around the huge city without knowing French, but I do remember seeing the Eiffel Tower and my mother talking to people in Yiddish.

After several days, we boarded a train for Rome, and after a day or so in the Italian capital, it was another train to

---

Above: Hesh Troper.

Naples, where we boarded a small Israeli ship, the *Negba*, which had been among the first reparations payments from Germany to the new State of Israel.

The *Negba* was already full when we boarded. In addition to a small group of North American youth making aliyah, including several from Toronto, there were Europeans, probably Holocaust survivors, and Moroccan Jews, part of a larger exodus then beginning. I don't recall interaction with the Moroccans. I believe they ate separately. Anyway, few passengers likely felt very social for most of the five-day voyage. The small ship was hit by a major storm and bounced around the Mediterranean like a cork for four days. Many passengers, me included, became seasick. The storm delayed our scheduled Friday-morning arrival until after dark. I recall standing with my mother at a crowded railing and looking into the darkness, straining for that first sight of land. All of a sudden there was one light, then another and another. The ship broke out in celebration. Staccato whistles and shouts from among the Moroccan women mingled with a spontaneous eruption of *Hatikvah* by Europeans and North Americans. All the while, the ship seemed to be heading directly into an expanding constellation of lights, the bejewelled cityscape of Haifa rising out of the water and climbing the seaward slope of Mt. Carmel.

Somewhere amid all those lights on shore was my brother. But a reunion would have to wait. The ship would not dock until after Shabbat, but on board the sense of joy was unbroken. We were in Israeli waters. My mother held me close as the *Negba* laid anchor in Haifa's outer harbour. I looked up at her. She was not crying, but there were tears streaming down her face.

———————————

Background: Hesh Troper, age nine, in Israel, 1951.

The Inspiration of Israel in Every Note I Play

BY DANIEL DOMB

It was 1954, and Haifa was buzzing with excitement over the arrival of the Israel Philharmonic for a series of concerts at Armon Concert Hall.

Music filled my family's life; I heard chamber music played in our home every evening, featuring the legendary Russian cellist Nikolai Mutman. I was already studying violin, but one night Mutman let me play the open strings of the cello. It gave me goose bumps, and my dream of playing the cello began.

When we went to hear the Israel Philharmonic, there was my dream in front of me: the virtuoso French cellist Paul Tortelier. I was mesmerized.

The weeks rolled on, and then the most incredible news arrived: Paul Tortelier had fallen in love with Israel and was moving with his family to live at Kibbutz Ma'abarot. My family excitedly discussed whether we dared to ask for an audience with this great man. We often drove by the kibbutz on our way from Haifa to Tel Aviv, and one day, without warning, my father turned in through its gates. Soon my mother and I were sitting in front of the kibbutz's secretary, telling him all about my desire to play the cello and my life's wish to study with the great member of their kibbutz, Paul Tortelier. The secretary clearly thought we had a lot of chutzpah to make such a request, and was disinclined even to let us talk to him. But we prevailed, and after hearing me play the violin, Tortelier announced that he would indeed, for the first time in his life, teach a beginning student.

Now, many years later, when I start my day by tuning my cello, my thoughts turn to those early days in Haifa: to Mutman, who first let me play the strings of the cello; to the vibrant musical life in Haifa; and of course to Tortelier, in his days at Kibbutz Ma'abarot.

Postcript: Daniel Domb became principal cellist with the Toronto Symphony Orchestra in 1974. His solo appearances have included the New York Philharmonic and recitals in Carnegie Hall.

Left: After studying earlier with the French cellist Paul Tortelier, Daniel, left, is reunited with his teacher at Jeunesse Musicales, Mt. Orford, Quebec, 1959.

Lights of Freedom

BY EDNA DISHY

Every year, when I light the first candle of Chanukah, surrounded by my three sons and six grandchildren, I think back to the first time I celebrated Chanukah in the land of Israel.

I lived as a child in Egypt, where being Jewish was no easy task. I vividly recall walking to school and having other children call out insults. We were never allowed to walk by ourselves, especially not at night. But when I was fifteen, three weeks before the start of Chanukah, my family moved to Israel. I will never forget the thrill of being able to stand together in our home and light the candles in full view of the neighbours. But an even more amazing experience was yet to come.

After lighting the candles I went for a walk with my two sisters, Chana and Saleen. We had been walking for a few minutes when a truck full of teenagers passed by and invited us on board. My sisters and I looked at each other, not sure what to do. We heard Hebrew being spoken, and that was enough to reassure us, so we jumped onto the truck.

Soon we arrived at the centre of town, and everyone jumped out of the truck, laughing and singing. We saw that the town square had been lit with huge torches to symbolize Chanukah candles, and it was filled with hundreds of teenagers in a festive mood. Some people sang or played musical instruments, while others began to dance.

At first I just stood there, unable to move. Was this allowed? Then, suddenly, I was in the centre of a group of people dancing the horah. For a moment, I actually felt frightened. Then I saw that all the people encircling me were smiling and happy. All of them were Jews, the brothers and sisters I had for my whole life longed to see. In the midst of all this excitement and celebration, I realized that I was free. I was a Jew, and no one here would ever condemn me for it. I had never felt so proud.

*Right: Edna Dishy, loving
her new home in Israel, 1956.*

It Was an Exciting Time

FROM A CONVERSATION WITH ALLEN STERN

I would say that my underlying reason for immigrating to Israel in 1966 had more to do with my career as a pilot than with my Jewish background. It was the exciting prospect of going to a relatively young country that I thought needed me, although I also thought it would be a very comfortable environment for me as a Jew. So, I trotted off to see the Jewish Agency in Toronto, and in a short time they found a position for me.

One of the exciting things about being in Israel in those years was that it was still a developing country, in terms of technology in agriculture, and many other industries, so the work I was doing – spraying crops by airplane – was considered a very, very important profession. You have to spray the length of the field and fly into the wind, and so, in many of the fields, there was no option except to cross the border into Jordan. The Israel Defence Forces sent us armoured vehicles, and to protect us they would position them in the field while we sprayed.

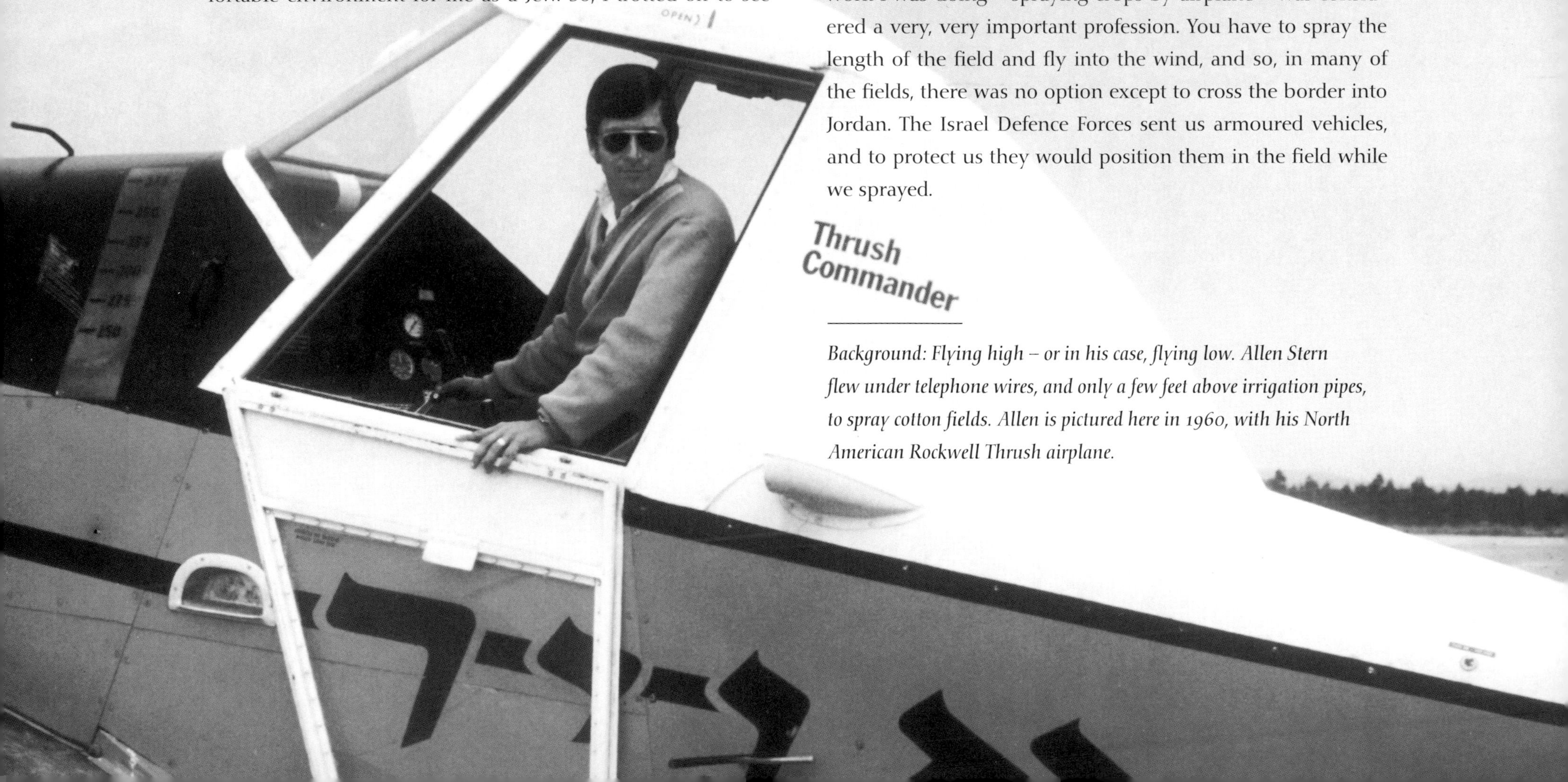

Thrush Commander

Background: Flying high – or in his case, flying low. Allen Stern flew under telephone wires, and only a few feet above irrigation pipes, to spray cotton fields. Allen is pictured here in 1960, with his North American Rockwell Thrush airplane.

Their Enthusiasm for Life!

BY MICHAEL G. SHULMAN

I had just spent five days in London in 1959, meeting my late grandfather's family for the first time, when my cousin Bob exclaimed, "You cannot think of returning to Toronto without visiting Israel!" I had just finished a three-and-a-half-month bicycling trip through Europe and was anxious to return home and tell all my stories, but within forty-eight hours I was on a student flight to Israel.

When the pilot announced, "Ladies and gentlemen, on the left side of the aircraft you can see the lights of Tel Aviv," it was a very emotional moment. Several people began to cry, and a number of young men congregated at the back of the plane to say prayers.

Once through Security at Lod International, I was directed to a Tel Aviv–destined bus. On the bus I met a friend from London, who suggested I stay with him at a cheap hotel in central Tel Aviv, off Dizengoff Street. Joseph, the owner, was a gruff little elderly man, who would wake us up each morning with a huge breakfast of fresh vegetables, cheese, coffee, and sweet rolls, accompanied by amazing personal stories.

D. Lou Harris, who was known in Canada as "Mr. Israel," was a family friend, and he quickly arranged a number of wonderful introductions for me. Murray Greenfield was the head of the Association for Canadians and Americans in Israel, which is not to be confused with the Association for Americans and Canadians, which he also ran, and for which he changed the sign on the door when an American visited. Murray was an expatriate from Brooklyn who had emigrated permanently to Tel Aviv, and for two days he drove and talked me non-stop around Israel in his old beat-up Peugeot. A dynamic Carl Alpert, head of the Technion, showed me just what could be accomplished by energetic, technically creative immigrant students. Eddie Gelber, a former Torontonian many decades my senior, excited me with his passionate vision for this young country.

In all, I spent two weeks in Israel, and I was intrigued and amazed to find how comfortable and at home I felt there. There was a rather naive freshness to the people – an extraordinary, outspoken pride in their accomplishments. They were full of enthusiasm for life. This trip as a teenager gave me a keen awareness of our Jewish history and culture and began my commitment to its continuity.

Above: Michael Shulman, age nineteen, visiting a remote Bedouin camp near Jericho, 1959.

The Greatest Contribution Is Yourself

BY RABBI REUBEN SLONIM

In 1948, upon the declaration of the new Jewish state, the publisher of the *Toronto Telegram* asked me to visit Israel and write a series of articles. At the time I was the rabbi of Beth Tzedec Synagogue and not yet on the staff of the newspaper, but I saw this as a great opportunity. I had the privilege of interviewing David Ben-Gurion, Moshe Dayan, Golda Meir, Moshe Sharret, and Abba Eban, among other worthies.

The *Telegram* wanted my reactions to the state as a Jew and as a rabbi. Since I had the official status of a visiting journalist from Canada, all doors were open to me. In those days, Israel wanted to reach the hearts and minds of Jews, especially those in North America, and this was an opportunity for them.

I was wonderstruck by Israel. In fact, in my book *Both Sides Now*, the title of the first chapter is "Wonderstruck." It was amazing to see Jews as citizens of their own state with the mechanisms to run it. It was as new and wonderful to Israelis as it was to me. Everybody acted as though they were celebrating a wedding. In a way they were. They were marrying the kind of bride they'd always hoped for.

After my first visit to Israel I was invited to become an associate editor and Middle East correspondent to the *Toronto Telegram*. Over the years I interviewed Ben-Gurion a number of times, and his first question to me was always, "When are you coming to settle in Israel?" But when my daughter married an Israeli and moved to Israel, he said, "You don't have to come any more. I have the best you have; your grandchildren will be Israelis."

That was the great watchword: settle in Israel. It is all right to contribute funds, but the best contribution is yourself. You must come to live here and build the land, especially if you have the language and the tradition and you have been loyal to that tradition all your life. Ben-Gurion was right!

Above: Rabbi Reuben Slonim, standing, and Abba Eban, Israeli foreign minister at the time, enjoying the moment, Toronto 1960.

Israel Exists in Sault Ste. Marie

BY MORLEY TORGOV

When I was a kid in Sault Ste. Marie, I was convinced that Palestine was created by the Manischewitz people. I imagined the deserts consisted of millions of acres of matzoh crumbs, and that the Red Sea was red because it was filled with fermented Concord grapes. I imagined, too, that Palestine was a land only religious fanatics would want to visit. After all, didn't our fathers repeat at every Passover, "*Next* year in Jerusalem; *this* year business is too good here at home"?

It was a joke . . . and it wasn't a joke. Our parents were immigrants from Eastern Europe upon whom the twentieth century had bestowed more than their share of catastrophes. By the early forties their fortunes had improved, and the saying "It's tough to be a Jew" was now recited more out of habit than hardship.

Then two things happened. Our local rabbi, claiming tenure, refused his critics' demand that he resign his post because he'd fallen behind the times. Not long after, disputes arose among the three trustees overseeing the construction of the congregation's first synagogue.

Both issues – the rabbinical employment contract and the building project – split the forty-odd Jewish families into two bitterly opposed camps. At the height of these controversies, High Holiday services were held in two separate locations in town. God, gazing down at the worshippers, must have wondered if they, too, were an invention of the Manischewitz people.

I exhume these memories because fractiousness has always been a part of our makeup. Despite Israel's wonders and accomplishments, an age of sweetness and light has yet to shed its glow upon us Jews. In the meantime, Israel, and Jews everywhere for that matter, are sharply divided on questions of Middle East peace and religious influence in government.

But here's the good news: Both Jewish communities – Israel's and Sault Ste. Marie's – have survived and are here to stay. In our shared experiences and characteristics, we are one. It requires no great stretch of the imagination to declare that Israel exists in Sault Ste. Marie, and Sault Ste. Marie exists in Israel.

Above: Morley Torgov, Sault Ste. Marie, c. 1944.

A Dream Come True

BY SELMA ZEITLIN SAGE

The summer of 1947, when I was fifteen years old, coloured my entire life. I spent it at a Hashomer Hatzair "training" camp. The purpose of the camp was to prepare young people to settle in kibbutzim and fight for freedom in Palestine. Although most of the group with whom I trained left hurriedly and clandestinely for Palestine, I stayed behind to study, take graduate degrees, raise a family, and pursue a career in Jewish education. When I was finally able to live in Israel, during that golden time after the 1967 war, I found that many of my group had been killed. Those who had survived were toughened and seemed to have aged beyond their years. Yet I envied them the years they had spent sharing the birth of Israel, difficult though they were.

I feel I have touched Jewish destiny in my lifetime. In the summer of 1996, I travelled Israel's sacred soil with my oldest granddaughter, walking where the prophets walked, in a Jerusalem authentic and golden. I feel privileged to have lived the dream that came true, and I pray that I shall be able to share the reality of that dream with each of my grandchildren.

Below: Selma Sage, right, with friend Carole Seiler Greenleaf at the Hechalutz "training" camp in Wappingers Falls, New York, 1947.

Ken Skolnik writes, "In 1965 I was a young man with a passion for Israeli folk dance, and I had to go to the source. At first it seemed strange to me that a Canadian folk dancer knew as many Israeli dances as the Israelis did themselves, or even more, until it was explained to me that a key thrust of Israeli folk dance was to forge cultural and emotional ties with the *chutzniks* [those from outside Israel]." Here, Ken Skolnik, left, leads a group in an Israeli dance workshop.

"**I** am a child of Holocaust survivors," writes **Frank Dimant**. "I am deeply involved in both the Zionist and general Jewish community. One of my most important commitments is to Betar, a Zionist Youth Movement, affiliated with the former right wing Herut Party in Israel.

"In 1967, I led a group of ten Betar volunteers to serve in the Six Day War. We were the first group of North Americans to come to Israel's aid.

"We were proud to visit the Kotel [Western Wall], once again a part of Israel. After the war our group went to lend our assistance to Kfar Szold, in the Galilee, a settlement badly damaged in battle. It was a cultural shock for this left wing kibbutz to welcome us, as we were Orthodox.

"Yet within days of our working side-by-side with the kibbutzniks, mutual respect was achieved. It also changed the policy of Kfar Szold, which, until this time, had only accepted non-Jewish volunteers." Pictured above is Frank Dimant, right, publisher of B'nai Birth's *Jewish Tribune*, shaking hands with **David Bar Ilan**, publisher of the *Jerusalem Post* (owned by Torontonian Conrad Black).

"**F**or my father, **Teddy Richmond**," recalls **Anne Richmond Golden**, "Israel was the symbol of the 'truth by which he ordered his being.' He believed completely in the worth of the Jewish People and had full confidence in their continued existence, both in the Diaspora and in Israel. He was very conscious of being part of a generation that had been witness to the death of a great period of Jewish history and the beginning of another, and viewed the creation and growth of Israel as a miraculous rebirth.

"He made many trips to Israel with my mother, Florence, and participated in numerous missions, several of which he led as head of Israel Bonds and the United Jewish Appeal, and as the Jewish National Fund Negev honouree. Each trip filled him with renewed commitment, enthusiasm, and optimism. He treasured hearing and meeting the great and colourful personalities who built Israel: Chaim Weizmann, Itzhak Ben-Zvi, David Ben-Gurion, Abba Eban, and Golda Meir. I remember him telling me about visiting Golda in her famous kitchen, and how impressed he was that she made and poured the tea herself!"

Michael Rosenberg, who survived World War II as a hidden child, and his wife, **Lily**, also a Holocaust survivor, first visited Israel in 1963. He writes, "We found ourselves sitting in a café and staring at passersby, trying to recognize someone we might have once known from our shtetl [Eastern European village]. And then a bus pulled up, and I recognized a woman I went to school with in my home town of Shevoyetz, Poland. Until that moment, I hadn't known she was still alive. It was an emotional reunion. On this same trip, my wife attended a reunion of women she had known in the camps."

"**I**srael and I have a special relationship," writes **Lindsay Gold Weiner**. "We were both born in 1948. As a participant in the Rabbi Eugene Weiner Hamilton Israel Summer Institute, I travelled to Israel in 1964 on the SS *Israel* on a study program with other high-school students. The most spiritual and profound moment of our trip came as we arose at 5:00 AM to watch our entry into the port of Haifa. That first glimpse of Israel, that mysterious yet familiar land, brought overwhelming tears to my eyes, and an unexpected joy to my heart. Never will I forget the incredible experience of the sunrise on our left and Israel on our right. The highlight of the trip for me occurred coincidentally on my sixteenth birthday, when our group spent a remarkable two hours with David Ben-Gurion." In the photo, Lindsay is second from the left in the back row of those seated.

Soldiers celebrating at the Western Wall after the Six Day War.

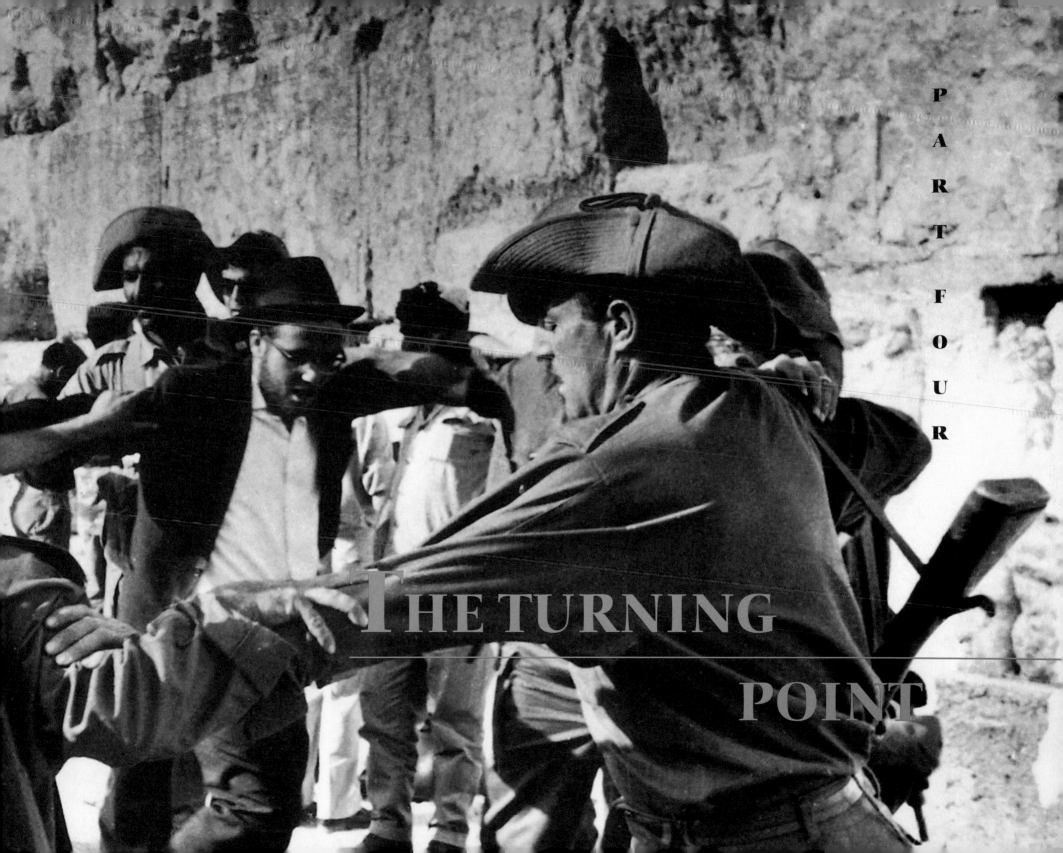

The Turning Point

The Making of a Campaign

FROM A CONVERSATION WITH BEN SCHNEIDER

I recall very distinctly what happened in 1967. I was executive vice-president of the United Jewish Welfare Fund at the time. On June 4, a national meeting of the United Israel Appeal was called in Montreal to discuss the implications of the continuing threat of war between Israel and its Arab neighbours. A delegation of about twenty-five Torontonians went to Montreal that Sunday morning, including Sam Sable and Ray Wolfe, Max Tanenbaum, Stephen Berger, and Morris Kaufman. They represented much of the top campaign leadership in the UJA at that time.

There was a motion made by some of the older leadership at the meeting, which was held at the Montefiore Club in Montreal, that we raise an additional ten million dollars for Israel above and beyond our 1967 UJA campaign. It was the young turks at the meeting, particularly those from Winnipeg and Murray Koffler from Toronto, who recommended that we raise twenty-five million dollars. Despite the objections of some older men (including, by the way, the late Sam Bronfman, who served as chairman at the meeting), the goal of twenty-five million was approved. The Toronto delegation

then went into a private session and raised a total of $875,000 within ten minutes.

The next day, war broke out, and the response by the Jewish community was amazing. By word of mouth and telephone, we arranged an emergency meeting on June 5 at the Park Plaza Hotel. This meeting attracted about two hundred people, and we raised two million dollars in a little over an hour. When we came out of the meeting we were swamped by the press, who wanted to know what had happened. The leadership was always reluctant at that time to seek or get publicity for the fund-raising activities of the Jewish community. We made it very clear that the money raised was to support Israeli resettlement programs

Above: Ben Schneider, left, and Al Green, breaking the ground for the new Lipa Green Building in Toronto that houses UJA Federation and many other Jewish community organizations, 1982. Ben, as always, works with the home front to help Israel in times of crisis.
Facing page: Israeli Prime Minister David Ben-Gurion brings admirers to their feet in enthusiastic support, Beth Tzedec Synagogue, 1968.

only. The total raised in Toronto in 1967 represented a high-water mark in Toronto fund-raising for Israel.

The Yom Kippur War in 1973 found the community better organized to cope with an emergency. When a delegation from Israel – led by then-treasurer Pinchas Sapir, Leon Dulchin, and the commander-in-chief of the armed forces, General Haim Laksov – came to town for a few hours, Murray Koffler, the campaign chairman that year, organized a last-minute meeting at the Skyline Hotel. About 2,500 people came out, and we conducted actual fund-raising at the hotel that lasted almost four hours. We raised a total of twenty-six million dollars for the Israel special campaign that year.

Throughout the 1960s, there was a constant flow of Israeli leadership visiting Toronto, including Ben Zvi, Golda Meir, Moshe Dayan, David Ben-Gurion, and a whole array of military figures. Whenever these Israeli leaders came to Toronto, we were sure to have massive turnouts to hear them speak. When Ben-Gurion was scheduled to come, he stopped in Montreal first. A group of sixty men rented a plane and flew there to bring him and his wife, Paula, to Toronto. A meeting was held at Beth Tzedec Synagogue to which the community was invited under conditions of very tight security. There was a lineup waiting for admission that stretched around the corner and halfway down the block. By the time the doors were closed, every seat in the sanctuary was occupied and there was no standing room left.

Of all the visits and meetings that were ever held in Toronto, what stands out most is the response to the wars in 1967 and 1973. These were emotionally charged and reflected a great concern for the survival of Israel.

The Six Day War

The Six Day War, in June 1967, was a turning point both for Israel and for Toronto's Jewish community. Within six days, Israel was transformed from a country on the verge of being "driven into the sea" into a military power that successfully repelled the forces of three invading Arab armies, from Egypt, Syria, and Jordan. In addition to giving the Israeli army buffer zones between itself and its Arab enemies, the Six Day War also led to the reunification of Jerusalem after nineteen years, as well as access to religious and historical places in biblical Judea and Samaria. Like Jewish communities everywhere, the Jews of Toronto rode the roller coaster of emotions associated with the war in 1967: from the sense of near-desperation as Egypt's President Gamal Abdal Nasser evicted UN peacekeepers from the Sinai and mobilized his troops for attack, to the tremendous pride felt over Israel's swift and decisive victory on the battlefield. The Jews of Toronto wept with every Israeli loss and celebrated with Israelis when the *shofar* (ram's-horn trumpet) was blown at the foot of the liberated Western Wall.

Making the Tourists Feel Safe

BY HARVEY WEINER

Thirty years ago, on my first trip to Israel, our itinerary brought us to beautiful Caesarea for a three-day visit.

While we were enjoying lunch at an outdoor café, we couldn't help but notice the continuous stream of army tanks going by. We jokingly remarked that, in order to make the tourists feel safe and protected, the same tanks probably just kept driving around and around the block.

After lunch, we arranged for a game of golf at a course that was lovely, but extremely noisy! Airplanes were flying overhead every few minutes, and as every golfer knows, that can be very distracting, especially while trying to putt! Then, when we were on the twelfth hole, the greens-keeper drove up and insisted that we finish our game quickly, since the course was about to be closed. Surprised, but trying to be courteous, we did as he asked.

When we returned to the clubhouse, we discovered the reason the course was closing: many of the employees would be going into the army the next day. Even then, we accepted these explanations as normal activities of Israeli life. After all, this was our first trip to Israel!

Little did we realize that Israel was on the eve of an amazing historical event. By the next day, we were on an airplane home – the Six Day War had broken out!

Below: Harvey Weiner, in front of the Shrine of the Book, Israel Museum, Jerusalem, 1967.

The Six Day War

A Wife's Story
BY ROSE SHTIBEL

When war broke out on June 5, 1967, I had airplane tickets for me and my daughters to come to Toronto. Fate changed my plans. My husband went into the army to fulfil his duties, and I ran with our daughters, Barbara and Iris, aged eight and two, to hide in the shelter in the basement of our building. The war sirens immediately reminded me of my childhood in World War II.

During the six days of the war, we spent a lot of time in the shelter. All of the women became very close. We were united, and we shared our fears, tragedies, and hopes. Every day neighbours were notified that a husband or father had been killed or wounded.

For sixty days after the war began, I did not hear from my husband. I worked hard in the overcrowded hospital and tried to live day by day. One day I answered the doorbell and saw a female officer at my door. I immediately concluded that my husband was dead, and I fainted. When I finally came to, the woman assured me that my husband was all right. She had been in the same military unit and told me that he sent regards and would be home soon. I considered myself very lucky.

Life changed in Israel after the Six Day War. Before, people considered others according to their country of origin. I was Polish. Others were Romanian, Hungarian, or Moroccan. The moment the war broke out, we were all Israelis united against the same enemy.

A Husband's Story
BY ADAM SHTIBEL

I was a child survivor of the Holocaust and remained in hiding in a village in Poland until December 1947. By 1967 I was living in Israel with my wife and our young daughters. I'll never forget the morning of June 5, 1967. I sent my wife and children to join the others in the basement shelter of our building, and I left

---

Above: Adam Shtibel, Jericho, June 1967.

Left: Rose Shtibel, in her bacteriology laboratory at Kaplan Hospital in Rehovot, c. 1967.

to join my army unit. I was ready to fight for the existence of our country, Israel.

I was stationed in Jericho for sixty days, during which time the process of exchanging prisoners took place. My duty was to be the personal driver to the military governor. I was driving him in a private car, a white Lark, which I disguised by covering it with dirt, mud, and sand so that it would not stand out. Our unit was responsible for bringing the occupied city of Jericho and the surrounding area to a livable state. When we first arrived there, we were shocked to see it looking like a ghost town. We were to make sure the water supply was safe and that the area had electricity.

Our unit was stationed in a house which belonged to King Hussein of Jordan. Very often, high military officials such as Moshe Dyan would come for meetings with the military governor. I was trusted to be present at all their important meetings, and I was proud to be of service to these senior officers. Today, I wish only that the dream of peace would become a reality.

_____

Background: "This exchange of prisoners," writes Adam Shtibel, "took place on the Allenby Bridge in 1967. The military governor was always present during these exchanges, and as his driver, so was I."

"**I** lived in Israel from 1967 to 1973," writes **Ira Teich**. "In that time I served in the Israel Defence Forces during the Six Day War and in the Tank Corps during the Yom Kippur War. One small event stands out particularly in my memory. In 1967, two months after the war, I was sitting in the back of an army pickup truck, travelling from my base in the southern Sinai to El Arish. Near El Arish, in the doorway of her small house, stood a young Arab girl, about six or seven years old, dressed in a bright red dress. As I passed, she looked at me and smiled. I waved to her and returned the smile. She responded with a wave and a sweet ear-to-ear grin. At that moment a woman appeared at the door. With the back of her hand she struck the child across the face. I can still hear that resounding slap and see that child falling down against the door post and onto the ground. And I will always feel some guilt for her pain. I cannot help thinking that somewhere there is a thirty-seven-year-old woman who received an early education in hatred." Ira Teich is pictured here in Israel, 1967.

You Don't Have to Be Jewish to Be a Zionist

FROM A CONVERSATION WITH DOUGLAS BASSETT

I can remember my grandfather Bassett, my father's father, telling me that he came over to Canada from the north of Ireland and was discriminated against by the Anglo-Saxon hoi polloi. So I grew up with prejudice, not against me personally, but you always heard about it. And you always heard about persecution of the Jews. Growing up in Sherbooke, Quebec, for instance, my Jewish friends were discriminated against. People would say, "Boy, do they ever look Jewish." I used to pull down my fly and say, "I'm just as Jewish as they are!"

I made my first of three visits to Israel in May 1961, at the time of the trial of Nazi war criminal Adolf Eichmann in Jerusalem. My parents had been there several times before; Israel is a holy land to the Christians and Muslims, as well as to the Jews. I was looking forward to the trip. My father was the publisher of the *Toronto Telegram* at the time, and our correspondent, Rabbi Reuben Slonim, was reporting on the trial on a daily basis.

There weren't any Holocaust museums in those times, you just heard about these bloody atrocities. It was hard to believe! I, as a Canadian, a Christian, thought it was just horrific. I was seated no further than thirty yards from Eichmann. It was just an unbelievable experience. Eichmann's

face was very hollow; he was dishevelled, and he didn't look like a person who was capable of doing what he did. He put on a good act, but it didn't fool the Israeli justices.

In 1982 I toured with Dan Perry of the Nature Reserves Authority. We went right through the north of Israel and into Lebanon. Bullets were flying all around us. It was a little nerve-racking, to say the least.

It's difficult for people who have not been to Israel to understand that Israel's enemies are so close. It's as though we are standing at the corner of Bay Street and Front Street in the city of Toronto, and our enemy – who wants to destroy our families and our country – is up at Yonge and Eglinton, with big guns pointed at us. They're also to the west, at the CNE, and they're out there on Lake Ontario. People just don't understand that: Israel's enemies are on all sides and are so close!

I have come to realize that you don't have to be Jewish to be a Zionist. I think everybody is entitled to a homeland, and to live in peace there.

Above: Douglas Bassett, 1990s.

Rafi

BY SHEILA RICHLER LANCIT

In June 1967 I was an eighteen–year–old student visiting Israel with my family, "in love" with a young man named Rafi, who worked on mine demolition. On our "dates," we would throw hand grenades into empty fields, collect empty bullet casings, and pick up young hitchhikers from Germany, France, and America in an army Jeep. Every time we passed soldiers, we would stop the Jeep and get out and cheer them.

After I returned to Canada, I didn't hear from Rafi, and I wrote to his friend Yossi to find out why this seemingly sincere young man hadn't written. Yossi replied that Rafi had been seriously injured while detonating a mine. He had hundreds of metal splinters in his body and was totally blind; the injuries had also affected him emotionally. I felt useless, far away in Canada, until finally I decided to call the Combined Jewish Appeal to canvass in their college division so I could be of some help. Thirty years later, I am still canvassing. And I still remember Rafi – the last I heard of him, he was in America, learning how to use a seeing–eye dog.

Above: Sheila Richler Lancit and Rafi on the beach in Tel Aviv, 1967.

Mandy Sharf writes, "This photograph was taken at the Straits of Tiran. I'm standing on a gun that had been placed by the Egyptians to stop Israeli shipping from going up the Gulf of Aqaba. This was a provocation for the Six Day War in 1967."

Menachem Begin and **Moishe Dayan**, on the balcony of the historic King David Hotel, Jerusalem, August 1967, caught in a private moment by **Libby Rosenberg**'s camera. Perhaps they are discussing their recent victory.

An ICBM missile, captured from Egypt during the Six Day War, displayed during a parade in Israel commemorating the twentieth anniversary of Independence. Photographed by **Harold Green**.

The Toronto Jewish community rallies for Israel to show their sympathy and support during the Gulf War, Beth Tzedec Synagogue, 1991.

PART FIVE

ORT ISRAEL

A SENSE OF
MISSION

Operation Exodus

The Road to Freedom

BY WENDY HERMAN EISEN

I was born in Toronto a few years before the birth of the State of Israel, into a family imbued with Zionistic ideals. My parents, Alice and Bernard Herman, worked tirelessly to raise funds for a country called Palestine.

A personal allegiance to Israel was formed in 1966, when I travelled there with my parents. It was strengthened five years later, during a leadership mission to Israel under the auspices of Montreal's Combined Jewish Appeal.

My commitment to Israel was permanently forged in the mid-1970s, when I joined the global campaign to liberate Jews from the Soviet Union. It was then that I became acutely aware of the significance of Israel as a homeland for Jews who had no place else to go.

"Next year in Jerusalem" became the cry of Soviet Jews whose religious and cultural initiative, stifled for six decades under the rule of communism, was revived by Israel's victory in the Six Day War. That cry became mine, as I, and fellow members of the "Montreal 35s," took to the streets in protest.

The Montreal, Toronto, and Winnipeg 35s were part of an international activist women's group for Soviet Jewry. Named in 1971 for a thirty-five-year-old Soviet Jewish female prisoner, the group advocated for the right of Soviet Jews to emigrate to Israel.

The inalienable right to repatriate to one's homeland was guaranteed by the 1948 United Nations International Declaration of Human Rights and reinforced in 1975, when delegates from thirty-five nations met in Helsinki, Finland, to draft the Helsinki Accords. Among its many assurances, this agreement included a commitment to humanitarian concerns and the right to family reunification.

Above: Moscow, Yom Ha'atzmaut, April 1988. Left to right: Yuli Kosharovsky, a refusenik for seventeen years, Wendy Eisen, Irving Abella, and Vladimir Kislik, another long-term refusenik. Facing page: Operation Exodus. Wendy Eisen greets new immigrants from the former Soviet Union at Ben-Gurion Airport, October 1990.

As a signatory to the Helsinki Accords, the Soviet Union and its authorities were obliged to accept official invitations sent from Israel, requesting emigration visas for Soviet Jews.

Some Jews who applied received permission to emigrate, but most such requests were denied. Those refused emigration visas became known as "refuseniks."

Strained American–Soviet relations made it increasingly difficult for Jews in the West to communicate with refuseniks. The Soviets did their best to squelch the burgeoning aliyah movement by jamming telephone lines and Western radio broadcasts, and through a vociferous campaign of anti–Israel propaganda in the Soviet press.

As global advocacy for Soviet Jewry escalated, my commitment intensified. I recall my feelings of compassion, when, in 1975 in Jerusalem, I met Avital Sharansky. The desperate young woman spoke passionately about her husband, Anatoly (Natan), whom she had left in Moscow one day after their marriage. She clung to the promise made by Soviet emigration authorities that he would soon join her in Israel.

At that time Avital could not have imagined Natan's activity on behalf of human rights would lead, in 1977, to his arrest and subsequent prison sentence – and separate them for nine painful years. Nor could she have imagined the extent of the global campaign that would evolve on his behalf.

As East–West relations eased by the spring of 1978, nine Jewish prisoners, sentenced in the 1970 Leningrad trials, were released from prisons and labour camps. The interviews I conducted with them in Israel prompted me to record their gruelling experiences in *Jewish Voices from the Soviet Gulag*, published by Keren Hayesod in Jerusalem.

At no time did I feel the passion of Israel more dramatically than in December 1978, when I travelled with a fellow activist to the Soviet Union. In the privacy of cramped apartments, the refuseniks spoke of their dream of aliyah – and of how it was eluding them. As our tear-filled eyes met, we discussed their plight and devised plans to secure their release.

When I moved back to Toronto from Montreal in 1981, I continued to work on behalf of Soviet Jewry through the Toronto 35s and the Canadian Jewish Congress. Our committees linked synagogues, churches, and charitable organizations with individual refuseniks and prisoners. We co-ordinated

Above: Poet Irving Layton leads a Passover freedom march on behalf of Soviet Jewish prisoners, April 1980. Wendy Eisen, centre, represents Ida Nudel.

marches, rallies, demonstrations, petitions, letter-writing campaigns, and hunger strikes. We implored parliamentarians and other prominent Canadians to wield their influence with Soviet officials.

In the late 1980s, after two decades of pressure from the free world, the Iron Curtain began to part – and Soviet Jews commenced their long-delayed journey home.

But activists could not yet cease their efforts. For many long-term refuseniks, like Elena Keis, Israel was still an illusion. When several Canadians met with Keis in April of 1988 in her Leningrad apartment, we decided that her poignant poetry might be the vehicle by which the Toronto Jewish Women's Federation could champion her case. Elena Keis's poems sparked an energetic international campaign. Within six months she held a tearful reunion with her family in Israel.

On that trip I shared Israel's fortieth anniversary celebrations with eminent refuseniks in a small flat in Moscow. During the festivities, Jewish Agency chairman Simcha Dinitz telephoned from Jerusalem. "All of Israel is together," he declared, "hoping for an end to the problems in our country. We have just lit forty torches on Mount Herzl. We are with you in your struggle – as you are with us in ours. We are one people."

The ultimate victory for Soviet Jewry activists came on October 26, 1989, when an El Al flight arrived in Tel Aviv carrying 205 Soviet Jews. What had begun as a trickle in the early 1970s had become an exodus of historic proportions. To date, Operation Exodus has brought almost one million Soviet Jews to their historic homeland.

The magnitude of the success of the Soviet Jewry rescue movement inspired me to write a book about the role of Canadians in the global struggle. *Count Us In: The Struggle to Free Soviet Jews* was published in 1995 by Burgher Books.

On October 18, 1995, David Berger, Canada's ambassador to Israel, hosted an event at his Israeli residence for Canadian Jewish leaders, Israelis, and dozens of former refuseniks and prisoners who had gathered to celebrate the book's publication. At that moment, I felt a closing of the circle around Diaspora Jewry, Soviet Jewry, and Israel. I felt exceedingly proud to be a Jew.

Above: Wendy Eisen and the 35s served typical "soviet prison fare" during a demonstration in Montreal, October 1979.

Their Struggle for Aliyah Was Our Struggle

BY GENYA INTRATER

I was born in Moscow and came to Palestine at a very young age. The language at school was Hebrew, but at home we spoke Russian. My parents insisted that I read all the Russian classics in our library. When I said to my father I would rather spend the time learning Spanish or Italian, since Russian was a language spoken behind the Iron Curtain and therefore useless, my father, a Moscow intellectual, exclaimed, "How can you say that? You will be able to read Tolstoy, Dostoyevsky, and Pushkin in the original!" And he was right.

When the exodus of Jews from Russia began, I was a student at the University of Toronto, not really aware of the great significance of this event until the Israeli consul from New York came to Toronto to see me. He told me that Soviet Jews, who had been the "Jews of Silence," were now starting an aliyah movement, demanding their right to emigrate to their ancestral homeland. He also told me that the Soviets, while assuring the world that Jews could go to Israel for the purpose of family reunification, had created the classification of "refuseniks" – those forbidden to leave the country until their knowledge of state secrets became obsolete. These refuseniks were fired from their jobs and made into pariahs because their

requests for emigration were interpreted as acts of disloyalty to the communist state.

Some refuseniks were sentenced to prison terms on trumped-up charges and became "Prisoners of Zion." The refuseniks and the Prisoners of Zion were very visible because of their demands for the right to aliyah. Their only hope was support from abroad.

The Israeli consul told me that my knowledge of the Russian language could be put to good use. He gave me a list of names and phone numbers, and suggested that I telephone refuseniks and families of Prisoners of Zion. The calls were to give them moral support, but also to get information about their activities and needs and the persecution they were experiencing. Another reason was to let the KGB, who were monitoring the calls, know that Western democracies were aware of these people and their plight and that their stories were being publicized

---

Above: Ida Milgrom, left, mother of Anatoly Sharansky, Barbara McDougall, middle, then minister of external affairs, and Genya Intrater, right, making representation to the government of Canada on behalf of Soviet Jews. Ottawa, March 1987.

Soviet dissident Anatoly (Natan) Sharansky, left, is escorted by U.S. Ambassador Richard Burt after Sharansky crossed the border at Glienicker Bridge in Berlin, during an East-West spy and prisoner exchange, February 11, 1986.

in the media all over the world, discouraging the government from any attempt to make them "disappear."

For political reasons, the Israeli government was reluctant to telephone the refuseniks from Israel. Someone like me, fluent in Hebrew and Russian, calling from Toronto, was considered to be the right candidate for this task. Thus began my work on behalf of Soviet Jews, primarily to support their right to aliyah.

In 1973 I was among the first Westerners to go to Moscow, Leningrad, and Kiev to visit refuseniks. Meeting those brilliant scientists and professionals – out of work, living in constant danger of being arrested and sent to the Gulag, totally dependent on us for their livelihood and support of their struggle for aliyah – made a profound impression on me. I knew then that I would dedicate every moment of my life to save them. After all, I had been born there, too.

A great hero of the aliyah movement was Anatoly (Natan) Sharansky, whom we affectionately called Tolik. Right after their wedding, his wife, Avital, was allowed to leave, and I met her in Jerusalem. I promised her I would do everything I could for her husband until he could join her in Israel.

At that time I was the head of the Soviet Jewry movement in Canada. I used to telephone Natan and his friends and then disseminate their information. I was also in touch with Avital wherever she was. We organized petitions, demonstrations, sit-ins, and hunger strikes. We lobbied our governments and met with representatives of the thirty-five nations who had signed the Helsinki Accords.

Sharansky, a very effective aliyah activist, was sentenced to thirteen years for spying. The outrage of this unjust sentence

reverberated all over the free world. After nine years in the Gulag, he was exchanged for a Soviet spy and joined his wife, mother, and brother in Jerusalem.

All through the nine years of Natan's incarceration, his Toronto family and I telephoned his family in Moscow every weekend. Their every visit to Natan, his letters, his hunger strikes, and every word he told them, were immediately publicized worldwide as a result of these phone calls. We did what the refuseniks and Prisoners of Zion told us to do. "The fate of Soviet Jews does not depend on the KGB; it depends on you," said Natan during one of our telephone conversations. We took these words very seriously.

On television, the world witnessed the triumph of Natan's homecoming and his reunification with his beloved Avital. They became the proud parents of two daughters and at last were able to live a normal life in Jerusalem.

Above: Avital and Anatoly Sharansky share a special moment at Ben-Gurion Airport, 1986.

"**I** am the supervisor of the Community Integration Program (CIP) of the Jewish Immigrant Aid Services (JIAS) at the Bathurst Jewish Centre," writes **Ludmilla Felik**. "I arrived in Canada with my family in 1988, having emigrated from the former Soviet Union to Israel eleven years earlier. When we first moved to Canada, we were alone, without family or friends. Several years later, a Canadian friend invited me to help prepare a Chanukah celebration for recent Russian immigrants. As a person who speaks Hebrew and Russian, I could be a great help. This event was the beginning of it all. I learned about the Toronto Jewish community and became part of it, largely through the efforts of **Susan Goldberg** and **Marsha Slavens**. Only then did I begin to feel at home in my new surroundings, and I wanted to help those who were in the same predicament I had been in, only a few years before.

"We, the CIP staff and volunteers, try to involve people in Jewish culture. Many immigrants in the program did not have the opportunity to identify themselves as Jews in Russia, since synagogues were closed and they were not permitted to study Hebrew or to learn about Judaism. Here in Canada they are free to express themselves, and we help them to do this."

Ludmilla Felik, right, is shown with her husband, **Alex**, and daughter, **Galit**.

"**T**he Russian aliyah to Israel," recalls **Gerald Sheff**, "reached its height in the early 1990s, with as many as four planes full of immigrants arriving daily. However, I witnessed a much different scene in 1974. In those early days, the Russian aliyah was just a trickle, and people never knew when planes were going to come in. On the night we were leaving Israel to come back to Toronto, we met a group of Russian *olim* in one of the holding areas of Ben-Gurion Airport.

"There were a couple hundred people, frightened and full of apprehension. We felt invasive with our fancy clothes and cameras. There was no commonality at all until some of us started singing *Shalom Aleichem*. Some of them started humming, because they didn't know the words, and some started crying and embracing and dancing. They danced with us, we danced with them, there was kissing and hugging, and it was like crossing a bridge of a hundred years. It was really amazing. I still find it emotional all these years later."

Gerry Sheff, right, is pictured with Prime Minister **Yitzhak Rabin** in Jerusalem.

SECTION II

Taking Action

How Na'amat's Adopt-a-Child Began

BY LOUISE CORNBLUM

The year was 1960. My husband, Murray, and I were on our first trip to Israel. When we arrived in Haifa we phoned the staff of Omna, a Pioneer Women/Na'amat residential care facility for abused or traumatized children. We arranged to have shoes bought for every child.

The next day I was kneeling in front of a chair at Omna, buckling leather sandals onto one little pair of feet after another, smiling into curious eyes and loving it. I didn't realize then that the children were not really smiling back.

Murray and I began to walk from room to room with the staff, surrounded by an escort of little boys who solemnly watched our every move. One in particular stayed close to me, his eyes riveted on my face. I felt his longing, his need for recognition. On impulse I knelt down and extended my arms to him, and without hesitation he threw himself against me, hugging with all his might.

Suddenly all of the other children leaped on me, all trying to embrace me at once. I was thrown back against a wall,

and there I sat on the floor, hugging and hugging as the tears rolled down my face.

I asked myself, what kind of people work here, to neglect these children so badly? Then I looked up at the faces of the staff. They were crying as much as I was. It wasn't their fault. Years of abuse are not quickly overcome.

Later they told me that the first little boy was named Eres. No family ever came to visit him. He was never taken home for Shabbat. Perhaps that was why he was so eager that the visitor from abroad should notice him. I felt completely helpless. What could I do, in Canada, to help him?

Someone had the answer for me. Sylvia Mirsky (who had been one of the founders of Toronto Pioneer Women in 1925)

Above: Yitzhak Rabin, left, then Israel's minister of defence, with Murray and Louise Cornblum at the Na'amat March for Peace, 1988.
Facing page: Louise Cornblum, buckling new sandals onto little pairs of feet at the Omna Care Facility, 1960.

had also visited Omna that summer. Sylvia was a dynamic woman whose devotion to Israel had included travelling there from Toronto in the spring of 1948 to stand with the new state's defenders on the front line.

Sylvia suggested that people in North America could financially adopt children who, like Eres, needed Na'amat's care. This would be a spiritual adoption of a symbolic child, not of any specific child. The "parents" would gain their sense of participation by knowing that they were sharing significantly in the cost of caring for a child in need.

This is how "Adopt–a–Child" was born. For Murray and me, it was perfect. We became the first "spiritual parents." In our hearts, the child we adopted was Eres.

Actions Speak Louder than Words

BY MURRAY KOFFLER

This year my family and I celebrate forty years of involvement with the State of Israel. We feel very fortunate to have been able to play our small part in so many exhilarating and creative ways.

My first introduction to Israel was in 1956. I'd joined the UJA study mission from Canada and was so enthusiastic that I agreed to be chairman of the pharmacy division of the UJA campaign that year. It was a stimulating experience, one that resulted in yearly, sometimes twice–yearly, trips to Israel. Along with this came a firm commitment to the growth of the State of Israel. My wife, Marvelle, and I have worked on its behalf ever since.

Perhaps the most rewarding experience for Marvelle and me has been our involvement with the Weizmann Institute

of Science, recognized as one of the major scientific research centres in the world. In the early 1960s, Meir Weisgall, then its president, visited Toronto and asked me to establish a committee of Weizmann friends and supporters from Canada. This led to the establishment, in 1963, of the Canadian Society for the Weizmann Institute, which I chaired until 1984. I became a member of the board of governors of the institute itself in 1974 and am currently its chairman emeritus.

Above: Murray Koffler, after receiving an honorary doctorate in Philosophy from the Weizmann Institute, is shown standing proudly in front of the Koffler Accelerator Building on the institute's campus, 1976.

Marvelle and Murray Koffler, August 1991.

In 1988 Marvelle helped establish a committee known as Women for Science. This initiative, now operating in Israel and nine other countries in the Diaspora, has been extremely successful in expanding interest in the Weizmann Institute and in research related to women's concerns.

I've also been involved in Israel's economy. In 1975 I led the Canadian mission to the second Economic Conference in Jerusalem, which focused not only on investment, but also on how to bring practical experience from abroad to aid Israel's developing economy. I led by example, with the opening of the first Superpharm retail pharmacy in 1978, modelled after Shoppers Drug Mart. My son Leon, who lives in Israel with his wife and three sabra (Israel-born) children, oversees Superpharm, which now boasts over sixty retail outlets.

Sports and recreation – in particular the development of the Israel Tennis Centres, an initiative supported by friends from all over the world – is yet another exciting area in which I've had the pleasure of working.

Each time my family and I visit Israel, we have the joy of seeing some of the initiatives we have helped bring to fruition.

Above: Murray Koffler chatting with Golda Meir, Israel, 1976.

Tennis, Everyone?

The Canadian involvement with the Israel Tennis Centre was born in 1977 when Ralph Halbert, Lionel Schipper, Alex Fisher, Harold Green, and I realized that tennis would be a natural medium to bring children together in Israel. We hoped that tennis could become the means for children of diverse backgrounds and cultures to learn that they had more in common than they thought. In fact, because our main purpose was to work with children, we eventually dropped the "tennis" from our name and are now known as the CICC, Canada–Israel Children's Centre.

Now we have thirteen centres across Israel and over 120 coaches, among them more than twenty who were coaches and tennis instructors in Russia. Five thousand children a day come to our centres, including over a thousand Russian immigrants. We have special programs for Bedouin children in Beersheba and a program for children in wheelchairs. The Israel Tennis Centres were awarded the Israel Peace Prize – not for sports, but as recognition of the social impact that tennis has had on Israel. It was a great honour to receive that award.

Above: The ribbon-cutting ceremony for the Canada–Israel Tennis Centre. Left to right: Budgie and Joe Frieberg, Norma and Lester Rosenberg, and Reuben Josephs.

Below: Enthusiastic Canadian fans at the Israel Tennis Centre, 1991. From left to right: Joe Frieberg, Ken Moore, Harold and Miriam Green, Malka and Al Green.

That Was the Way He Felt

My husband Phil's first trip to Israel was in 1952, when he accompanied the Canadian Maccabiah team as chargé d'affaires. He found it to be such a profoundly exciting and stimulating experience that he went on to visit Israel forty times in several capacities involving different and extremely worthwhile Israeli causes. As a member of parliament he was proud to represent Canada at the state funeral of Prime Minister Levi Eshkol. When president of the Canadian Zionist Federation for twelve years, he chaired its one and only convention ever held in Israel, in 1976. When the busloads of delegates arrived at the Hilton Hotel we greeted them with our freshly made snowman – the weatherman had obliged the Canadians with one of Israel's rare snow falls!

During his term as mayor of Toronto, from 1963 to 1966, Phil was privileged to receive many Israeli dignitaries, who were so pleased to be welcomed by the Jewish mayor of such a vibrant and sophisticated city.

I accompanied Phil to Israel about thirty times, and was always astonished to see such amazing progress and tremendous changes taking place. Over the years I watched the Western Wall's visiting space develop from a narrow alley to the vast expanse of the great square that it now is.

In 1982 Phil wrote to the Israeli government, asking them to send him a flag that had flown in the Knesset; he had already received a Canadian flag that had flown atop Parliament Hill. When his time came, he wanted to be buried with both flags covering his casket, symbolizing the two countries that he loved and served so well. I put those flags in safe-keeping until I fulfilled his wishes on November 30, 1995. That was the way he felt.

Above: Min and Phil Givens.

Left: Israeli and Canadian flags together, as Phil Givens wished.

A Magical Learning Experience

FROM A CONVERSATION WITH JACK ROSE

In the mid-sixties I was very involved with a Jewish Young Leadership Development program, which is what first stimulated my interest in going to Israel. I finally arrived in Israel at the end of May 1967, only to witness great movements of tanks, military machinery, and personnel through the entire country. It was no shock to me when the Six Day War began on June 6. Yet the Israelis I was with exuded such confidence that I felt surprisingly safe. My dedication to Israel deepened on this trip, and I was set on a life-long path of commitment to its well-being.

It was thrilling for me to be in Israel during the signing of the Jordanian agreement (pictured below) to begin the peace process in October 1994. The Israelis and Jordanians were all mingling happily. It was a very emotional moment. *Left to right, seated: Prime Minister Yitzhak Rabin, President Bill Clinton, Prime Minister Abdul Salam Majali of Jordan. Behind Prime Minister Majali stands King Hussein of Jordan. Shimon Peres stands on the far right.*

As president of the United Appeal of Canada in 1975, I had an ex officio seat on the board of the Jewish Agency, of which Keren Hayesod is a part. That began a long term, which only recently ended, in June 1997. This was a magical learning experience for me. I sat and argued and resolved issues with some of the giants of the Jewish world. *Left to right: Israel's President Yitzhak Navon, Phil Granovsky, Jack Rose.*

Menachem Begin, who had just become prime minister, asked at a Keren Hayesod meeting if the Jewish Agency would undertake an urban-renewal program that subsequently became Project Renewal. Phil Granovsky and I asked Mr. Begin if he would launch the worldwide campaign on a visit to Canada. Knowing that we had to have a totally different kind of approach for this project, we decided to twin Canadian cities with cities and communities in Israel. Toronto was very supportive and its program became one of the most successful urban-renewal projects ever undertaken. This photo was taken when Prime Minister Menachem Begin visited Ottawa to kick off Project Renewal (International) in 1978. *Jack Rose is on the left.*

Project Renewal

BY ADRIENNE OFFMAN

In 1979 Menachem and Aliza Begin came to dinner. In her husky voice Aliza Begin told me her husband had come to propose a daunting task for all of us in the Diaspora: Project Renewal. In Israel there were communities that had made little economic and social progress since their settlement in the late 1940s and early 1950s, and we were being asked to provide not only our dollars to these communities, but also our hands-on expertise in guiding their renewal.

Our first community was Beit Dagan, situated across from Lod International airport. It had garbage thrown on the roads and piled in yards, and a subculture of drugs and violence. No one wanted to live there, let alone venture out at night.

Many years later this has become a real community: it is free of drugs, and children go to college, serve proudly in the army, and return to settle and rear their own families. They know how to hold their heads up high because of the progress the community has made.

There were years of heated discussions between us, in which our cultural and language differences appeared. For instance, we were funding a community centre, which we North Americans believed should have a multi-purpose social

hall. Beit Dagan representatives envisioned a room much like a theatre. We couldn't understand this and resisted for a long time. They wore us down and we finally agreed. A community centre was built that became a magnet for people from the entire region, is financially independent, and, through its activities, won a cultural award for Beit Dagan.

It is a privilege to be a Zionist, not only in heart and pocketbook, but also through work with the citizens of Israel themselves. Certainly, the renewal of neighbourhoods was our target and great results were achieved. But perhaps our greatest accomplishment is that through our contact with the people *we* renew our own identity with Jews throughout the world. Thus, we owe our thanks to those who have allowed us to participate.

Above: The pioneering first Toronto committee for Project Renewal, at Beit Dagan. Included in this photo are Toronto committee members Marty Goldberg, Irving Granovsky, Alan Reitzes, Steve Ain, Adrienne Offman, and Michael Benjamin, along with their Israeli counterparts, mid-1980s.

Teddy and I

BY WILLIAM DUNPHY

As a Christian with an appreciation of the deep Jewish roots of my religion, I still get the same feeling every time I go to Jerusalem: I am always profoundly aware of being in a truly holy place.

My several visits over the past two decades began with a letter from the mayor of Jerusalem in 1980. Teddy Kollek invited me to become a member of the Jerusalem Committee, an international advisory group to the mayor and the municipality of Jerusalem. Its more than seventy members included former diplomats, retired Supreme Court judges, distinguished architects and urban planners, philosophers and theologians, historians, artists, and writers. What they had in common was a love of the city, combined with urgent concern for the restoration and preservation of its ancient sites and civic planning for the future. I was honoured to join this distinguished group.

Soon afterward I flew to Jerusalem to attend my first plenary session of the committee. I had gone a few days early to spend time with my old friend Emil Fackenheim, who had recently made aliyah with his family. Just before sharing a Shabbat supper with them, I was surprised to get a call from Mayor Kollek: "Tamar and I would be pleased if you would

join us for dinner at the close of Shabbat." When I asked for his address, he replied, "Take a taxi and tell the cabby you're going to Teddy's for dinner." At sundown the next day I followed his advice, hailed a taxi, and told the driver I was going to Teddy's. The driver said, "Okay," flipped on his meter, drove me to a modest low-rise apartment building, and pointed to the floor where the mayor lived. Thus I came to join that select circle of the mayor's friends privileged to call him "Teddy" – at last count there were many thousands!

Recently I have become involved with his Jerusalem Foundation, which raises funds for cultural, educational, and health-care projects benefiting all residents in both East and West Jerusalem. At a meeting of its international council in November 1995, I experienced the tragic and traumatic events following the assassination of Prime Minister Rabin. Teddy and others there were his personal friends, and I was moved by their reminiscences.

Above: In the chancellor's office at the University of Toronto, as Teddy Kollek receives an honorary doctorate, November 1995. Left to right: Dr. Ralph Halbert, Dr. Teddy Kollek, Dr. Bill Dunphy.

A Woman Called Intrepid

BY CHARLES PACHTER

My mother, Sara Pachter, was born in 1915, and she declares proudly, "I'm not eighty-two. I'm sixty-seven U.S.!" A first-generation Canadian and a child of the Depression, Sara was blessed with abundant energy. She was always on the run, championing causes and organizing events. She was a member of the Canadian Council of Christians and Jews, active in B'nai Brith, the Holy Blossom Temple sisterhood, and charity bazaars. But what was to become her abiding passion and later life's work – leading tours to Israel – began by chance.

In 1959 a troupe of Israelis – the INBAL dancers – were performing at the Royal Alexandra Theatre in Toronto. After one performance my mother invited the entire company to our house for coffee and her coveted *mandelbroit*. The troupe broke into an impromptu barefoot ballet in our living room, and their haunting dance rhythms made an impression on all of us, but none more so than on Sara, who had discovered her breakaway connection to an exciting new world. Thirty-eight years later, my intrepid mother has led more than eight thousand people, in the course of 135 trips, to Israel.

Here's a story about Sara. She is checking a group into the posh Laromme Hotel in Jerusalem. She finds out that the hotel is short four rooms. The manager is firm, saying nothing can be done. Sara asks those without rooms to relax and wait in the coffee shop while she and her friend Sally Libman go for a stroll near the hotel. They arrive at the Wailing Wall. Sara finds a crumpled note at her feet that has fallen from a crack in the wall. She places the note back in the wall, then thinks, "What harm can it do to write a note?" So she does, and it goes like this: "To whom it may concern: I am a tour leader from Canada, and I need four more rooms at the Laromme. Do you think perhaps you could do something? P.S. My friend Sally sends regards." They stick the note in the wall and walk back to the hotel. When they get there, they are told that four more rooms have suddenly become available. It is a miracle!

My mother's motto is "Have plane, will travel," and this passionate pied piper's commitment to Israel has always been unconditional. Governments have come and gone, policies have been criticized and defended, crises and tragedies have occurred, but Sara remains loyal. Put simply, she loves Israel, its people, and the joy of discovering it time and time again through its five decades of rebirth and its painful and triumphant growth.

Above: Sara Pachter in Israel, 1994.

Sara's one hundredth trip to Israel: On the steps of the Church of the Holy Sepulchre in ancient Safed, October 1991.

Through the Eyes of ORT

FROM A CONVERSATION WITH RUTH DRUXERMAN

Give a man a fish, and he eats today; teach him how to fish, and he will never go hungry." This motto has been the guiding force behind all of ORT's (Organization for Educational Resources and Technological Training) work for the last 118 years. Helping young people to lead independent, self–reliant lives has a great appeal for me, and I can scarcely remember a time when I was not involved with ORT.

I am fortunate that my husband, Alven, and I have had the opportunity to travel to Israel many times over the years. We feel we have shared in the joy of watching its growth and development. In 1985 we attended the groundbreaking cere–monies for the magnificent ORT Braude International Institute of Technology in Karmiel in the Galilee. What a thrill it was to know that ORT in Canada helped raise $2.5 million to help build this state–of–the–art institution.

But after thirty–five years of volunteering for ORT, no–thing can surpass the delight I felt when in 1987 I raised the Canadian flag at the expanding campus at Karmiel. With the increased Russian immigration to Israel during Operation Exodus, the population of Karmiel doubled. The school was in the right place at the right time. I feel proud to be part of this organization that helps people to help themselves!

Background: Ruth Druxerman, National Karmiel Building Campaign chair, raises the Canadian flag for the first time at the ORT Braude International Institute of Technology in Karmiel in 1987, as Baruch Venger, mayor of Karmiel, looks on.

At the opening of the Canadian Zionist Youth Program Centre in 1982 are, from left: **Zave Ettinger, Joe Tanenbaum, Phil Givens, Jack Israeli,** and **Colonel Ben-Ami Cohen.**

Syd and **Annette Bearg** chatting with Prime Minister **Yitzhak Rabin**, right, in 1983. Annette was chair of the UJA Campaign Women's Division that year. Syd is one of the most devoted supporters of Boys Town, a school that combines Orthodox Jewish studies with learning a trade. He was their 1982 honouree.

Ensuring a Healthy Climate

FROM A CONVERSATION WITH GERRY AND TOOTSIE HALBERT

Tootsie: Over the years, Gerry has put in hours and hours of work for Jewish causes. His first comment when he came back from a mission to Israel very shortly after the birth of our daughter in 1962 was, "I have to make sure the climate for the Jewish community is a healthy one for my child to be brought up in." He is still saying the same thing today. Only now it's for our grandchildren.

In 1994 our whole family went to Israel to celebrate Gerry's receiving an honorary doctorate at the Hebrew University of Jerusalem. This was presented to him because of the variety and depth of his accomplishments in the Jewish community.

Gerry: My being involved with Israel is no surprise, because both of my parents were committed Jews. My father always had a love for Jewish life, the synagogue, and everything to do with it. My mother, on the other hand, is extremely athletic. She loves sports. These two loves were connected when I became involved in the Canada Centre in Metulla.

I was president of the United Israel Appeal of Canada (UIA) from 1992 to 1995. The UIA honours each of their presidents at the completion of their term. In my case the UIA decided to create an annual scholarship for youngsters in the north of Israel so they could learn to skate on the rink at the Canada Centre. Whether they are sabras or children from Russia or even from Iraq, the Canada Centre is a place where they can interact as members of Israeli society.

Left: Prime Minister Menachem Begin launches Project Renewal at the opening UJA dinner of the 1979 Toronto Campaign to an enthusiastic response. Left to right: Prime Minister Menachem Begin, Gerry Halbert, and Tootsie Halbert. November 1978.

Above: At the opening of the Olympic-sized rink at Canada Centre in Metulla, 1995. From left to right: David Goldstein, Gerry Halbert, Mayor Yossi Goldberg, Jeff Budd, and Toronto hockey great, Frank Mahovolich.

Left: At the dedication of the Gerald Halbert Park and Observatory Plaza on Mount Scopus, looking out toward the Dead Sea. This was built in Gerry's honour as the Jewish National Fund 1986 Negev Tribute recipient. Left to right: daughters Michelle and Wendy, Gerry and Tootsie, a Canadian embassy official, Moishe Rivlin, JNF world chairman, and Avraham Harman, chancellor of the Hebrew University of Jerusalem.

A Dream to Be Realized

BY ALVIN B. ROSENBERG

I was raised with a Zionist outlook. My mother was president of Toronto Hada–ssah. My father was an ardent Zionist, and I remember going to a Zionist convention before I was ten years old.

Perhaps due to my short service in the Royal Canadian Air Force during World War II, I was approached by the late Samuel Zacks in 1948 to recruit a group of young Jewish men to defend Israel. I recruited Irving Matlow and Robert Eisen, but I was not able to go with them to Israel, because my wife and I were expecting our first child and my family persuaded me it was more important to remain at home.

I finally went to Israel in 1960 when I led a study mission as UJA chairman. It was on this trip that I first heard of the Dead Sea Canal project, whereby Mediterranean water would travel through a canal and a pipeline to the Dead Sea. This would not only generate clean electric power, but would open up vast areas of the interior to industry, housing, and recreational resorts. In 1977 I formed the Dead Sea Canal Corporation with a board of directors that included Ray Wolfe and Murray Koffler, and arranged with Israel Bonds to dedi–cate its sales to the development of the canal. Millions of dollars were raised, but all of it even–tually went toward other worthwhile projects in Israel. Unfortunately the politics are such that it seems unlike–ly the canal will ever be built.

I have always been and remain prepared to spend the rest of my life building the canal, but even if I never have the opportunity, I hope it will be built some day and that the power generated by the project will be used to make the Negev bloom.

Above: Alvin Rosenberg, 1980.

Left: Three generations were represented at the 1949 Osgoode Hall graduation. The member of the graduating class was Alvin B. Rosenberg, with his father, Henry Rosenberg (class of '23), and his grandfather, Jacob.

The Highest Degree of Charity

BY MURRAY GOLDMAN

Growing up in Glace Bay, Nova Scotia, I always heard the adults in shul (synagogue) wish each other, "Next year in Jerusalem." By the time I'd moved to Toronto and raised a family, my longing to go to Israel could no longer be ignored. In 1967 I went as a volunteer in the Six Day War. I was assigned to harvest potatoes on a kibbutz.

During the early seventies I began to read *Pirkei Avot* (Ethics of the Fathers). I learned that the highest degree of charity in Judaism is to help others help themselves. I had been searching for meaning in my life, and believed I had found it. I would try to make the world, especially my world, Israel, a better place.

I became directly involved in Israeli business. I invested in Clal, a major industrial conglomerate, and in late 1973 was appointed to the board of directors. This obliged me to attend quarterly meetings, which was a great excuse for me to go to Israel four times a year. It opened a whole new world for me, including becoming a Jewish "beer baron."

In 1974 National Brewery Ltd., the sole beer company in Israel, was in financial trouble and about to shut down,

throwing seven hundred people out of work. I spoke to Labatt's in Toronto, and they eventually agreed to buy the company, but only if I did it with them as a joint venture. So I became chairman, and National Brewery turned from a ramshackle operation into a modern, efficient brewery, whose best-known brands are Macabee and Goldstar.

Many people have asked me why I've never made aliyah. My answer is that although I have always been deeply involved in cultural and business affairs in Israel, I was told by Pinchas Sapir, Israel's first finance minister, "We don't want you to live here, Goldman. Go back to Canada, and with G–d's help make lots of money and send it here, together with your sons, to build our state!"

Above: Murray Goldman, left, enjoying lunch with Shimon Peres at the Netanya Brewery, 1984.

The Value of Higher Education

Ralph: My initial contact with Israel dates back to 1960 when I was part of a United Jewish Appeal study mission where we learned about Israel both from the standpoint of the land and the people. Later I was asked to become involved with the Canadian Friends of the Hebrew University in Jerusalem. Before doing that I wanted to visit the university, which my wife, Roz, and I did in 1963.

Roz: We toured the university and we were hooked.

Ralph: Our association with Hebrew University has lasted for many, many years. We have always believed that higher education brings great value to a country through its people. I was chairman of the International Board of the Hebrew University from 1993 to 1996. I know that for both of us one of the best aspects of being connected with the institution has been the Halbert Centre for Canadian Studies, which is co-sponsored by the government of Canada and Roz and myself. It began with a faculty exchange program in 1978 between Hebrew University and universities across Canada and has grown to support joint research projects and conferences with their resulting publications. Recently a graduate and postgraduate student-exchange program was begun. This centre is unique in that it is the only one that the government of Canada supports for Canadian studies. This two-way network has been most beneficial to both countries.

Roz: It's been a tremendous experience in our lives. Ralph has given a great deal of himself. He has also received a lot, and now our children, too, are committed to Hebrew University.

Above: Ralph Halbert, left, chairman of the board of the Hebrew University, joins Mayor Ted Kollek of Jerusalem, who was awarded an honorary doctorate at the University of Toronto graduation ceremonies, 1995. Ralph received an honorary doctorate from the Hebrew University in 1984.

Left: Ralph and Roz Halbert, right, signing the academic-exchange program that they endowed between the University of Toronto, represented by its president, George Connell, centre, and Jerusalem's Hebrew University, represented by its president, Amnon Pazy, 1978.

Ralph: It's enriched all our lives enormously.

Roz: Of many stories, there's one that's not very important, but it's quite humorous. Just after the Yom Kippur War, a gala was held at the Knesset with Golda Meir. The Israelis were anxious to make this an especially uplifting meeting. They wanted us to dress up in long gowns, but the only long garment I had with me in Israel was a flowered robe borrowed from my sister, Marilyn.

Now at that time this was not a very typical thing for me to do – I was very shy and conservative in those days – but I decided to get dressed up in that robe. I put on my high heels, my pearl earrings, and my sister's housecoat, and away I went. It was a beautiful evening, and when I went through the receiving line to meet Golda Meir, she exclaimed that I looked like a breath of spring in my floral gown!

———

Below: On a visit to Toronto in the early 1970s, Prime Minister Golda Meir is greeted by Roz and Ralph Halbert. Also present, left to right, are Israel's consul general, Abba Gefen, and Israel's ambassador to Canada, Epi Evron.

Alexandre and **Jeannine Raab** admire the vigour of the new rose seedlings at their experimental farm in Benyamina, Israel.

Alexandre Raab writes, "As we celebrate the fiftieth anniversary of the rebirth of the State of Israel, my joy transcends my personal connection to the historical roots of my people. The rebirth of Israel was not only glory for the survivors of our Hebrew ancestors but a victory for human decency over evil. Personally, I am committed to supporting the State of Israel and believe that so should all people of goodwill."

What's Going to Happen Next?

I arrived in Canada in 1950 and have lived in Toronto almost ever since. J. Irving Oelbaum introduced me to the Toronto Jewish community and made me understand about an ethical commitment to Canada *and* to Israel. He explained to me that we Jewish people in Canada have two obligations: one to the country where we live, and the other to Israel. That has remained my philosophy for all the years I have lived here.

I worked for everybody – UJA, JNF, and other such organizations – but I worked equally for both Jewish and non-Jewish institutions. About 1957 I became involved with Israel Bonds of Canada. I started in a modest way, but it developed into more and more of a commitment. Everybody was helpful, and I worked very diligently. Eventually, I became involved in the organization internationally. I was in Israel for an Israel Bonds Mission right after the Six Day War and also after the Yom Kippur War, and on both occasions I met Yitzhak Rabin. We arranged to bring him to Toronto to speak at a fund-raiser and I introduced him as the future prime minister of Israel. Very shortly afterwards he *did* become prime minister. Another time, I introduced Shimon Peres before a small gathering and six months later *he* became prime minister. Soon after, I was at an Israel Bonds Conference and Mr. Peres said to me, "I heard you were going to be here, so I arrived earlier than usual because I want to know what's going to happen next."

My favourite accomplishment – an on-going project that I started with Gideon Hausner, who was the chief prosecutor at the Eichmann trial, and Minister Moshe Kohl – is Massua ("the Beacon"). Massua is a unique school located in Natanya that has provided 250,000 Jewish and non-Jewish students from around the world with an understanding of the Holocaust and why it happened.

I have been involved with Israel Bonds for over forty years, and on October 21, 1990, a very great honour was bestowed on me. A tribute dinner was held for me, and I was presented with the highest award given by the bond organization worldwide – the Golda Meir Award. It's very special that someone from Toronto should receive this, and I am very proud of it.

Above: Prime Minister Shimon Peres, left, Genia Grossman, and Alex Grossman, at an Israeli Bond Conference in Jerusalem, late 1980s.

A Family Affair

BY LYNN ALBERT

As a young girl I was introduced to Israel at the dining–room table. Our discussions always involved Israel – the Bond campaign, knitting for the Hadassah Bazaar, Hillel, B'nai Brith. The feeling of pride that my family shared took hold when my father, Dave Bronstein, went to Israel to cover the Eichmann trial for the *Toronto Telegram.* His passion for Zionism served as an example for his children and grandchildren to follow.

I believe that the best way we can repay Israelis for allowing us to share in their feelings of love and commitment is by raising funds. And the nicest part of fund-raising is that, for us, it's a family affair including my mother, sisters, brothers–in–law, aunts, uncles, husband, and sons. We're a hands-on family and have organized plant sales, bowlathons, walkathons, telethons – you name it – and, of course, the Hadassah Bazaar.

My first trip to Israel was a UJA Young Leadership mission that included the thrill of meeting Golda Meir. My love for her grew even more when I realized that she smoked as much as I did. Noting the big box of matches she carried, I gave my gold Dunhill lighter to an aide to give to her. Within minutes "security" had stepped in and totally dismantled the gift. I'm not sure if they ever even gave her the parts!

Today my children continue the legacy established by my parents and have all gone on to take leadership roles in the community and share my love of Israel.

Below: Raising funds can be fun! Here's a "Trivia Night" arranged by this bunch of "beauties": from left to right, Penny Fixel, Marlene Savlov, Barbara Bernstein, Andie Marcus, Lynn Sigel, Lynn Albert and Bonnie Levy.

Arnold (Bucky) Epstein remembers that "following the 1973 war, a major fund-raising event was held in New York at the Waldorf Hotel. Abba Eban was the guest speaker, and he broke down and cried as he spoke of the war. We at the head table all stood for him as he approached. As Eban walked by he noticed my badge stating that I was from Toronto. He stopped to say how wonderful Toronto had been during the crisis."

Nathan Hurwich has been working for Israel since he was twenty, and helped found the Jewish National Fund in Canada in 1948. In 1974 he established the Toronto chapter of Bar-Ilan University. He has made numerous trips to Israel, but especially recalls the visit when he was honoured there by Bar-Ilan late in 1974: "Instead of sending out invitations to the event, several ads with my photograph were placed in the newspapers. I was surprised to see so many people show up. It was a most memorable experience." Here, Nat is shown on the right, with his wife, **Roey**, and **Professor Emanuel Rackman** of Bar-Ilan University.

The Cost of Conflict

With this photo, **Irving Ungerman** has captured the feeling of what it was like to be crammed into a Hercules plane transporting soldiers in the Yom Kippur War. Irving was part of the 1973 delegation, as was George Cohon, sent to observe the final stages of the war.

A Magical Moment

BY GEORGE COHON

In the final stages of the Yom Kippur War, I was on a bus with a group of about twenty other civilians heading from the Suez back to an Israeli airfield, where the plan was for us to catch a flight to Tel Aviv. Suddenly, we went over a big rock in the dirt road. The bus cracked down hard, and oil was going everywhere. We, on the other hand, were going nowhere.

So there we sat with armies all around us, helicopters and transports flying overhead. Earlier that day we had stood by the Suez Canal and looked across its waters toward the smouldering Egyptian tanks that had been abandoned during the battle of China Field. It had been an unforgettable sight.

We were rescued eventually by Israeli soldiers and put on a military transport plane. And on that plane an extraordinary thing happened. There were no seats – it was a big Hercules transport – and the soldiers, of whom there were about five hundred, were crammed in like sardines. Every soldier sat on the floor with his legs around the man in front of him. They were all tired and dusty and battle-weary. We, the civilians, sat among them.

The war had been a stunning victory for Israel, and now, on the Hercules, everyone was talking – about the war, about going home, about friends and family. But for a second there was a lull in the hubbub, so that one voice – that of a young soldier at the front of the plane – stood out from the rest. Then there was a shout from an older man, also a soldier, from the rear: "Josie!"

The older soldier and Josie were father and son – neither had known the other was on the plane. In fact, neither had known the other was even alive until that moment. But there was no way they could move, for there wasn't an inch of space. So the soldiers at the back hoisted the father over their shoulders, and the soldiers at the front did the same with the son . . .

It was a magical moment.

– excerpted from To Russia with Fries *(Toronto: McClelland & Stewart, 1997).*

Above: George Cohon, left, with Yitzhak Rabin, 1979.

Surgeons in the Midst of War

FROM A CONVERSATION WITH ALLAN GROSS AND FRED LANGER

When the 1973 Yom Kippur War looked imminent, a meeting was called by a group of Toronto doctors looking for surgeons – plastic, thoracic, abdominal, orthopaedic, or neuro, all the types most needed for trauma – who would be willing to volunteer their services in Israel. A list of volunteers was sent to the Israeli government, and that seemed to be the end of it.

A couple of weeks into the war, however, the Israeli Medical Association recognized that the only people surviving injuries from shrapnel, shell fragments, or bullets were those with orthopaedic injuries; people who were hit in the chest or abdomen were much less likely to survive. This meant that Israelis had a mounting need for orthopaedic surgeons. So they put out a call.

We think they chose us because they reasoned that if we were working full-time at university-affiliated hospitals, we couldn't be too bad. And, as doctors recently out of residency, we were certainly used to long hours. The Israeli consulate in Toronto called and said they would like us to go to Israel right away. They were desperate. We said okay; after all, we had made the commitment, we were young, and it sounded like a great adventure. We had to be in New York

to catch a special El Al flight that was taking people to Israel for the war – soldiers, surgeons, intelligence agents. So we dashed home to pack.

"My wife, Penny, wasn't there," Allan recalls. "She was at school, so I just wrote her a short note and left it on the pillow. I remember that Fred and I were sitting in New York, waiting to board the El Al flight that nobody was supposed to know about – it was uncharted and unregistered – when my wife had me paged over the intercom. She was a bit surprised, to say the least, by what we were doing. Needless to say, so were we."

We arrived in Israel and were met by the deputy minister of health and some high-ranking officers, who told us that while the Israelis had suffered many casualties in the first week or two of the war, they were now winning, taking back a lot of territory, but also picking up hundreds of Egyptians on the field with orthopaedic injuries. The place we surgeons

Above: Shortly after arrival in Israel in 1973, with a group of surgeons and one lone nurse. Allan Gross is in the second row, wearing a turtleneck, and Fred Langer is in the front row, wearing plaid pants.

could do the most good was the prisoner-of-war hospital. Some of the Americans actually refused and were sent home. We agreed to go.

A hospital in Tel Aviv had been converted into a POW hospital. There was a helipad there, and the casualties were being flown in daily. We worked twenty-four hours straight, then were off for twenty-four hours. The POWs (particularly the Egyptians) were very grateful for the care they got, not at all belligerent or hostile. We found the work rewarding.

After two weeks we were transferred to the Sinai to work at a field hospital. We were flown there in planes from World War II, and for the first time felt real fear. The field hospital was like a M.A.S.H. unit. We slept in tents, but the actual operating rooms were in bunkers. It was around the end of September, and during the day the temperature reached about 35° Celsius, but at night it dropped below freezing. The blankets were thin, and we'd go to bed wearing every stitch of clothing we had.

We were there for about three weeks. We actually had to be inducted into the army and given uniforms and ID, because if we had been captured by the enemy and found carrying a Canadian passport, they'd have assumed we were spies and might have executed us on the spot.

Once, in the Sinai, we had to go on a convoy crossing the Suez Canal to visit a field hospital, which put us in Egyptian territory, though at the time it was held by Israelis. Just the day before, we had been taken out to a rifle range to learn how to fire an Uzi – just in case! We were working much harder in the Sinai than we had in Tel Aviv, and sometimes to the buzz of overhead missiles. We heard about some terrible

isolated incidents, too; one where a casualty brought in from the field dropped a hand grenade, killing himself and his rescuers. So we knew that anything could happen. We never slept really soundly.

The five weeks we spent in Israel were an incredibly emotional time. We saw things you just never see, such as the time we saw a rabbi davening (praying) behind the field hospital. We didn't realize what he was doing at first, but then we saw all these caskets – the guys they were getting ready to ship back home. A lot of people died in the war, many of them doctors. That was because, when Israelis were injured in the field, trauma units were flown in by helicopter to resuscitate them, and sometimes the helicopters were shot out of the sky. Nevertheless, as Fred told the *Toronto Star*, "Ours was not a

_____

Above: In the Sinai. This is the mess tent where staff ate their meals. Allan is on the left.

Allan Gross, standing second from right, with a group of medical workers and soldiers on the Egyptian side of the Suez Canal.

courageous act. The front-line troops made tremendous sacrifices and suffered terrible losses in the early going. We were observers, able to walk away at war's end. The real hero in my family was my father, Al Langer, who served in the 1948 War of Independence."

"When you're there, in that situation, life is treated very differently," says Allan. "The Israelis are much tougher and more fatalistic than we are. If somebody gets hurt, they get hurt. If they get killed, they get killed. As practical as that might be, I don't think we could ever be that fatalistic."

Below: an Israeli Defence Forces tank on the Israeli side of the Suez Canal.

The Yom Kippur War

The Yom Kippur War of October 1973 had a devastating impact on Israelis. The surprise Egyptian and Syrian attack, and the early Arab military successes, shattered Israeli confidence in their political and military leadership, a confidence that was only partially re-established by the ultimate success of the Israel Defence Forces (IDF) in reversing the situation on the battlefield. Toronto's Jewish community shared the shock felt by Jews everywhere over the surprise Arab attack, especially as it occurred on the most sacred of Jewish holy days. As it always had in the past, Toronto Jewry rallied to Israel's defence during the 1973 war.

A Wall and a Watchtower

BY BERL BESSIN

I n 1967 I was studying at Yeshivat Kerem B'Yavneh, the first of the *yeshivat hesder* at which Israeli students combined Torah study with military service. In May, as tension built toward the Six Day War, the study hall was slowly emptying of students who had heard their coded call-up notices over the radio. I, too, wanted to serve, but I had no military training and could only volunteer for civil defence. At that time, a question in the Talmud came to mind: "*Dilma dama dehahu gavra samuk tefei?*" ("Is it that someone else's blood is more red than yours?"). Why should the Israeli students fight for Israel and the Jewish people, while I, just because I was born in Canada, did not?

So in 1970 I enlisted for a two-year stint in the Israel Defence Force. I served in the Nachal, a regiment set up primarily to work in and defend border settlements. In the fall of 1972, the Israeli government under Prime Minister Golda Meir decided to establish such a settlement on a ridge overlooking the Jordan valley, a place to be known as Gittit. It was to be built literally overnight, in the same way early settlements

were built in what was then the British Mandate of Palestine. Those settlements were known as *choma umigdal* (a wall and a watchtower), for when they were founded, there was little else in them but tents.

As a reward for good service, I was assigned to a squad that consisted of the Nachal regiment colonel, the commander of the Central Army, and me, a sergeant from Ottawa. Despite the illustrious members, we had the task of fencing in about fifty metres of the new settlement. There we were, the three of us, pounding angle irons into the rocky terrain, and then joining them with barbed wire. By dawn, we were tired and cut, but finished – and proud to have been part of this unique chapter of the Return to Zion.

Above: Sergeant Berl Bessin, foreground, pounds angle irons and fence posts into the rocky terrain to build a barbed-wire fence, 1972. The colonel pictured with him is the commander of the Nachal.

A stand-off during the Yom Kippur War: Israeli soldiers in the foreground and Egyptian soldiers in the background. Between them are UN troops, Suez City, November 1973.

Out of Harm's Way

BY BARRY CAMPBELL

Our host in Israel promised my parents he would find my friend Eric Maldoff and me a good kibbutz to stay on, out of harm's way when we visited Israel in 1970. "You'll both be safe at Gesher Haziv."

Our summer home on the kibbutz, on the Mediterranean just north of Naharia, was a small, wooden hut in an open field – no running water, no electricity, a chair, a table, no beds, just a couple of mattresses on the floor. We were exhausted and grateful to lie down for the night.

The Katyusha rocket hit twenty feet from our front door just before midnight. Shouts woke us. Momentarily knocked out by the shock wave of the blast, or too deeply asleep from exhaustion, we heard nothing until the kibbutz guards came to get us out. Eric had some small pieces of shrapnel in his leg, no big deal as it turned out. I was fine, but in a daze as we were led to the shelter with the women and children and the steel door was closed behind us. Shaken, and, oddly, shivering in the heat, we sat down on hard wooden benches in the dark and waited.

As my eyes adjusted, I realized that our below-ground shelter doubled in good times as the kibbutz synagogue. We

could hear rumbling outside and the sound of tracked vehicles – ours I hoped. It was then that the chilling thought came to me. How many times in our history had Jews sat like this in a synagogue, hoping that no harm would come? I was scared and angry.

At daylight, we headed back to our hut. There were holes in the walls where the shrapnel had sliced through, cutting the legs off our chair and whizzing by us as we slept on the floor. On the theory that lightning doesn't strike the same place twice, we cleaned up and moved back in!

Gesher Haziv had never been attacked before, and there was some animated discussion amongst the kibbutzniks about a possible link between our arrival and the incident. Our nervous host reappeared, determined to take us to a safer place, but we wouldn't leave.

Above: Barry Campbell and his wife, Debra, 1996.

A Fact–Finding Mission

FROM A CONVERSATION WITH MAX SHECTER

In 1973, towards the end of the Yom Kippur War, Leon Kronitz, Phil Givens, Frank Dimant, and I went to Israel to develop a full and complete report on current conditions that would hopefully inspire confidence in Canadian Jewry to travel to Israel. It was a moving and emotional time. We flew over with volunteers who were returning home to fight in the army. During one twenty-four-hour period, we flew from Jerusalem to Syria and then travelled by automobile to Egypt, where we crossed over the famous bridge that had been set up to allow the Israeli troops to advance into Egypt and keep the Egyptian Second Army of some ten thousand men at bay. We were given the privilege of actually seeing these men and were taken to Kilometre 101, where preliminary peace talks

between Egyptian and Israeli military representatives, under UN auspices, had just been held. We felt fortunate to have been in Israel then.

In spite of the tension in the air, there were still some light moments. While we were in Syria the weather was very hot, and we had stopped for lunch. As we sat, partaking of the delicious canned rations provided by the Israeli army, Phil said, "What I would give for a cold Coke right now!" As he said this, an army Jeep pulled in from the road, and one of the Israeli soldiers stuck his head out and said, "Anybody here want a Coke?"

Above: Max Shecter, left, eating army rations with Frank Dimant, centre, and Leon Kronitz, November 1973.

Don't Be Afraid to Cry

BY DAVID GOTFRID

Yom Kippur, October 1973. I was nineteen and visiting Detroit with some friends, with no thought of spending the holy day in shul (synagogue). When my friend's mother woke us up to say that war had broken out in the Middle East, I blurted out to all my friends that I was going to Israel.

After arriving there some weeks later, I was assigned to Kibbutz Nahal Oz, in the Negev. As the bus started out, it stopped to pick up three soldiers. One of them sat across the aisle from me. He was nineteen. He had been in the Sinai when the war began and was now going back after three days of leave. He was one of the lucky ones in his unit to survive the original attacks. Until then I did not know why I had made the decision to go to Israel. I was not aware of any Zionist feelings. Now it was clear. Israel was my country, and if nineteen-year-old sabras (native-born Israelis) could risk their lives, then I could at least tend their fields.

About ten days later I read that Rabbi Plaut was in Jerusalem with a group of Toronto tourists. I decided that I would make my way to the Holy City on Shabbat to say hello to my congregational rabbi. The only way to make the journey was to hitchhike. Eventually I was picked up by a family recently arrived from South Africa. The father was telling his children about the War of Independence as we passed by the burned-out tanks that dot the roadside in a perpetual memorial. His children were not interested, but as he was about to give up in frustration, I asked him to please talk on. As the car climbed the hill, and I started to get my first glimpse of Jerusalem, I tried to fight back the tears. Sensing this, my driver said, "Don't be afraid to cry. It was my reaction the first time I laid eyes on Jerusalem."

Above: David Gotfrid, and his wife, Marilyn Schipper Gotfrid, in Israel, 1995.

"**D**uring the festival of Chanukah, our UJA study group travelled to the Sinai, to the Bar Lev line at the Suez Canal," **Jack Gwartz** remembers. "While visiting with Israeli soldiers in their bunkers, we witnessed an unusual and moving sight — the lighting of a very special Chanukah menorah. It was composed of a series of artillery shells, set in a row and lit with oil. On the other side of the canal, we could see the Egyptian soldiers in their positions."

Marv Roebuck, **Jack Gwartz**, **Judy Gwartz**, and **Mara Roebuck** at Yamit, a new city being built on the sand near the sea, during a UJA Young Leadership Mission in May 1974. "We visited with young families newly settled into this beautiful city, excited and optimistic about their future," recall Jack and Judy. "We lunched on 'chicken in the bucket' as the sun and sand warmed our bodies. Little did we know that Yamit would eventually become a part of Egypt, and all those families would be uprooted and relocated to another part of Israel."

The 1972 UJA study group standing on top of a bunker in the Sinai. Left to right: **Gerald Shear**, **Lionel Robins**, **Jerry Friedman**, **Jack Gwartz**, **Jack Chisvin**, and **David Marks**.

Sharing Their Talents

Building Jerusalem's City Hall

FROM A CONVERSATION WITH JACK DIAMOND

I have a long family connection with Israel. My great–grandfather was chief rabbi of Finland and later chief rabbi of London. His sister went to Palestine back in 1881, where she established the first wine co-operative in Israel. She is buried on the Mount of Olives, and her gravestone reads, "Here lies the modest wife" – a very nineteenth–century sentiment. A different branch of my family has been living in the Middle East since the nineteenth century, when the whole area was part of the Ottoman Empire. More recently, some of my relatives emigrated from South Africa to Israel at about the same time I came to Canada, in 1964.

But even though I had a family connection, and though there is a strong bond between Israel and the Jews of South Africa, I didn't feel a personal pull toward Israel. In 1967 I visited Israel for the first time, as a convenient stopover on a trip home from South Africa. What a revelation! This was about three weeks after the Six Day War had ended, and the tanks were literally still smoking. I spent several weeks in Israel and felt an extraordinary affinity for the country.

Several years later some Canadian developers became interested in launching a project in Tel Aviv, and I went with representatives from Olympia and York to investigate. It happened that we also had a meeting with the city engineer from Jerusalem. He pulled out some photographs and an architectural model and said, "Why don't you take these back to Toronto?" About three years later an informal competition was held among three or four architects. Our firm, A. J. Diamond, Donald Schmitt and Company, won the contract.

Having reviewed the city engineer's plans, I went to see Teddy Kollek, the mayor of Jerusalem, and outlined some concerns. The site for the city hall straddled a ridge dividing the

Above: Mayor Teddy Kollek of Jerusalem, left, Jack Diamond, chief architect of Jerusalem's City Hall, centre, and Paul Slavens, founder of the Jerusalem Foundation of Canada, 1995.
Facing page: Jerusalem's new City Hall, main building at the Safra Square entrance.

city. To the west was Jaffa Road and Jewish Jerusalem, and to the east, the Damascus Gate and Arab Jerusalem. We wanted the building to be accessible to both and to fit in with the generally low–scale city structures which are consistently built of Jerusalem stone. We banded sections of the building with alternating colours of rose and sand limestone. Contrasting fine metalwork – a device used by the Ottomans – was painted in a traditional Arab blue. We wanted to create a building that would reinforce the sense of continuity of Jerusalem.

Building the city hall in Jerusalem was a fascinating process. During the construction we really had a sense of Israel's antiquity. We were excited when we uncovered relics from the Crusades. The archaeologist we consulted said that since these were only from the eleventh century, and not truly ancient, we should record the find but continue build-

ing. Later, we found a very serious piece of antiquity: a Herodian stone that was part of the third wall of the Temple. That stopped work for two or three days. Discovering the location of the third wall would make it possible to determine the exact site of Christ's burial, but in the end the experts decided that the stone was not in its original location; it was believed instead that the Crusaders had cannibalized the wall from somewhere else to use in their construction.

We always work with a local firm wherever we build around the world, and in this instance our joint–venture partners, Kolker, Kolker, and Epstein, became good friends. We are doing other projects with them as a consequence. Among them is the new building for Israel's foreign ministry, on a site opposite the Supreme Court.

I will normally be on one of our foreign sites three or four times a year. During the construction of the city hall, however, I was in Jerusalem eight times in thirteen months, and at times it was exhausting and stressful. A meeting that would take one hour in Toronto takes two hours in Israel. There is a joke that says it is impressive that, out of the twelve thousand professionals in Israel, there are twelve thousand doctors . . . twelve thousand architects . . . and everyone is an expert!

Nevertheless, building Jerusalem's city hall gave me goose bumps. There have not been many times in three thousand years of history – particularly in the last two thousand years – when a Jewish architect has built in Jerusalem. It's possible that my ancestors were stone cutters or carpenters, and here I am, two thousand years later, still doing much the same thing.

Left: Looking down the Pergola, Jerusalem City Hall, south side of Safra Square.

The Mission

BY DUBI ARIE

In the early morning of June 5, 1967, smoke mushroomed from exploding grenades, land was swallowed up by artillery, and machine-gun bullets tore into the attacking Israelis. In the midst of the fighting, I heard the shrill, piercing sound of the shofar, preceded by the long-awaited words over a transistor radio *"HaKotel beyadenu"* ("The Western Wall is in our hands"). When I heard the shofar, I felt the spark of an idea that would lead me to the creation of the mission in my life.

I was born on August 4, 1939, in Warsaw, and my mother, Sara, spent the next four years running from the Nazis with my older brother, Isahar, and me. At the end of the Second World War, we immigrated to Israel, where my mother died three years later. Orphaned, living in Kibbutz Shaar HaGolan, I began the life of a pioneer, artist, and paratrooper. Serving in the Six Day War, the War of Attrition, and the Yom Kippur War, I felt there had to be a reason why I survived, and this belief led to the creation of *The Mission: Under the Wings of God and the Shadow of Amalek.*

I moved to Toronto in 1974 to find thinking space, and spent thirteen years learning, sketching, and planning, and the next seven years working on my canvas. *The Mission* is an artistic composition consisting of seven panels measuring nearly 38.5 by 7 feet that pictorially tells the story of the Jewish People from Creation to the Birth of Israel. It highlights the milestones in Jewish history and parallels the events of my life and that of the Jewish People.

Above: Artist Dubi Arie in front of The Mission, *an oil on canvas in seven panels, which tells the story of the Jewish People.*

Like Family

BY SOREL ETROG

My family emigrated from Romania to Israel in 1950 when I was seventeen. My sister, Zipora Gendler, and most of my family still reside in Israel, as did my late parents.

In the spring of 1959 I was privileged to have a chance meeting with Samuel J. Zacks at the Rose Fried Gallery in New York. Sam saw one of my painted wood constructions, asked my name, and bought the construction on the spot. He asked me to bring it to Toronto. Where was Toronto, and who was Sam Zacks?

That was a turning point in my life and career. Sam and Ayala's home in Toronto, with their world-renowned art collection, was an inspiration to me, and an education. Many important scholars, historians, artists, musicians, and actors were regular guests in their home.

Ayala, a native of Jerusalem, and an active member of the French Resistance during World War II, met Sam in Basel in 1946 at the International Zionist Congress. Sam was representing Canada as president of the Zionist Organization of Canada. Shortly thereafter, they married in Toronto. Sam and Ayala held many important positions in the arts: Sam was president of the Art Gallery of Ontario, and Ayala served on the International Board of Governors of Museums.

Ayala and Sam were intimately involved with all matters relating to Israel. They welcomed into their home many Israeli delegates visiting Toronto, including Meir Weisgall of the Weizmann Institute. In 1963 the Zackses brought together a group of distinguished Canadians whom Weisgall invited to become involved with the Institute. Their response was overwhelming; many made outstanding contributions to the Institute and continue to do so today.

Ayala was active in many organizations, such as Hadassah-WIZO, through which she helped to build the Hadassim School and Youth Village for refugee children. Sam and Ayala assisted in the archaeological digs at Hazor, which were supervised by the world-renowned archaeologist Yigael Yadin. They later built the museum that bears their name and houses the great discoveries from that dig.

I will always remember a visit I made to Sam's office. There was Sam, on one phone with the Art Gallery of Ontario,

Above: Sorel Etrog, centre, with Ayala and Sam Zacks, 1959.

on another phone connected to the stock market, all the while drafting a document for Dr. Chaim Ganzu, director of the Tel Aviv Museum, seated nearby. Sam then turned to me, asking, "Why did you stop talking to me?"

In the late fifties there were numerous people in Toronto connected to Israel. They showed their support and identification with the Jewish State in various ways.

Sophie and Archie Bennett had their own unique approach. Every Friday evening, for kiddush (the blessing over the wine) and supper, they opened their home to many Israelis in Toronto, introducing them to family and friends. The *haimish* atmosphere, and Sophie's warmth and generosity, made everyone feel welcome. We sat around the enormous, candlelit table and enjoyed an abundance of superb food.

Sam and Ayala Zacks, who were related to the Bennetts, took me there the first time. "You will enjoy it," said Sam. "It's a

place where you'll meet other Israelis, where young Israel is the topic of discussion and debate."

Discussion and debate was Archie's domain. He was an intense and philosophical man, a rabbi without tallis or tefillin, yet deeply spiritual. He could talk, and sometimes lecture, on virtually any subject: Israel, Toronto, the world – always challenging, like a boxer. Archie was also a compulsive walker. I had the privilege of seeing him at his best, one on one, as we walked and fought.

I cherish, as I am sure many others do, my memories of Fridays at the Bennetts'.

Above: Sophie and Archie Bennett, 1959.
Left: Sorel Etrog, left, Michael Sela, centre, and Ayala Zacks Abramov gathered at the Weizmann Institute for the dedication of a painted-bronze sculpture by Sorel Etrog entitled The King and Queen, *created to honour the memory of Sam Zacks, 1972.*

Sorel Etrog writes: "Ammunition Hill, now known as Givat Eshkol, was the site of some of the fiercest battles that took place between the Israeli and Jordanian armies during the Six Day War. In the early 1970s, when I was commissioned by the mayor of Jerusalem, Teddy Kollek, and art collector Nathan Cummings to create a sculpture for the battle site, trenches and battle-marked fields were still visible. However, it was not to be a memorial, but rather a sculpture of rejoicing – a celebration.

"The idea of a Hassidic head was first suggested by Nathan Cummings. I made a maquette and brought it to Mayor Kollek, who approved it. A year later the sculpted twelve-foot Hassidic head was shipped to Jerusalem from Italy, and the dedication took place in 1972."

Here, Mayor Teddy Kollek, far left, and Nathan Cummings, centre, unveil the Hassidic head on Ammunition Hill.

In September 1978, **Leo** and **Andrea Fine** and their four-year-old son, **Stephen**, went to live in Jerusalem for eight months during Leo's sabbatical year. While Stephen spent time in a nearby *gan* (kindergarten), Leo and Andrea volunteered in the archaeology department of the Israel Museum. Here, Andrea is reconstructing ancient pottery from shards found at various digs.

It Happens to Every Jew

BY GARTH DRABINSKY

In 1988 I arrived in Jerusalem at 4:00 AM for my first visit. Concerns over negotiations to obtain the Canadian rights for *The Phantom of the Opera* were banished by the overwhelming sensation of five thousand years of Jewish history. As I drove through the darkness, with the cool, dry, fresh air on my face and the sweet fragrance of flowers in the air, a tear trickled down my cheek. It happens to every Jew, I am told, arriving in Israel for the first time.

My guide asked me where I wanted to go. "The Wall," I answered. I was deeply touched to be at the Wall, bathed in a golden light at dawn, with Jews praying in dozens of dialects. My visit to Israel was one of the deepest emotional experiences of my life.

Below: Garth Drabinsky, right, with architect Moshe Safdie on the roof of Safdie's Mamilla Development in Jerusalem, 1994.

A Downhill Battle

BY GERALD B. COOPER

In 1974, when my wife, Kathy, and I were newlyweds, we took a long trip to Israel. While there, I befriended a kibbutznik who had served his army-reserve duty on skis! Qualified Ontario ski patroller that I was, I decided to volunteer for the patrol at Mount Hermon.

In the midst of a blizzard, Kathy and I arrived at the ski area of Mount Hermon. By a great stroke of luck I encountered my kibbutz friend, and within minutes was accepted as a volunteer ski patroller. We patrollers spent all the next day digging out the chairlift – by hand!

The skiing was incredible: deep powder in huge bowls, with a view of the Mediterranean. In one week I assisted more injured skiers than I had in an entire season at home.

Kathy and I returned to Mount Hermon when the snow had melted. We took the chairlift to the top and were astonished to see the idyllic ski hill littered with abandoned tanks!

Above: Gerry Cooper and a kibbutznik friend at the base of the Mount Hermon ski area, March 1975.

Isaac Stern, violinist, left, **Zubin Mehta**, musical director of the Israel Philharmonic Orchestra, and **Lily Barr** of the Canada Israel Cultural Foundation, at the Maureen Forrester and Friends concert, which raised funds for CICF Endowments, 1980.

Harmony in Black and White: "To the eye, the event was not only a fusion of harmonies but a checkerboard of colour, for the **Israel Philharmonic Orchestra** wore black jackets and the **Toronto Symphony Orchestra** wore white." – *The Toronto Star*

On March 16, 1989, the Israel Philharmonic Orchestra and the Toronto Symphony Orchestra, conducted by Zubin Mehta, played to a sold-out house at Roy Thomson Hall to raise money for the endowment funds of each orchestra. The highlight of the evening was when the two hundred members of both orchestras combined to play Symphonie Fantastique, Opus 14, by Hector Berlioz.

Aliyah

A Legacy of Love

BY LILY SILVER

I t was always my husband Nathan's dream, even as a boy in Poland, to live in Israel. To attain this goal, he worked for a year on a *hachsharah* (model communal farm), and by 1933 hoped to realize his ambition. But it was not to be, not then. He went to Canada instead, and his dream didn't come true for forty years.

We'd visited Israel several times, of course, and after a lifetime of activity in the Revisionist Zionist (Herut) movement, it might have seemed only natural for Nat and me and our children to make aliyah. The strongest impetus, in fact, came from our children, Debra, Joey, and Bonnie, who urged us to translate their upbringing (day school and Betar Zionist youth movement) into reality, at least for one year. Shoel, our eldest child, remained at university in Toronto.

We arrived in the summer of 1973. This was a fateful year, as it turned out, for that October brought the Yom Kippur War. It disrupted school for the children, but by December our youngest daughter Bonnie's Hebrew accent was indistinguishable from a sabra's (native-born Israeli's). The Yom Kippur War, coming so soon after we arrived, the terrorism, and, much later, the Gulf War, with its heart-stopping Scud missile

attacks, led many of our friends to wonder how we could live in Israel; life in Toronto cannot prepare you for the tensions here. Yet we never contemplated leaving. If anything, we grew stronger in our belief that this was our land, and we were a vital part of it.

Over the years we have lived here, our children have married and now have children of their own. We've made solid friendships, too, not the least of which was a close friendship with the late Menachem Begin, his wife, Aliza, and their family. We were especially privileged during the years Mr. Begin was prime minister to share in many of the exciting and history-making events of his career.

Above: Their smiles say it all, as Nathan and Lily Silver are honoured by the Ezrath Nashim Hospital in 1989. Since they made aliyah in 1973, they have always made visitors feel welcome in their home in Jerusalem.

Facing page: A view of Kibbutz Kfar Blum in the Upper Galilee, 1944. The kibbutz is named after Leon Blum, the Jewish prime minister of France from 1936 to 1938, and again in 1946, after surviving Nazi wartime incarceration.

the founder of the Revisionist Zionist movement, and his wife, Johanna, from New York, stopping en route in Paris for a solemn ceremony at the airport, and then continuing to Israel. We walked from the sea to the highway, with thousands of people lining both sides of the street in absolute silence.

Nat's last twenty-four years were spent in his beloved Israel. His funeral in April 1997 was attended by Israelis of all religious denominations and political persuasions, as well as friends and relatives from Canada. Eulogies were delivered by Benny Begin, Menachem's son, and by two other close friends, a Conservative rabbi and a Haredi rabbi. That may seem unusual in these days of tension among Jews, yet nothing could have been more appropriate. Nat was a Conservative Jew, but he felt comfortable among *roshei yeshivot* (heads of religious academies). Our Israel – to paraphrase a slogan of Canadian unity – includes all sectors of society. That was the principle Nat lived by. If we succeed in passing that legacy on to our children and grandchildren, we will, in some small way, have brought something positive with us from Canada to Israel, and left our new land a little better than we found it.

I still thrill to the memory of seeing Anwar al-Sadat standing in the doorway of the Egyptian plane at Ben-Gurion Airport, twenty years ago. I can hear the welcoming roar of the crowd, and feel the honour we all experienced as he greeted each of us personally. Those were heady days: the signing of agreements on the White House lawn, the first visit to Cairo. And who can forget seeing Mr. Begin receive the Nobel Peace Prize?

I also carry an earlier image: the day in July 1964 when we travelled with the bodies of Vladimir (Ze'ev) Jabotinsky,

Left: Enjoying a moment together are Lily and Nathan Silver and former Israeli president Zalman Shazar, left.

John R. Devor

BY DAVID DEVOR

One of the greatest thrills of my late father John Devor's life was representing the Zionist Organization of Canada at the inauguration of the Knesset in August 1966. Alongside my mother, Mildred, also an active Zionist, he was one of 120 representatives from Jewish communities throughout the world.

After a trial year in Israel, during which we experienced the Six Day War, the family completed aliyah in 1969. Sadly, my father had so little time to enjoy the realization of his dream.

Left: Mildred and John Devor, both active Zionists, moved to Israel with their family in 1969.

He was a wonderfully multifaceted man, whose life carved a broad swath of influence. Rumour had it that his earlier travelling for the famous Weston's Biscuit Company was merely an excuse; his real object was to give his voluntary effort to organize Judean clubs. This meant wherever Weston's biscuits were in great demand, the Young Judea thrived.

Aliyah

The return of the Jewish People to biblical Eretz Yisrael, the Land of Israel, and the idea of "ascending" (aliyah) to Zion – the ideal nation envisioned by Judaism – is the driving principle of Zionism. Since the start of modern political Zionism in the last decades of the nineteenth century, hundreds of thousands of Jews from all over the world have immigrated to the Land of Israel and participated in the building of the Jewish state. Since its founding in May of 1948, Israel has successfully absorbed more than two million Jewish immigrants, thereby fulfilling its Zionist mission of "ingathering the exiles."

Homecoming

A Mother's Story

BY LILA GOLDENBERG JULIUS

Home is not necessarily where you hang your hat, or where your family is. Home is where you are most yourself. My family and I came home to Israel twenty-five years ago. We came for a summer holiday – all seven of us, each with a suitcase light enough to carry – with the thought that if things went well, if jobs looked promising, we might come back another year. What we found was Neve Ilan, a *moshav shitufi* (something like a kibbutz), with work in my husband Robert's and my professions. The members were willing to take us on as candidates for a trial year, and we thought, we're already here; why go back to Toronto?

We ran it by the kids. The three younger ones thought it would be an adventure. Our fifteen-year-old daughter, Frances, wasn't so sure. "How will I say goodbye to my friends? Who'll pack my things? What about music lessons?" My husband went back to finish up his job, rent the house, and send some of our belongings. We told our oldest daughter she could go back

to help. "Why does she get to go and not me?" said her twelve-year-old sister. So they both returned to Toronto, while the rest of us started learning Hebrew.

We stayed on the moshav for six years, lived in and around Jerusalem, and eventually bought an almond and olive farm in the Lower Galilee. Our children number six now, and the youngest is in the army, like his sisters and brothers before him. Our oldest daughter returned to Toronto with her husband to study, and the rest have set up homes around Israel.

The three younger ones were right. It *has* been an adventure. And the right thing for us to do.

Above: Lila Julius with her brother Leon Goldenberg at her home in Moshav Kfar Kisch, 1992. The sign reads "Julius Family, Robert and Lila."

A Daughter's Story

BY FRANCES JULIUS FRIEDLAND

It was with mixed emotions that I tried to digest the news my parents delivered one day in the summer of 1972. I was fifteen, and with my four brothers and sisters had come to Israel for a six-week holiday. Our parents told us that they had decided to stay. I was scared, yet excited.

Life in Israel proved to be quite different from the image evoked by travel posters and the lively songs from the Israeli Song Festival. The first year was the hardest. I was enrolled in a rural high school. I thought I knew Hebrew reasonably well, but found I didn't understand one word of my first class. Later I found out it had been a biology lesson.

I learned Hebrew that first year, slowly and painstakingly, with the help of two good friends: one was a classmate, the other was an American from my moshav, who sat with me each night and translated the whole day's worth of class notes from my school friend.

Although getting used to life in Israel was difficult, there were many unexpected pleasant surprises. A popular slogan circulating about the country at that time was "Israel Is Real." I found that to be true. Life in Israel *is* more real. It's a sentiment difficult to convey. Just as Israelis are considered unsophisti-cated, more "raw," so too are friendships, relationships, and life in general. There is less pretence and more sincerity. Life is based on real values.

I married an Israeli and we came to Canada to study. Now, fifteen years and two children later, we're still here. My heart is in Israel and I believe one day my family will be, too.

Dedicated to the memory of my friend Gila Ben-Or.

Above: The summer we arrived, 1972. Left to right: Mona, Frances, Lara, Jamie, and Terry.

The Israeli Spirit

FROM A CONVERSATION WITH ELAYNE WORTSMAN

We chose United Synagogue Day School for our daughter Stacey's schooling for many reasons, but mostly because we felt it was important for her to be raised in a Jewish environment. Years later, after her first year of university, Stacey expressed a desire to visit Israel. So off she went for the summer in June 1986.

Stacey stayed with relatives and fell in love with the country, the people, and especially the Israeli attitude toward life. She felt so comfortable in Israel that she asked us if she could continue her university education there. We agreed that living on campus for a year would be a great learning experience for her.

Stacey came to realize that she wanted to stay and make her home in Israel. We asked her to come home for a year and gather her thoughts, but we made it clear that if she really wanted to go back we would support her decision. She worked in Toronto for a year, and then in May of 1988 she made aliyah. Stacey is now married and living in Israel, working for Bank Hapoalim, and is the mother of beautiful sabra children.

I now understand why life is so difficult for Israelis. Because their sons and daughters are called up for army service when they reach age eighteen, Israelis must live for each day. Their children are their most prized possessions. It really hits home when you see your daughter say goodbye to her husband as he goes off to military service, rifle in hand. As a wife and mother, I know how Stacey must feel, and she must truly have "the Israeli spirit."

Above: Stacey, Elayne Wortsman's daughter, celebrates at her sister's wedding with her husband, Gil.
Left: Stacey and Gil's two sabra children, Oren, left, and Tal, 1997.

Edith Sefton writes, "In the late 1970s the Toronto chapter of Parents of North American Israelis (PNAI) was born. We are not a fund-raising group or a political group; we are simply people with a vital interest in Israel. Our life blood is there: our daughters, our sons, and our grandchildren.

"At first we were very much a support group, but over the years we have evolved into a group of parents concerned with all the everyday things in Israel, events and circumstances not reported in the media. Many we see firsthand during our frequent visits for bar and bat mitzvahs, weddings, and the births of our grand-children. We recognize the realities when our offspring go into the army. All these joys and fears are shared with other PNAI members, and that is why our group exists.

"PNAI has connections with similar groups in Australia, England, and other countries. Religious and political differences among the members are meaningless. Our bond is the interest and concern we all have for our children living in the State of Israel, and this has led us into an understanding and appreciation of one another, no matter what our backgrounds or our beliefs. It is a wonderful feeling."

Here, Edith Sefton is seated beside Vernon Turner, the Canadian ambassador to Israel, 1984.

Mark Adler writes, "During my first visit to Israel in 1974, when I was twenty, I spent eight weeks on an archeological dig at Tel Dan. Upon my return to Toronto, I sought out everything Israeli. It was then I discovered a world hitherto unknown to me, of Zionist summer camp, *kenim* [clubhouses] and *rudiki am* [Israeli folk dancing]. I vowed to return to Israel as an *oleh* [immigrant], and after two more visits during university, I did.

Following five months at an absorption centre, learning Hebrew, I volunteered for army service, ending up in an armoured infantry unit that was totally non-English speaking. Most of the Hebrew I learned there (not to mention Arabic and Russian) was not for polite conversation! Upon release from the army, I married a Canadian *olah*, and we lived in Ramat for the next eight years, until post graduate study brought us back to Toronto. To quote Yehuda HaLevi, 'My heart is in the East, while I am in the West.' "

Mark Adler, in the foreground, is shown here enjoying the natural beauty at Benias, 1975.

"I made aliyah with my wife, Reisie, in August 1973," writes **Ted Miller**. "Before six weeks had elapsed, we found ourselves in a country at war. We sought ways to contribute our medical skills and counted ourselves lucky to be allowed to volunteer as drivers for the staff of Hadassah Hospital, since bus service was severely disrupted. I finally found part-time work, filling in for a home-care doctor who'd been drafted. In the following winter there was a prolonged call-up, draining the hospitals of much of their younger medical staff. One day a medical corps officer showed up at the absorption centre in his neatly pressed uniform, asking if I could fill in at Sha'arei Zedek Hospital while he and some of his colleagues did reserve duty. Thus began my medical career in Israel."

"In 1973 I was on sabbatical in Israel," writes **Joe Rezek**. "The kibbutz on which I worked, Lochamai HaGetiot, was chosen during the course of the Yom Kippur War as a temporary cemetery for soldiers killed in the north. It was there, standing in the cemetery, seeing the graves and the distraught relatives, that I understood the cost of being a Jew in Israel and how alone we were. I decided that I had to try to live there, and in 1975 my family and I officially made aliyah."

Akiva Skidell was born in Poland, and after immigrating to Canada as a teenager, he graduated from the University of Toronto, fluent in six languages and with a degree in mathematics. He served as a radio operator and interpreter in World War II, and after the war recruited crews for nine "illegal" ships that brought thirty thousand Jews to Palestine. During Israel's War of Independence he was a major in the Israel Defence Forces.

After the war, he settled with his wife and growing family at Kibbutz Kfar Blum, and became an inspiring and influential mathematics teacher.

Akiva Skidell is shown here visiting the *Exodus 1947*, in Baltimore, Maryland.

Harris Gulko writes: "'A farmer in Palestine' was the answer I gave as a youngster when asked what I wanted to be when I grew up. I was born in Toronto in 1927, the son of a dedicated Zionist, and by the time I was twelve I was selling Jewish National Fund stamps to raise money to plant trees in Israel. I organized a parade down Yonge Street to protest the British White Paper policy while I was still in my teens.

"As a teenager I was heavily involved in Zionist youth groups, and as an adult I worked for the United Jewish Appeal and the Jewish National Fund. From 1953 to 1963 I was the Ontario executive director of JNF and then went on to be the national executive director for the next sixteen years. My wife, Blanche, and I, with our youngest daughter, Sharon, made aliyah in 1979. From 1984 on, I was the international director of the Ezrath Hashim/Sarah Herzog Memorial Hospital, and am now a private consultant in fund-raising and public relations."

Emil Fackenheim writes: "I was born in Germany, ordained a rabbi in Berlin in 1939, and after incarceration in Sachsenhausen concentration camp, I moved to Aberdeen, Scotland. In 1940 I was interned by the British because I was German-born and sent to Canada, where I was placed in an internment camp. After my release I commenced studies at the University of Toronto, received my doctorate in 1945, and went on to serve as rabbi of Congregation Anshei Shalom in Hamilton for five years, ending up as a professor of philosophy at the University of Toronto.

"I made aliyah in 1983 after being appointed visiting professor at the Hebrew University in 1981, and I continued to teach there until 1987. In 1998 I plan to retire to write my memoirs (I have written twelve other books on religious and philosophical subjects) and to ponder the future of Israel – in particular, of Jerusalem."

SECTION VI

Moments in Time

The Nature Reserves

Wild About Israel

FROM A CONVERSATION WITH ROBERT BATEMAN

I saw my first *canus lupus* – the grey wolf – in the wild in Israel. I think everybody would be surprised to hear this about Robert Bateman, the famous Canadian wolf painter!

It was Michael Levine who got me to go to Israel. He had been saying that they had heard of me there and that some of the Nature Reserves people could show us around. I suppose I shouldn't say this, but Israel was not on my shortlist of places to visit. There are so many wonderful places for nature in the world, and my calendar is always so booked. But I thought, I guess I'll go; the history will be a little interesting. When I got there, I realized I had been totally wrong – the natural wonders in Israel are magnificent. It should be a major destination for nature lovers.

The whole trip was dedicated to these wonders. We first headed down to Eilat, stopping off at the large staging area to observe the spring bird migration. It was wonderful, because there were so many of them coming through. This is the main pathway for a huge number of birds that have wintered down in Egypt and the rest of Africa and are now making their way back to Europe. They have to come up through the Jordan

valley, and all the birds funnel in through that very narrow causeway of greenery. There are many more trees on the Israeli side than on the Jordanian side, so there is more vegetation for the birds, more insects for them to eat, and more water to drink. And the Israelis seem intent on keeping it as a good natural corridor for them. I heard that every Israeli

---

Above: Dan Perry, director general of the Nature Reserves, left, Birgit Bateman, with one of the Nature Reserve's guides, and Michael Levine, seated, viewing the Dead Sea from the cliffs above.

Facing page: Robert Bateman's painting of a magnificent Israeli leopard in the wild. It appears in his book Natural Worlds.

military airport has a military ornithologist, because it's important that they avoid mid–air collisions. A collision between a stork and a low–flying fighter jet can be fatal for both bird and pilot.

I did two paintings in Israel, both of which are in my latest book. I have one spread with a painting of an Israeli leopard and another of an ibex with Masada in the background. I didn't actually see any leopards in the wild, but we were right in the area the leopards frequent, as well as the hyrax, furry little creatures which are the main food of the leopards. It's a balanced relationship between the predator and the prey.

It's to Israel's credit that they have room not only for the prey species like the little hyrax, but for the predators as well. I brag about Israel every time I give a talk, that such a little country (8,000 square miles) should have leopards and wolves living wild and free, while in vast America, according to some pressure groups, there isn't room for wolves in Wyoming (96,000 square miles). And of course, Israel also has a breeding program with the ambitious and wonderful idea of trying to get every animal mentioned in the Bible – wild asses, antelopes, ostriches, the oryx and the ibex, and others – reintroduced and living in Israel. I found it

all most impressive – the people, the thoroughness of the program, and the amount of care.

I believe that 13 per cent of Israel is set aside as nature reserves, which is a prodigious amount for a little sliver of a country where land is so precious. And I've been told that every Israeli military officer must be a trained naturalist, because they know that the desert is so precious and easily damaged. As I say in my lectures, can you imagine a world in which every military officer had to be a trained naturalist? It could change the world in a matter of months! I think it's a wonderful, wonderful model for the rest of the world to follow.

Above: An ostrich in the desert nature reserve.
Left: An Arabian oryx, one of the animals of the Bible that has been brought back to Israel, in its natural habitat.

The Holyland Conservation Fund

FROM A CONVERSATION WITH SKIP SIGEL

Douglas Bassett, Thor Eaton, David Goldstein, and I looked at the agenda for the ensuing session of the Prime Minister's Economic Conference in Tel Aviv, and elected to "jump ship." We hired a car and headed to Jerusalem, to the office of our friend Yehuda Raveh, then a young but already prominent attorney, practising law with his father–in–law, Gideon Hausner, who had prosecuted Nazi war criminal Adolf Eichmann.

In Jerusalem we met Yehuda's friend General Avraham Joffe, the managing director of the Israel Nature Reserves Authority. The NRA was created in 1948 with the mandate to protect all of nature's living things in Israel: in the sea, in the deserts, or in the skies. General Joffe had brought along three Jeeps and NRA scouts, and we took off for a tour that was to last for the rest of our stay in Israel.

We covered the country from top to bottom, ducking rocket fire at the "Good Fence" on the Lebanese border in the north, visiting the sports complex Douglas's father, John Bassett, had build in the Negev, and then on to Eilat in the south. We were there at the height of the bird migration from Europe to Africa, and we observed this migration along with many professional and amateur photographers from around the world, at a superb bird–watching centre constructed by the NRA.

We returned to Jerusalem with a sense of belonging to a special group of dedicated people, and a commitment to help–ing our new friend expand his work for the NRA. Thor was an experienced member of the World Wildlife Fund, and with his support we developed the Holyland Conservation Fund in Canada. With the energy and support of David and his gang of nature lovers, along with the support of Doug, Thor, and many others, the work of the NRA carries on, and its efforts continue to be crowned with success.

Left: Skip Sigel, enjoying the outdoor life in Israel, 1985.

"We saw a giant canyon with this exquisite monastery carved into the canyon wall," writes Skip Sigel. "It is known as the monastery of silence. It was built not long after the Crusades and is still in use."

Memories of Prime Minister Menachem Begin

BY RABBI BARUCH FRYDMAN-KOHL

Two memories of the late prime minister Menachem Begin stand out in my mind.

Mr. Begin had revived a tradition established by David Ben-Gurion, of convening a Tanach (Bible) study group in his home on Saturday evenings.

On one such evening, my wife, Josette, and I were enjoying tea and cookies following the study session, when we went over to read the citation of the Nobel Peace Prize awarded to Mr. Begin and President Anwar al-Sadat of Egypt.

Beside the document hung a family picture of the Begins' granddaughter holding a sign that read: *"Yesh li et hasaba hatov beyoter ba'olam"* ("I have the best grandfather in the world"). As we were remarking about the juxtaposition of the citation and the photograph, Mrs. Begin overheard us and said, "Why not? He seeks peace for her future, and the love of family gives him strength for the nation." The connection between the personal and the political was never more clearly articulated.

My second memory is of a meeting in the prime minister's office with a group from the United Jewish Appeal Rabbinic Cabinet. Mr. Begin spoke about the war in Lebanon and then invited questions. I asked him about Israel's neglect of Ethiopian Jewry. Mr. Begin expressed his deep concern about the situation, saying he would not rest until he could reunite the black Jews of Ethiopia with the Jewish people in Israel.

Years later we discovered that Mr. Begin initiated the efforts that eventually culminated in Operation Moses and Operation Solomon, the airlifts that brought the Ethiopian Jews to Israel. This undertaking showed the depth of Menachem Begin's concern for the Jewish People in all their dispersions and variations.

Above: Rabbi Baruch Frydman-Kohl, left, is greeted by Prime Minister Menachem Begin. He had been invited to attend one of Begin's traditional Saturday evening Bible study groups, Jerusalem, 1980.

The Reunion

BY JACK KUPER

When the war that had made me an orphan was over and I came out of hiding, I fled Poland in the company of other child survivors. Along the way, fate intervened. While they braved the British blockade to Palestine, eventually reaching the shores of Eretz Israel, I found an uncle, followed him to Brussels, and ultimately ended up in the safety of Canada.

As the years tumbled on, I often thought of my pals enshrined in the pages of my photo album. Their memory haunted me like a grim shadow. Every Arab terrorist bullet that snuffed out a life made me think it was meant for me. Although the mere mention of the Jewish state elevated me to new heights, I made no move to set foot there. That is, until the summer of 1970.

Landing in Tel Aviv with my wife, Terrye, I expected to see my comrades of yesteryear dancing the horah. The breathtaking land tugged me and powerful hands sprouting from the ancient soil gripped my ankles. Stay, Yankele. This is where you belong.

Back in Toronto, I resigned from my cushy advertising job, sold our car, and rented our house and farm. My mother-in-law implored me to reconsider, but Terrye stood by me. Our three youngest looked forward to the adventure, but

fourteen-year-old Ellen called us Zionists. Neighbours were baffled. "Why are you going? Canada is your country."

Once we were settled in the Merkaz Haklita in Jerusalem's Katamon district, I launched a search for my Zionist comrades. One inquiry led to another until I was directed to a kibbutz between Tel Aviv and Haifa. One blistering Saturday, we piled into the car, and I steered our new Opel to Maanit.

"Do you know who I am?" I smiled at the familiar face of the man who answered the cottage door. He sized me up. "Show me your photographs," I said. A seated woman looked up when we entered. I recognized her as well. He reached up to fetch a dust-covered album from the top of a bureau. The focus of the first page was a photo of four youngsters in mixed army gear, brandishing weapons. The two seated in the foreground held a crudely painted

Above: Jack Kuper (Yaakov Kuperblum) stands on the left beside Pinchas Zając. Seated are: Itzchak Ruchlajmer, left, and Motel Liwer (the partisan). They were photographed in 1946, in Poland, dressed in military gear and holding a sign in Yiddish that reads "Our Future."

Yiddish sign, proclaiming, "Our Future." I pointed to the one standing to the left, with a pistol tucked in his belt.

"You're Yaakov?" His gasp tore his wife away from her sewing machine.

"You're the one who hungered to play accordion," she said.

The first pages of the album could easily have been mistaken for my own, but what followed was radically different: bulldozers clearing land, houses in stages of construction, kibbutzniks harvesting fruit, tanks in the windswept desert, young soldiers at the Suez Canal, celebration at the ancient Wailing Wall.

Over lunch in the clamorous communal hall, I encountered others from my group. They shook my hand with hazy memories and fogged eyes. I introduced Terrye, my children.

"What happened to you? Where have you been?" they asked.

An older version of Itzchak, the stamp collector, now in overalls and rubber boots in charge of livestock, was summoned to our table. Benjamin, the fellow we had nicknamed "Professor," soon appeared. When I inquired about Motel the partisan, Pinchas Zając, now a mathematics teacher, told me, "Motel is a big business man in Haifa. He sells tractors."

Several were no longer alive: one had been murdered in an ambush, another had stepped on a mine.

"I always felt guilty for deserting," I confessed to Pinchas, the one I felt closest to. "Your silent stares when I left have pursued me through life."

He swung an arm around my shoulders, pulling me towards him. "Don't you realize what that was all about, Yaakov? You found family and we were jealous."

– Excerpt from Jack Kuper's book, After the Smoke Cleared (Toronto: Stoddart, 1994).

Background: Jack Kuper in the shaded courtyard of East Jerusalem's American Colony Hotel, 1970.

Guarding Continuity

BY KURT ROTHSCHILD

In this century we have experienced the greatest threat to our Jewish existence and yet also the greatest opportunities granted to us after two thousand years of exile. My personal life and communal involvement are a reflection of this traumatic period. We are faced with a constant challenge to work for the continuity of our people and Israel.

I was born in Cologne, Germany, into an Orthodox family rooted in the life of German Jewry. At the age of sixteen, after Hitler had been in power for three years, my parents sent me to the safety of England to work and study.

In 1940, together with other young German Jewish men, I was shipped to Canada and placed in an internment camp. The British had categorized us as "enemy aliens," and the Canadian government of the time did not change our designation for two years. This episode had an abiding influence on my life and that of all those who shared the two years behind barbed wire in New Brunswick and the province of Quebec.

Following my release from internment camp, I attended Queen's University

in Kingston, where I obtained a degree in Electrical Engineering. Thereafter, I established a national multi-trade contracting firm, headquartered in Toronto. At the same time, I considered it a priority to be actively involved in Jewish causes in Israel, Canada, and the United States.

Some twenty years ago my wife, Edith, and I established a home in Jerusalem, where we spend several months a year. For many years I have made it a custom to visit the military cemetery on Mount Herzl on the day before Yom Kippur. I wander alone, or with one of my grandchildren, among the graves of the thousands of young Israeli soldiers, many of them born in the countries of exile, who gave their lives for the defence of our precious homeland. Every year I stumble upon new graves. It is my time to identify with them and reflect on the immense heroic sacrifices that brought about the founding of the State of Israel and which continue to safeguard its security.

Above: Kurt Rothschild and his wife, Edith.
Left: Kurt Rothschild, right, receiving the Jerusalem Prize for Jewish Education from Israeli president Ezer Weitzman at Beit Hanasi ("the President's House"), June 1997.

The Conversation

BY HOWARD ADELMAN

T he most exhilarating event of my many visits to Israel occurred, surprisingly, in a surgical waiting room in 1980.

While I was consulting a retired Israeli for an article I was writing, he began to experience chest pains. Because he had a heart condition, I took him to the nearest hospital, Tel Hashomer. Once he was safely in the emergency department, I heard the name "Nguyen" over the intercom, summoning a doctor to Surgery. That sparked my curiosity, because I had been involved in Operation Lifeline, which had encouraged private sponsorship of Indochinese refugees to Canada. I knew that Israel had taken in eight hundred refugees, and I wondered whether Dr. Nguyen was one of them.

The hospital was then housed in a series of Quonset huts, and I set out to find Surgery. When I got there I discovered that Dr. Nguyen was expected shortly, and after he arrived, I spoke with him briefly. It turned out he was the leader of the first four hundred refugees who had arrived in Israel. Their resettlement had generally gone well. The doctor couldn't talk any longer, but suggested that, if I had time, I should wait for him.

Sitting on the bench in the waiting area was a boy, also Vietnamese. Unlike Dr. Nguyen, he did not speak English, but he seemed to know some Hebrew. My Hebrew was terrible; despite having studied it for years, I had never spoken any, except for the odd phrase. However, as I was determined to speak to this boy, I decided to give it a try.

I learned that the boy was twelve, had arrived in Israel ten months earlier, and was waiting for Dr. Nguyen to operate to remove the sixth finger on his hand – which he proudly displayed. His flight from Vietnam had seemed to him an adventure rather than a terrifying ordeal, even though he had not been with his parents. As we talked, it became clear that he was fluent in Hebrew. I suddenly realized we had been talking for forty minutes. Fearing that my Israeli friend would come out of the emergency department and find that I was not there, I rushed away. Only then did I realize that I had been speaking Hebrew all that time without thinking about it.

I never did meet Dr. Nguyen again, and I cannot remember the boy's name. But I won't forget him or our conversation. And, though I have tried, I have never been able to converse in Hebrew since!

Above: Professor Howard Adelman has worked with Canada's department of foreign affairs on the issue of Palestinian refugees in the West Bank and Gaza.

Scout's Honour

FROM A CONVERSATION WITH ROBERT ENGEL

I was born on March 26, 1923, in Berlin, Germany. I was a Boy Scout in Germany, but I couldn't stay in the Scouts after Hitler came to power, because they were soon taken over by the Hitler Youth. Shortly after, I joined a Jewish Scouting movement called Maccabi Hatzair. In Israel there is still a very small movement by that name. (In Canada, it's known as Young Judea.)

After Kristallnacht in 1938, there was a push to get Jewish children out of Germany. This program – called Children First! – was started in England, supported by Quakers, and then spread to other countries. England took ten thousand children, Holland two thousand, and France and Belgium took some as well. My mother registered me in the program, and I was selected to go to Holland, where I was placed in a children's refugee camp in Eindhoven. It was run like an orphanage.

When I was in Holland in 1939, Dutch Scouts came to the camp and made a camp fire for us. We were so happy to be visited by other young people instead of elderly ladies. We shook their left hands in the traditional Scouting handshake, and told them we had been Scouts in Germany and Austria. They said, "Why don't you start your own group?" And we did, with their help. But when the Germans occupied Holland,

the Scouts were outlawed immediately, along with the Girl Guides, the Communist Party, the Masons – anything international.

A woman who was the former head of the Dutch Refugee Committee in Eindhoven eventually helped me find a Jewish family to stay with. When the Dutch Scouts formed a resistance cell, I became a part of it. I was arrested in 1942 and shipped to the Westerbork concentration camp in Holland. It served as a labour camp where people worked until being transferred to an extermination camp. One thousand people were shipped out per week. I was put to work at the camp and remained there until Liberation.

I came to Canada in 1951 and lived in Montreal for twenty years before moving to Toronto. In 1956 I started my own company, importing goods from Israel, which necessitated my travelling there at least twice a year. I had become a Scoutmaster in Montreal, and on my second trip to Israel, back in 1958, I asked one of the manufacturers there if he knew someone involved in Scouting, because I wanted to visit

Above: Some of the Canadian contingent at Israel's 50th Anniversary of Scouts, 1969. Robert Engel is standing second from the right.

a very emotional moment for me when I presented our flag. I had been liberated by the Canadian army in Westerbork, and because of that, Canada has always been tremendously dear to me. To march in Israel behind the "Canada" sign, with the Canadian flag in front of us, was very special for me.

When I see those Scouts in Israel, or when they come to Canada every year with the Friendship Caravan, and they dance and sing in their Israeli uniforms with the Star of David, for me that's the ultimate sign that Hitler didn't win the war.

Top: Marching proudly behind the "Canada" sign, Robert Engel, second row right, parades with the Canadian Boy Scouts and Girl Guides at the 1969 Israel Scouts Jubilee celebrations held in Israel.

Background: A moment of reflection for a Canadian Scout and Guide at the Western Wall, 1969.

un Israeli troop. He checked around and was able to arrange a meeting for me with a Scout leader.

This Scout leader and I became friends, and he explained to me that Israel had a big problem in scouting. Children are taught that Scouting is a worldwide movement, but since Israeli children could not cross the border to shake hands with Arab Scouts, they needed to reach out to other friendly countries. There was an association of friends of Israeli Scouts in Britain, France, and America, and he wanted me to start the same program in Canada.

In 1963 we brought two Israeli Scouts over to visit Canada for the first time. In 1969 a Canadian contingent of twelve Scouts and Guides went to the Golden Jamboree of Jewish Scouting in the Holy Land. (The first group of Scouts had been started in 1919 by British officers.) It's a tradition in scouting that at the end of your visit to a foreign country you present your country's flag to the host country as a gift. It was

I Met the Challenge

BY MANNY ROTMAN

After being alone for about two years following the passing of my wife, Goldie, my depression and restlessness pushed me to consider a change of environment. At that time I had already completed about half of my obligations for a degree at the University of Toronto, and it crossed my mind that a year's study abroad, in a warm climate, would take me away from the bitter winter cold and could change my mood for the better. I mailed letters of introduction to several universities, and eventually I was accepted by the Hebrew University of Jerusalem as a part–time student.

I arrived in Israel on September 9, 1977. I had hoped to get accommodations at the Hebrew University dormitory, but they felt it would be undesirable for a sixty-eight-year-old to be among a group of young students, so I rented an apartment at 4 Disraeli Street. About two months later, a thief broke into the apartment and stole my best clothes and many precious things. The suffering of my losses, though, was a small price to pay for running off as I did into the unknown, leaving my family behind. During this period, Ruth, who was to become my second wife, came to Israel on a Na'amat trip. We

discussed marriage and decided to advise the family of our intention.

Studying my university subjects in Hebrew was not as easy as saying my prayers, which I had learned long ago in Poland. This was because prayers don't need interpretation. At the university I found Hebrew conversation the most difficult. In the main, though, students, as well as the professors and their assistants, were most helpful and respectful.

Learning to speak, read, and write Hebrew almost fluently, and satisfying the academic requirements of two universities – well, I consider these to be among the greatest achievements of my life. Thank you to the Hebrew University and thank you to the University of Toronto.

– Manny Rotman passed away on December 27, 1997.

Above: Manny Rotman, at one of the five gates of Israel's Supreme Court in Jerusalem, May 1995.

Standing Upright

BY RABBI RAPHAEL MARCUS

Every day of my life in my morning prayers, I petitioned the Almighty: "... and may you bring us in peace from the four corners of the earth and lead us 'standing upright' (*komemiyus*) into our land."

Well, when I was seventeen, for me at least, those prayers were answered. I'd finished my Jewish high-school education and was travelling to Israel for further study. The event that would irrevocably change my life began on the El Al flight with the clapping, the singing, the heartfelt emotion. I was brought "standing upright" in peace to Eretz Yisrael, just as it said in the prayer.

In my first year at Yeshiva Kerem B'Yavneh, where the Torah, the word of G-d, is studied, I arose early and retired late every night, immersed in my studies with a depth and intensity I had never before felt. Why? In part, because of my two Israeli roommates.

There were cultural differences between us. In our room there were about thirty hangers in the closet, five filled with the clothing of my two roommates, and twenty-five hangers filled with my clothes; it didn't take long to dawn on me that clothes left in a trunk and not on hangers made for smoother international relationships. While we in Toronto talked about

subjects aside from our studies, the Israeli yeshivah students spoke only of two subjects: Torah scholarship and service to their country in the Israeli army.

One day my new Israeli friends suddenly left "standing upright" for the second commitment of our yeshivah: they left for army training and duty. They understood that our return to the land after two thousand years placed new obligations on our people and required us to make sacrifices of the highest order.

I shall never forget the sight of one of my Israeli friends returning from paratroop training. He could barely walk and was in obvious pain. He didn't leave his bed except for prayers and Torah studies – apart from the hour or so he held court with friends, sharing his experiences. It put my North American values into a perspective that is still with me.

Today, I am privileged to serve as rabbi of Congregation B'nai Torah, an Orthodox synagogue committed to the strongest ties with the State of Israel and to the unity of the whole Jewish community of Toronto.

Above: In the Old City of Jerusalem, Rabbi Raphael Marcus, right, celebrates Yom Yerushalayim with young Israelis, 1990s.

Hebrew: A Living Language

BY MAURICE BENZACAR

Even though it was not until 1971 that I first set foot on Israeli soil, Israel had been part of my "mental environment" since the 1940s. When I was a child in Morocco, my mother often said to me, "If I don't see Jerusalem with my own eyes, I hope you will see it for me." Every year, at the end of the Pesach seder, when we sang "*Leshana haba'a be Yerushalayim*," my heart flew over to Jerusalem.

I was a Zionist, as was everyone else in the community. Our Zionism came from our heart, our mind, our prayers. It was a mystical, spiritual, religious feeling which had always been kept alive in the Sephardi communities all over the world. It was quite different from the intellectual, political, left-wing Labour–Zionism of our brothers and sisters of Eastern Europe, but no less real or powerful.

May 14, 1948, the day of the creation of the State of Israel, is one of my dearest memories. I can still see all of us sitting around the radio, counting the votes of the UN Assembly. The relief, the pride, and the general sense of euphoria that we felt remain beyond description. Soon afterward, the Jewish Agency began sending representatives to Morocco to recruit young men and women to make aliyah to Israel. Those of us who stayed behind faced difficult times, because Morocco, an Arab country, could not have direct contact with Israel. So we were cut off from our dear ones who had left for Israel, since there was no postal service between the two countries. Every Saturday night, we would sit around the radio and listen to the programme *Kol Tsion la gola*, during which people who had settled in Israel sent greetings and encouraged us to make aliyah.

In 1957 I left my native land of Morocco for the first time. The offices of Hebrew Immigrant Aid Service and the Jewish Agency in Casablanca sometimes sent a few families to Canada and the United States to appease the Moroccan government, since the majority of the Jews left for Eretz Yisrael. With my wife and one-year-old son, I took off from Casablanca on an Air France plane to Paris, where we were making a stop to say goodbye to relatives. From there we flew on an El Al flight to New York.

How proud we were to be on an Israeli airplane. Coming from Morocco, an Arab country, it was a moving experience to walk over to an El Al counter in Orly, where I saw Israeli

Above: Maurice Benzacar, 1997.

hostesses, Israeli pilots, and the blue-and-white Israeli flag with the Star of David, displayed out in the open, for the first time in my life. Then I heard Hebrew over the airplane loud-speaker: "Welcome, fasten your seat belts . . ." It was wonderful. Imagine: Hebrew outside the context of prayer, a living language! I thought I would burst with pride.

In 1971, travelling with two close friends, I made my first trip to Israel. I met with my father and brothers for the first time in fifteen years. After landing at Ben-Gurion Airport, we headed straight to the Kotel (Western Wall), where we put on our tefillin. From Jerusalem we drove to Hebron to visit the tombs of our ancestors. We were so moved that we could hardly talk. So many thoughts were racing through our minds, so many memories: our involvement with the UJA, JNF, and the Zionist movement; our family who had not been granted this joy; the young soldiers who had given their lives so we could be there and live this moment of unspeakable pride, freedom, and gratitude to the Almighty who'd made it possible.

Below: Left to right: Maurice Benzacar, Jacques Perez, and Albert Bitton, in front of the Western Wall, 1971.

Passover in the Desert

BY ANNE TULCHINSKY

When I arrived in Israel that spring of 1979, the first thing my sons did was to take me around the hills of Jerusalem, where everything looked so lush and green, so breathtakingly beautiful.

After a relaxed Shabbat with the family, I went to the market. The variety of fruits, vegetables, and flowers was outstanding, especially the huge oranges, grapefruits, and strawberries. Along the streets of Jerusalem I saw signs of Erev Pesach (the evening before the Passover holiday): women washing windows and beating carpets, and bedding hanging on clotheslines. After a day of cooking it was time for the seder (the Passover meal). So many times I had repeated "Next year in Jerusalem," and now here I was!

The next day the adventure began. We prepared for our trip to the Sinai: packing food; freezing milk, juice, and water in huge plastic containers; preparing the sleeping bags, blankets, tents, and chairs. We left very early in the morning and finally reached Maagam. It was surrounded on three sides by mountains and on the fourth by the beautiful blue sea.

We set up our tents and swam to cool off. We shared the beach with a busload of tourists. A friendly Bedouin kept the beach tidy.

This great-grandmother had never camped in her life, and although the sleeping bag was soft and cosy, the ground was hard. I slept anyway. There were no facilities here; we washed in the sea, and when we ran out of water, we had to go to Neviot for more. The sense of isolation, even with others camped on the beach, was inspiring. The real joy of camping is that people have time to sit, talk, and relax.

The other campers came from many lands, including Germany and Russia. In the evening we could see and hear them around us, singing and dancing in the moonlight. It was wonderful to watch. The military patrolled the beach several times after dark, and we could see faint lights from across the sea in Saudi Arabia, and from ships slowly passing by.

When it was time to leave, we said emotional goodbyes to our new friends while we all packed up. As I looked around, I thought what a privileged experience it was for me to have camped in the Sinai on Passover.

Above: Schmooze time in the Sinai desert during the Passover camping trip, 1979. Anne Tulchinsky is seated, back row, far left.

Full Circle

BY YAFFA WISE

When Shelly and I were married in Israel on July 2, 1972, it was more than just a happy event for our families. For our mothers it was a reaffirmation of life and a triumph of the spirit.

My mother, Rivka, and Shelly's mother, Manya, grew up in Stopnitz in pre-World War II Poland. Their families were neighbours and shared many good and bad times together. During the war the two young women were deported to the same work camp. For three years they shared a sleeping bunk, cared for and supported one another, covered for each other when one was sick, shared food and clothing, and kept each other's spirits up.

After the war my mother's family went to Israel and settled on Kfar Shmuel, a moshav in the Ayalon valley. Shelly's family came to Toronto. Rivka and Manya wrote letters updating each other about their families.

I first met Shelly in the summer of 1962. In honour of his bar mitzvah, Shelly had been sent to Israel to spend the summer on Kfar HaYarok. Manya asked her old friend Rivka to check on her son, and naturally my mother took me along. I don't remember much from the visit; Shelly remembers a

skinny, eleven-year-old girl hiding behind her mother.

The second time we met, I was already in the army and Shelly was a student at the University of Toronto. To our surprise, Shelly and I discovered we had grown up listening to the same stories about Poland, both before and during the war. But we also found out that we had more than stories in common.

Shelly and I and our children, Tali, Yishai, Ami, and Nati, live in Toronto. However, I feel that my greatest accomplishment in raising my children has been instilling in each of them a love for Israel; they consider Israel home. All four children speak Hebrew and feel comfortable with Israeli culture. Now my life has come full circle, as our family is in the early stages of building a home in Israel, across the road from my parents on the moshav where I grew up.

Above: At Nathan Wise's bar mitzvah in 1992, the two friends are reunited. Seated, left to right, are: Manya, Shelly's mother, and Rivka, Yaffa's mother. Standing, left to right, are: Yishai, Grandfather Meyer, Tali, Nati, Grandfather Herschel, and Ami.

"I travelled throughout Israel about nine years ago with my then-eighteen-year-old son while researching a book," writes **Diane Francis**, pictured here in 1997.

"I was raised in Skokie, Illinois, a predominantly Jewish neighbourhood, where all my friends were Jewish and we were Zionists with a huge affinity for Israel.

"Both my children were touched by their contact with Israel. My son bought a Star-of-David pinkie ring on our trip and has never taken it off. My daughter travelled to Israel and spent eight months there. After working on a moshav, she attended a yeshivah and studied Talmud. I think that my great-grandfather, who came from Germany and was named Reichman, may have been Jewish – perhaps that explains my Zionism.

"In Israel I realized what an act of courage it takes to live among one's enemies, and I was amazed by what has been accomplished in only two generations."

Shelly Gwartz Allen with **Golda Meir** in December 1974. "A year after the Yom Kippur War," recalls Shelly Allen, "the United Jewish Appeal invited Golda Meir to speak to the Toronto community at large. What an honour it was for me to present her with flowers at a special luncheon at the Inn on the Park! Especially since that year in school I had written an essay on the woman I most admired – Golda Meir!"

David **Demson** is a professor of theology at Emmanuel College, University of Toronto. A long-time member of Canadian Professors for Peace in the Middle East and of the publication committee for *Middle East Focus*, Professor Demson has participated in and led several study missions to Israel. Those include a 1978 sabbatical at a Christian college near Jerusalem and a 1979 tour, during which this photograph of him wearing an Israel Defence Forces cap was taken.

"In 1977," writes **Mirial Small**, "I had the privilege of chairing the Canadian Hadassah-WIZO convention in Israel, attended by 650 men and women from across Canada. The most incredible event of the convention occurred at the closing banquet, at which Menachem Begin spoke, making the stunning announcement that he had invited Anwar al-Sadat to visit Jerusalem. While many of us were still in Israel, Sadat arrived for his historic visit.

"Four years later, Sadat's wife, Jihan, received our Hadassah-WIZO mission with grandeur and warmth at the Sadats' residence in Cairo, completing the circle that had begun in Israel." Pictured here at the Sadats' residence in 1981 are: **Madame Jihan Sadat**, centre, with Mirial Small and Mirial's husband, **Allen**.

Jim and **Heather Peterson** are shown here at Masada overlooking the Dead Sea, on their first trip to Israel in 1976. Jim returned in 1982 with a group of Canadian parliamentarians. "We met leaders from all parties and were among the first outsiders to visit Lebanon following Israel's entry. Two days after we left Beirut, Israel's ally, President Gemayel, was assassinated. Upon returning to Canada we reported on the hostilities that had wracked Lebanon."

The many faces of modern Israel.

THE
PRESENT

Gathering Our People

Judy Feld Carr and the Damascus Keter

Among the thousands of ancient Hebrew manuscripts held by the Jewish National Library in Jerusalem, one unique work remains hidden from public view. Its travels in the last decade of the twentieth century were shrouded in as much secrecy as its early wanderings. It left Spain in the mid-sixteenth century and made its way to Damascus, Syria. There it remained for hundreds of years, in the basement of a synagogue.

This veiled manuscript is the Damascus Keter ("Crown") or Codex, an exquisite compilation of the sacred books of the Jewish People – the Torah, the Prophets and Ketubim. By what Sephardi hand it was written is not known. Unlike most manuscripts, it has no colophon identifying either its scribe or the benefactor for whom it must have been written with such loving devotion, probably over a lifetime.

Until 1992, the outside world knew nothing of its existence. Were it not for a chance meeting, it might now be in the hands of the secret police of Syria, lost for all time to the Jewish People.

For some twenty years, Judy Feld Carr of Toronto had striven covertly to bring the hostage Syrian Jewish community out of the veritable prison that was its own country. The members of this community, with roots going back to the time of the Second Temple, had been forbidden to emigrate since 1948. For almost forty years they suffered unspeakable privation at the hands of the Syrian government. Only their deep commitment to Judaism and their hope of ultimate salvation kept them intact as a community.

By paying bribes to get "legal" passports, and paying more bribes to smugglers to spirit people across the borders, Judy had been responsible for the exit of 3,212 Syrian Jews.

Above: Judy Feld Carr, holding the Damascus Keter, which she rescued from Syria in 1993.
Facing page: As a result of her rescue by Judy Feld Carr, this Syrian "bubbie" was able to celebrate at her granddaughter's wedding in Israel. Judy, over a period of twenty years, rescued thousands of Syrian Jews.

This was no mass exodus, but rather one or two members of a family at a time – perhaps a father and mother and one child – to be followed years later by another child. It was an agonizingly slow and dangerous process.

In 1995, when virtually all the Jews had left Syria, Prime Minister Yitzhak Rabin sent a personal letter of commendation to Judy Feld Carr, which said, in part, "Words cannot express my gratitude for the twenty-three years of hard and dangerous work, during which you devoted your time and your life to the Jewish community in Syria. . . . The Jews of Syria who were rescued and the State of Israel owe you so much. . . . And the rest will be told in history books. Judy, the State of Israel salutes you."

By the early 1990s, while still negotiating and bargaining for exits for the few hundred Syrian Jews who remained, Judy had begun to turn her attention to the priceless articles of Jewish worship and study in Syria. Thus, dozens of printed volumes and the last remaining Torah scroll in Aleppo found their way to her home in Toronto, and from there to Jerusalem.

In the summer of 1992, on a visit to the laboratories of the Israel Museum, Judy watched as the last of the pages of the famous Aleppo Keter, used as a reference by the great Moses Maimonides, were restored. The curator happened to mention that scholars believed there was a Damascus Keter, although there had been no tangible evidence of it.

Back in Toronto, she set to work with her contacts inside and outside Syria to track down the book. She learned that, indeed, there was a Keter, which had been kept for generations in one of the city's synagogues. There, in a glass case, with frequently replaced dishes of water to maintain humidity, it had been venerated almost as a talisman. Only once a year – on Shavuot, the commemoration of the giving of the Torah to Moses and the Jewish People – was it ever brought out of its case and read to the congregation.

Through the Jewish "underground" that she had established, Judy inquired whether it would be possible to remove the book. She knew that the Syrians had made a detailed inventory of all Jewish religious artifacts and that anyone caught trying to take anything out of the country would suffer immediate imprisonment and the torture for which the Mukhabarat (secret police) were infamous.

One of her contacts said that he was prepared to risk removing the book from the synagogue, for he, too, believed that it would be a sin to leave it behind. However, he would not be able to take it out of the country, and he knew nobody who could. Without some workable plan to get it across the border, it was useless to remove the book. If the secret police were to visit the synagogue and find it gone, there would follow a house-to-house search of the entire Jewish quarter until the book was discovered.

Judy brought to bear all the intensive research skills that had served her so well over the past two decades, and which had led to the discovery of capable and willing go-betweens,

Above left: The magnificent Damascus Keter, its ancient text preserved on fragile translucent vellum.

couriers, and smugglers to bring out Jews. Now it was a Jewish book – inanimate, much easier to conceal – that needed rescuing.

Finally, Judy found someone she could trust who, by coincidence, was going to visit Damascus. She knew him well, but she had never before involved him in her clandestine work. She decided that it was best for him, as well as for her and her friend in Damascus, if he did not know how precious was the object she wanted him to transport. She told him only that a friend of hers in Syria wished to send her a present. She thought the present was a Jewish book of some description. Since the Syrians wanted to keep all Jewish artifacts in the country, it would have to be spirited out covertly. Would he do her a favour and take it from her friend? She would come and retrieve it from her new courier when he had got it safely out of Syria. He agreed.

Judy got a message to her friend in Damascus, advising him that he would be contacted and that he could safely turn over the book when he received the password. The friend quietly removed the book from its case in the synagogue basement and took it home, trembling lest anyone discover that it was gone.

But all went well. The courier arrived in Damascus and a secret meeting was arranged. The friend passed the book to the courier, who slid it under his coat. The courier then took a cab, but in case he had been followed by the secret police, he got out some distance from his hotel and walked a circuitous route the rest of the way.

Ten days later Judy met the courier and received the book. She then took a plane back to Toronto, nonchalantly carrying a black plastic shopping bag as she walked through the arrivals area. No one seeing her would have known how nervous she was or guessed that a priceless object was in her bag. She had rescued one of the most important sacred books of the Jewish People. Somehow, mystically, she had been given the *schut* (privilege) of rounding out her rescue of so many souls by rescuing the precious texts that had nourished those people – her people – for centuries.

Postscript: The Keter was presented by Judy Feld Carr and the former chief rabbi of Syria, Rabbi Ibrahim Hamra, to the president of Israel, Ezer Weizman. The ceremony took place at the President's House (Beit Hanasi) on March 19, 1998.

Left: The first man Judy Feld Carr helped to escape from Syria, shown here with his family, now all safe in Israel, 1979.

Gathering Our People

Since the State of Israel was created in 1948, a number of rescue operations have brought Jews from many countries of the world to a new life in Israel. These rescue operations were not simply an Israeli objective, but an aspiration and challenge for the entire Jewish People.

Operation Magic Carpet, 1949–1950
Nearly forty-nine thousand of Yemen's fifty-five thousand Jews were airlifted to Israel.

Operation Moses, 1984–1985
About seven thousand Jews from Ethiopia were rescued. Most walked to Sudan, where they were airlifted to Israel under a veil of secrecy.

Operation Solomon, 1991
Most of the Jews remaining in Ethiopia — some fifteen thousand people — were airlifted directly from Ethiopia to Israel on May 24 and 25.

Operation Exodus, 1990–1996
When President Gorbachev opened the doors of the Soviet Union and allowed Jews to leave freely, over seven hundred thousand Russian Jews came to Israel.

The Jews of Ethiopia

FROM A CONVERSATION WITH SIMCHA JACOBOVICI

I am the child of Holocaust survivors, and that, as well as my being Israeli-born, has given me a very strong Jewish and Zionist identity and a commitment to the Jewish People and their survival.

This attracted me to the plight of the Ethiopian Jews, once known as the Falashas. I didn't want to see a Jewish community annihilated while I was one of the people who watched in silence. As a Zionist, I was appalled that the Jewish community in general, and Israel specifically, was not doing everything it could to rescue this Jewish community. As chairperson of the North American Union of Jewish Students Network during my grad-school years, I had worked hard to bring attention to the plight of the Ethiopian Jews. Now, as a journalist, I had a means to publicize the issue.

In 1981 I wrote the first articles to appear in the secular press about the plight of Ethiopian Jews and the inactivity of Israel. The articles appeared in the pages of the *Globe and Mail* and the *New York Times*. There was an Israeli cabinet meeting to review the allegations, and Menachem Begin denied the charges. I noticed that as long as there was publicity such as my articles, there were rescue efforts, but when the publicity died down, so did the rescue efforts.

I tried to interest documentarians in making a film about Ethiopian Jews, but the obstacles seemed insurmountable. On the one hand the established Jewish community seemed uninterested in such a project, and on the other, there was a Marxist regime in power in Ethiopia. No Western film crew had ever gotten access to the Ethiopian Jews since the time of Haile Selassie. Finally, I decided to make the film myself. Had I actually known what I was getting into, I would never have done it.

I went to the library and checked out a book on documentary films, then began raising money. I financed the project with my credit cards and a grant from the Ontario Arts Council. In the end the film would cost about three hundred thousand dollars; however, I'd raised only about twenty thousand dollars when I began filming. Our film crew (me and four others) sneaked into Ethiopia, got to the Ethiopian Jews, filmed them, and smuggled the film out. Then we went to Sudan and interviewed Ethiopian Jews

Above: Simcha Jacobovici, producer of the award winning documentary film Falashas: Exile of the Black Jews.

Facing page: A Menmasseh priest in front of ancient Aramaic writing.

in refugee camps. I interviewed Sudan's ambassador to Washington and the Sudanese vice–president (who was later jailed for co–operating with the Israelis on the airlift of the Ethiopian Jews from Sudan). When we arrived in Israel, our film was almost confiscated, until I pointed out how it would look if I had been able to go in and out of dictatorships in Ethiopia and Sudan, only to have my film confiscated in democratic Israel.

Because I needed money to finance the final product, I actually ended up making several short films first. I made a half–hour film called *Falashas: Agony of the Black Jews*, which aired on CBC's *Man Alive* series, and one for the United Nations High Commission for Refugees called *Forgotten Refugees*. I also made a fifteen–minute piece for CBC's *The Journal*, and a fifteen–minute segment for NBC. With the money from NBC, I was finally able to finish a ninety–minute documentary feature called *Falashas: Exile of the Black Jews*.

Below: Simcha Jacobovici, on the far left, outside Nablus/Schechem on location during filming of Deadly Currents, *his award-winning documentary on the Palestinian–Israeli conflict, 1990-91.*

It was released in 1984 and went on to win several international awards, including a Certificate of Special Merit from the Academy of Motion Picture Arts and Sciences in Los Angeles.

Back then my film was not aired on Israeli television. However, it was screened in the Knesset. Israeli politicians were shocked to see the vice-president of Sudan admitting there were Ethiopian Jews in his country and that he didn't mind if they went through European countries in order to make their way to Israel. And that was what indeed finally happened. During Operation Moses in 1984 and 1985, the Falashas went from Sudan to Belgium to Israel.

I have made many films since then. Currently, I am completing work on a film about the ten lost tribes of Israel. We essentially used the Bible as a treasure map: "Where does the Bible say they went?" Our shooting took us to many places: to Tunisia, to Uzbekistan, and to the Afghanistan–Pakistan border. We landed at the Burma–India border and were greeted by the people from the tribe of Menmasseh, who live in the Indian states of Manipur and Mizoram and in Burma. Three thousand of them practise Judaism. They believe they are descended from the lost tribe of Israel named "Menashe." "Menmasseh" is thought to have evolved from that original tribal name. They wore yarmulkes, and the tzitzit (fringes) from their tallises (prayer shawls) peeked out from under their clothing. A bus ride, filled with Hebrew song, took us to their synagogue, where we all davened (prayed). I hope

our new film will raise the issue of these people as we raised the issue of the Ethiopian Jews.

I am very proud that our documentary on the Falashas was cited as being a catalyst for the airlifts of Ethiopian Jews. It influenced the Jewish agenda and that translated into action that saved lives. I think the Canadian Jewish community, and Toronto specifically, has played a great role in, and for, Israel, and I believe one of its noblest moments was the role it played on behalf of the Ethiopian Jews.

Above: Ethiopian Jews receiving medicine at a clinic set up by the Israeli Embassy, Addis Ababa, 1991.

The Money Lady

BY LORETTA TANENBAUM

In the fall of 1986 our family had the privilege of spending several months in Jerusalem. While our children studied and my husband worked, a part-time job fell into my lap. The American Association for Ethiopian Jews (AAEJ) needed someone to locate all Ethiopian *olim* (immigrants) who were post-secondary students and give them a one-time sum of money to help offset the cost of books, fees, or bus tickets. It was not a large cheque but it would help. I was to go to the registrars of all the universities and get lists of the Ethiopian students.

Word of the cheques spread around the Ethiopian community like wildfire, and life in our Katamon apartment took a new turn. I was deluged by letters and personal visits from new immigrants desperately seeking help. Over endless cups of tea, I learned to understand the halting Hebrew with the lilting Amharic accent, choking back my tears as I heard of mothers crossing the desert on foot with babies strapped to their backs, of attacks by the "shifta," of the people who did not make it to the refugee centres in Sudan. I dealt mostly with men, for the women were shy and not used to speaking out.

The decisions were sometimes hard to make. Were trade-school students included? What about yeshivah students?

And then there was the student who asked for an extra two hundred shekels to pay dorm fees so he could remain in school. He promised to pay it back at the end of the year. I gave it to him, and he did pay it back.

In the course of the months, the number of Ethiopians increased. I believe that as soon as they landed, someone whispered that there was a "money lady," and my apartment often became one of their first stops. They walked in my door with a need to talk.

The task of absorbing this immigration was enormous, and the cultural differences were wide. I knew that I was meeting people who were tenacious and determined, resourceful and hardworking. I saw a love of Israel and a deep faith, and I was humbled by their trust in me. When we left, a small delegation arrived at my door with flowers and some postcards with their names for me to remember them by. Indeed, I will never forget.

Above: Loretta Tanenbaum with friend Amnon from Ethiopia, Israel 1986.

They Are Our People

BY CECILY PETERS

As national president of Hadassah–WIZO of Canada, I had the privilege of playing a role in Operation Moses. The village of Hofim, supported by our Canadian Youth Aliyah organization, was chosen to be the main absorption centre for Ethiopian children. One of my most exciting memories was the phone call from Uri Gordon, world head of Youth Aliyah, to say that the children would be arriving there in a few weeks. It had to be kept top secret. On July 25, 1984, the first group of children arrived.

One of my many visits to Hofim stands out. As our buses pulled into the village, the Canadian flag was flown from the buildings in our honour. We were told the most touching stories of the 183 Ethiopian youngsters there. The children had seen so many deaths that even a sore throat would make them think they were dying. Six of them were sitting shivah (the seven days of mourning immediately following a funeral) the day we were there; they had just received word that their parents had died while trying to get to the refugee camps en route to Israel.

After having lunch with the children I made a speech that was translated into Amharic for them. I told them they had inspired us to return home and work even harder on their behalf, and ended with a prayer that they would soon be joined with their families. The children in turn performed several Israeli songs, danced, and sang in Amharic. It was a most memorable day for all of us.

Right: Standing, left to right, Ben and Ruth Wagman, Cecily and David Peters, Moses and Harriane Kronick, and Cyril Rotenberg. Seated are, Blanche Katz and Gertie Rotenberg.

Heroines of Aliyah

BY FRAN SONSHINE

I am a child of Holocaust survivors, ardent Zionists who made their way to Israel after World War II. They were part of the many groups who crossed the Italian Alps by foot and sailed the Mediterranean in dilapidated ships, only to be turned away by the British in Haifa. They were sent to a detention camp in Cyprus, where I was born. Still behind barbed wire two-and-a-half years later, we were finally allowed to go to Israel. In 1952 we joined the remainder of our family in Toronto, becoming Canadian citizens and starting a new life.

Throughout my childhood, dinner-table conversations revolved around Europe and Israel and what was happening there. I was always involved in Jewish youth groups, and as an adult I became very committed to Canadian Hadassah-WIZO.

In 1996 I had the good fortune to attend the first UJA Lion of Judah International Conference in Jerusalem. One of the events there made a lasting impression on me. It was hearing the profoundly moving stories of three women, symbolic of so many heroic women who have made aliyah. The first was Sarah Pachanec, who arrived in Israel in February 1994 following twenty-two months of siege and six months of living underground in war-torn Sarajevo. Seventeen years before she was born, her mother, Zaynaba, a Moslem, saved Jewish lives during World War II. Her deeds were not forgotten, and those she saved implored the Jewish Agency to rescue her and her family in 1994 from Sarajevo. Sarah's love for and gratitude to the Jewish people for their help in starting her new life in Israel became a part of her. She, her husband, and her daughter chose to convert to Judaism.

Another was the story of Gratzia Ibrahim. While in her twenties, she made aliyah from Syria. In her first escape attempt, while she was pregnant, she was captured by the Syrians and put in jail, where she gave birth. After her release, she, along with her child, again left Syria, this time successfully, thanks to the heroic efforts of Torontonian Judy Feld Carr, who helped more than three thousand Jewish Syrians make aliyah.

Above: At the UJA Lion of Judah International Conference in Jerusalem, 1996, are: left to right, standing, Libby Dwor, Bonnie Goldstein, Karen Morton, Ancie Fouks, Elsie Pape, Fran Sonshine, and Carole Grafstein; kneeling, Sondi Ritter and Vicki Campbell.

And finally we heard from Yardena Fanta. She was twelve when her parents and eleven brothers and sisters made aliyah during Operation Moses. She walked for thirty days from Ethiopia to Sudan, most of the time carrying her little sister on her back. They spent eleven months in a tent camp before boarding a plane to Israel. When they first arrived, they were astonished that Jews could have blue eyes and blond hair. Today, Yardena is studying for her master's degree at Tel Aviv University. She also works at counselling other Ethiopian *olim*.

Yardena's story is the thirty-five-hundred-year-old story of our Exodus from Egypt; the story of my own parents' crossing of the Brenner Pass in the dead of winter and living in tents in Cyprus; the story of the children of Youth Aliyah and the schools and absorption centres that I've been working with for all my adult life through Hadassah–WIZO.

How fortunate it is that the stories of these three women share the same happy ending as my own family's story – reaching a safe haven.

———————

Above: Yardena Fanta and Sarah Pachanec have been brought to Toronto so that other Canadians can hear their inspiring stories. Pictured in Yetta Freeman's garden are, left to right, Yetta, Shira Ozery, Yardena Fanta, Sarah Pachanec, and Aggie Mandel, chair of the 1998 UJA Federation Women's Campaign.

Moving Forward

My Wish for Israel

BY ART EGGLETON

In 1992 I met the late Yitzhak Rabin, then leader of the opposition. I was inspired by his dream of a better and safer Middle East. In 1994 we met again when, as prime minister, he came to Canada to begin the process that led to the historic free-trade agreement between our two countries, an agreement I eventually signed with Natan Sharansky, minister of Industry and trade. The year was 1996, but in fact I shared a bond with Sharansky from years before, when I was mayor of Toronto.

To publicize his imprisonment, I had chaired a birthday party for Natan in his absence, in co-operation with the worldwide committee working to have him released from prison in the former Soviet Union. After the party I supported rallies and sent petitions to every possible forum to draw the world's attention to his plight, and in the end we succeeded.

I have long admired the vitality, tenacity, and hard work of the Canadian Jewish community, believing they have played a significant role in the growth of Canada. I have visited Israel twice, and witnessed the dynamics of a country that rose from the ashes to become a sophisticated, high-tech,

leading player on the world stage. I also saw kibbutzim holding on to the salty grounds in the Negev and the threatened borders in the Galilee, where children sleep in shelters to be safe from missiles. I travelled the roads connecting one end of Israel to the other and realized not only how narrow this country is, but also how wide is the vision of its people.

Besides enjoying economic growth, despite five decades of distractions and struggle, Israel has also experienced growth in its political relations, much of which I attribute to Yitzhak Rabin. His tragic death had a great impact on me, and when I visited Israel in 1997, the first thing I did was to pay tribute to his memory by laying a wreath on his grave. I was amazed at how many Israelis visit the site daily, just to share a few moments with this great leader's spirit.

Above: Art Eggleton lays a wreath at Yitzhak Rabin's grave, Mount Herzl, Jerusalem, February 1997.
Facing page: Natan Sharansky, Israel's minister of industry and trade, left, and Art Eggleton, then Canadian minister of trade, at the historic signing of a trade agreement between the two countries, August 1996.

During that visit I participated in the ribbon-cutting and official opening of two Canadian-based franchises – Second Cup in Jerusalem, where I worked behind the counter, serving coffee to the nonstop flow of guests, and Saint-Cinnamon in Ramat Gan, where I put on an apron and kneaded dough like a pro! I also paid a visit to Haifa's Technion, the institute for technology, where, in a very touching gesture, a chair in Molecular Medicine Research has been dedicated to me. I regard this as a great honour.

That visit to Israel taught me much, and now, as Canada's minister for national defence, it serves me well. My greatest wish for Israel is to see the peace process that has begun there unfold in its entirety.

Contrasts

BY AL GREEN

We are in the egg business in Israel. I don't mean we keep chickens and sell eggs in the market. What we do is take eggs and convert them for use in commercially produced food such as baked goods. The business has grown large, and we currently process about forty million eggs a year.

A little while ago when I was in Israel I went to Hadera to visit the plant. I expected little bubbies (grandmothers) to be sitting cracking open eggs. But the plant is nothing like that – it is state-of-the-art in this field. The eggs are shipped to the plant in boxes of twelve gross: 144 eggs in a row, twelve layers deep. An automatic arm comes and picks up 144 at a time, then swings them to a machine that cracks them

and sends the shells in one direction, the yolks in another, and the whites in yet another. The yolks and whites go down a chute, automatically, into sealed containers. I was very impressed with the modern system.

Sitting at the bottom of these machines are four rabbis checking the yolks and whites to make sure they are pure. I couldn't help but notice the contrast of twentieth-century machines and old-world rabbis checking the eggs. Only in Israel!

Above: Al Green, right, presents Prime Minister Yitzhak Rabin with a mezuzah he hand-sculpted, Jerusalem, 1995.

Let Their Dream Become a Reality

BY SHIRLEY GRANOVSKY

Three hundred and twenty Soviet immigrants were flown from Budapest to Tel Aviv in June 1991, on a special El Al flight called "Keren Hayesod–United Israel Appeal Granovsky Exodus Flight." The naming of this Operation Exodus flight in our honour was a complete surprise to my husband and me, and we were overcome with emotion.

The flight also carried 130 participants to the World Conference of Keren Hayesod, which had begun in Budapest and was continuing in Jerusalem. But the *olim* took centre stage. Since I am fluent in Yiddish I could converse with some of the older *olim*. Although life had been difficult for Jews in the Soviet Union, they were feeling apprehensive about facing so many changes in their lives. These people arrived carrying their belongings in oversized blankets or sheets tied on top with a huge knot. Some of them brought their pets and even live chickens.

When the plane landed at midnight, there was a short ceremony. Masha Yarowitzky spoke on behalf of the *olim*. "My dear friends," she said, brimming with emotion, "this feeling of coming will never leave us. It is a very happy moment."

My late husband, Phil, addressed the *olim*, speaking about his own background. If his parents had not left Russia in 1920, he might have been one of those coming off the plane. "We wish you the best in your homeland of Israel," he added warmly. "We hope that everyone left behind in the Soviet Union will follow you."

This exodus validated Phil's devotion and hard work for Israel, the tangible culmination of everything he had strived for. We hoped that the *olim* would be able to meet the challenges they now faced and that their dream would become a reality.

Above: The Granovsky Exodus Flight, 1991. From left to right: Phil and Shirley Granovsky, with their daughter, Fahla, and son-in-law, Howard Irving.
Left: Phil Granovsky.
Right: Shirley Granovsky.

You Always Feel Welcome

FROM A CONVERSATION WITH EDWARD AND MARSHA BRONFMAN

Edward: My father was a founder of the Canadian Friends of Hebrew University in Montreal in 1944 and continued to be involved with the university for years. My parents were visiting Israel around Pesach (Passover) in 1955, and I went to meet them. I had very little feeling about Israel at the time. I knew I was Jewish, but Israel was very far away. When I arrived, we toured in a dusty old De Soto. My parents put me in the front seat with the guide and we drove all around the country.

I was there for no more than seven days, but it did something to me. I felt more deeply Jewish than I ever had before. There was no intifadah then. It was a completely different era. Israel was a very small country, and Jerusalem was a very quiet city. We could hear the recently arrived Yemenites singing throughout the night. We could also see the Western Wall from our window at the King David Hotel, but the area was heavily mined and you just could not go near it. I was told never to point a finger at the Western Wall, because there were concerns that the Jordanian soldiers stationed above it would fire at us.

Marsha: I was born in Moncton, New Brunswick, but we moved to Montreal in the 1950s, because my parents wanted their children to get a proper Hebrew education. I remember first encountering discrimination when I met some neighbours in the area. I stood up for myself, because I was always proud to be Jewish. My first visit to Israel came in 1967, just after the Six Day War. I had such a sense of safety and warmth and trust. We went to a kibbutz where I stayed for two months. I loved it there. When Edward discussed the Negev project that he was sponsoring as JNF Negev Dinner Honouree and mentioned this kibbutz, I could really relate to it.

Edward: It's Kibbutz Naot Smadar, just seventy kilometres north of Eilat. Eighty people moved down there from Jerusalem with their children in 1989, and now, in 1998, there are 110 adults and seventy children. They are strictly vegetarian and practise organic farming. They have all sorts of citrus orchards and are creating their own lake for water.

Marsha: Seeing all these developments was quite miraculous. There I was, back in the desert thirty years later. It brought my life full circle. It's like an old friend. You don't have to become reacquainted. You always feel welcome.

Above: Marsha and Edward Bronfman at Kibbutz Naot Smadar, 1997.

Pat Alpert, national president of Hadassah-WIZO, surrounded by WIZO children at a day-care centre in Israel. She says, "Each time I go to Israel, it nourishes my soul and reconfirms my commitment to its future."

The University of Toronto and Israel

BY HEATHER MUNROE-BLUM

In May of 1998, the University of Toronto offered a day of academic programs to celebrate our diverse and fascinating array of academic and research partnerships with Israel.

Our communities share much. Bonds of ideas, democratic development, cultural heritage, and promising futures are close to our hearts. In May of 1997, I had the wonderful opportunity, together with University Chancellor Rose Wolfe, to lead an academic mission to Israel to improve contact with our many alumni, to cement ties with leading universities, and to expand commercial collaboration linked to our research.

Our ties run deep. Beginning in the 1840s, U of T offered studies that paved the way for academic links to Israel. Over the last three decades in particular, we have significantly expanded our offerings. Today, we offer Canada's strongest array of research and teaching on subjects related to Israel. These include languages, literature, archaelogy, philosophy, religion, and social history, and related library and research resources among the best in North America. Using science to contribute to peace, we have established a program in molecular biology and thyroid cancer, involving nationals of many countries, rising above politics.

I have had the great privilege of visiting Israel regularly over twenty years for personal and professional reasons. The presence there of extended family, former students, and faculty colleagues adds to the call of the country. I never cease to be amazed by Israel, by the strength and depth of our many effective partnerships there, and by the overwhelming commitment of so many researchers, students, and friends to ensuring the highest quality of academic and national achievement. The achievements of our colleagues at the Weizmann Institute for Science, the Technion, the Hebrew University of Jerusalem, Tel Aviv University, Ben-Gurion, Bar Ilan, and others, reflect the dynamic spirit that pervades Israeli culture.

Building on successes to date, the University of Toronto is eager to further the ties that bind our two communities and in turn strengthen each of us.

Above: Mayor Teddy Kollek, Dr. Heather Munroe-Blum,
and Mrs. Kollek meet in Jerusalem, 1997.

Memories of Israel

BY LORNA JACKSON, MAYOR OF VAUGHAN

On April 27, 1993, the City of Vaughan, Ontario, and the City of Ramla, Israel, became twinned after three years of discussions with the Israeli consulate and visits from Ramla dignitaries to Vaughan. As the mayor of Vaughan, I, along with my husband, finally had the opportunity to visit Israel for the signing ceremony, which took place in Ramla. Our visit coincided with Yom Hashoah (Holocaust Remembrance Day) and Yom Ha'atzmaut (Independence Day). It was an experience that we will never forget – the history, the commitment of Israel's citizens, and, most impressive, the exceptional hospitality we received.

We visited the Holocaust Memorial on Yom Hashoah. I was impressed by the observance of a minute's silence at 11:00 AM. Everything came to a halt – the buses and taxis all stopped, and the drivers stood at the side of their vehicles. The city of Jerusalem fell silent. My most vivid memory is of the Holocaust Museum. Although there were hundreds of people inside, it was so quiet. The hundreds of candles reflected in a room of mirrors was a spectacular memorial to those who had lost their lives.

We also visited several kibbutzim. It was wonderful to see how the Jewish settlers had turned the arid desert into a beautiful, green, productive oasis. It was sad to see, however, that it was necessary for so many young people to be armed and ready for any eventuality, but I sensed that the young people of Israel are stronger for this training; they seemed so mature, self-confident, and dependable.

In Jerusalem, as in Ramla, we experienced the diversity of cultures. It was interesting to note how Jerusalem is an important centre for Judaism, Christianity, and Islam. Israel truly is the cradle of faiths for so many people. I applaud the Israeli government for retaining all religious sites and caring for them, thus preserving them for generations to come.

Despite wars, natural and geographic limitations, and having to accommodate so many newcomers, the country has developed and thrived.

Above: Celebrating the twinning of their cities are, left to right: Bernie Green, former councillor of City of Vaughan; Lorna Jackson, mayor of City of Vaughan; and Moshe Peretz, former mayor of Ramla, 1993.

A Mission with a Difference

BY VICTOR MONCARZ

B eing avid cyclists, my wife, Sharon, and I decided to organize a charity bike ride in support of Hadassah Hospital, part of the Hebrew University of Jerusalem.

Since this was the first trip of its kind to be done from North America, every aspect of it had to be designed from scratch. The route was chosen, the logo was designed, and Aufgang Travel handled the arrangements. By the time we left for Israel, thirty–six Canadians and three Americans – the oldest participant was seventy–five – had signed up to ride from the Golan Heights to the Hebrew University at Mount Scopus, a trip covering about 350 kilometres.

As we approached the Sea of Galilee from the north, the view was breathtaking. The Jordan and Beit Shean valleys were exceedingly hot but magnificent. The hills of Judea held a new and special meaning when we climbed them on bicycles. The trip culminated in a steep eight–kilometre climb from the valley just outside Jerusalem up to the Mount Scopus campus, where we were greeted by dignitaries of the university, the Israeli press, and a Ben & Jerry's ice cream cart. As we

reached the top I was overcome with a wonderful sense of accomplishment and pride. The Canadian ambassador, Norman Spector, summed it up best at the gala evening when he said that he normally does not accept invitations to such events but had to meet this "group of lunatics" who had challenged themselves to raise money for Israel.

Traversing the countryside on bikes gives one a different perspective of the land; every new rise has special meaning as one climbs it.

The ride also brought together thirty–nine people who might otherwise never have met. We still go riding together in the summer. By pushing ourselves to the limit, we learned the true meaning of commitment and perseverance.

Above: A stop for bike repairs. Left to right: Chaim Rockman, the guide, Fred Rosen, Victor Moncarz, crouching, and Stephen Sandler.

Left to right: Dean Adam Stabholz, Hebrew University, with Joel Edelson, Ken Lawlor, Stan Jacobson, Victor Moncarz, and Arthur Segal, at the completion of their biking mission, 1994.

Running Exercises

BY ALLAN OFFMAN

My most satisfying involvement with Israel was the establishment of a United Israel Appeal Canada network of projects, which answered social needs in vulnerable communities in Israel. These projects became a special source of interest for Canadian missions to Israel, as well as boosting local employment and enhancing living conditions in the relatively dangerous North Galilee and in new zones of high-tech industry.

For me, one of the most poignant and telling images of Israel is that of seventeen-year-olds doing running exercises around a soccer field, wearing heart-monitoring equipment prior to being registered for the Israel Defence Forces draft. Surrounding them are their emotional parents, aware that their children are entering a critical period in their lives. There is a message to North Americans in this scene: what a contrast to so many of our children, who are usually involved in selecting colleges and camps at this stage in their lives.

_____

Below: Allan Offman at the dedication in his honour of the Leo Baeck Allan Offman Sports Centre in Haifa, 1991.

Project Toronto

BY DAVID HOFSTEDER

Growing up in an environment steeped in Jewish tradition and history, I always revered Eretz Yisrael (the Land of Israel). But my experiences with the children of Project Toronto have strengthened my relationship with Israel in the most extraordinary way.

Project Toronto helps take underprivileged children from the streets and enrol them in schools. For example, the Yisraelov brothers were the three children of a recent Russian immigrant to Israel. They seemed nervous and never smiled. An investigation revealed that their mother had been unable to adjust to her new life and had committed suicide. Trying to earn enough to keep the family together, the father was away from home from early morning until late at night. A Project Toronto worker gained the trust of the father,

persuading him that the children could be helped by placing them in a dormitory in the north, away from the negative influences in their current setting. The children are now thriving.

I have witnessed the miraculous transformation of street children into ambitious, productive people, and the joy this has brought to them and their parents. While providing children with warmth and guidance and granting them the opportunity to discover their traditions, their history, and their G–d, my own ties to them and the land have grown exponentially.

_____

Above: A Project Toronto teacher and student.

Careful Cultivation

BY LUCILLE BENSKY

Emotionally disturbed children who have been victims of abuse and violence are offered rehabilitation at the Jewish Women International's Residential Treatment Centre.

While touring the Canada group home, the residential treatment component for boys fourteen to eighteen, we entered the room occupied by Aaron, one of the residents. We were struck by the beautiful floral arrangement adorning Aaron's bedroom wall and were told his story.

From very early childhood Aaron had spent his life in numerous foster homes and institutions. Now, a violent and destructive sixteen-year-old, he had been sent to live at the group home as a last resort. There was a good chance that, with his present aggressive and hostile attitude, Aaron would eventually end up in jail.

While receiving therapy he was sent to school, only to run away repeatedly. After several unsuccessful employment placements, one final opportunity was given to Aaron as an assistant at a florist's shop. He discovered a love of flowers and a creative talent for arranging centre-pieces. His employer gradually gave him more responsibility, and nine months later he was still there. Aaron is now planning to follow this artistic career after graduation from the group home with the hope of owning his own florist's shop one day.

Above: Jewish Women International (formerly B'nai Brith Women) honoured Lucille Bensky for her work in establishing Tay Sachs clinics in the 1970s and her connection with the Residential Treatment Centre near Jerusalem.

Gymnasts go through their exercises at the **Jordana Lokash** Sports Centre in Jerusalem, which gives Israeli children an opportunity for recreational and competitive training. Jordana was a young Torontonian who died in a tragic accident. The sports centre is a fitting remembrance of Jordana's love of gymnastics, Israel, and children.

Chaskel Davidson, holding his daughter, Joy, at Kfar Lam, 1952.

"In 1949," **Rosalie Davidson** recalls, "I went to a *hachshara* in Smithville, Ontario. There I met Chaskel (Charles), whom I married in June 1950. We made a commitment to make aliyah. In May 1951, we were finally sent to Israel to work on Kibbutz Giva. Shortly after the birth of our daughter, Joy, we joined a South African group at Kfar Lam. We felt very welcomed. To celebrate our twenty-fifth anniversary, we were able to return to Israel and relive our fond memories."

This picture was taken by the late Brian "Yitz" Davidson, Chaskel's brother.

Sam Ruth and **Nancy Dine Ruth** in the Golan Heights in 1991. Both are very involved in the Toronto Jewish community. Nancy spent eight summers studying at universities in Israel. Among her many community positions, she is a past-president of Holy Blossom Temple and an executive member of Arza Canada (the Zionist arm of the Reform Movement).

Amram Moyal recalls, "I was raised in a religious Sephardi family in Fez, Morocco. My father, Cantor David Moyal, taught me the melodies and traditions of Sephardic music, and we used to sing together, especially the Moroccan songs called 'Bakashot.'

"I moved to Israel with my wife in 1961 and served in the IDF. One night we were driving in a tank, and stopped to camp on a beach. I sang a song to my fellow soldiers – a popular love song. I will never forget that beautiful night, and now I use that tune for the kaddish.

"After we came to Canada in 1966, I helped to found Synagogue Magen David Sephardic Congregation and Minyan Sepharad Synagogue, serving as cantor for many years. I have sung for ten years at Beth Tzedec Congregation on Shabbat Zachor. I think it is especially beautiful to hear the Sephardi and Ashkenazi music together."

Amram Moyal is pictured here in his Israeli army uniform, 1962.

John Sereny immigrated to Israel in 1948, armed with a Hungarian glider-pilot's licence and dreams of becoming a pilot in the Israeli air force. He was assigned to the airforce, but as a truck driver, and later as the commanding officer's chauffeur. After the 1956 Sinai campaign, in which he fought, he emigrated to Canada and began a business career. "When my longtime friend Brigadier General Ya'akov Terner, now commander of the Israeli Air Force Museum, approached me to chair a gala fund-raising dinner for the museum in 1997, I threw myself into it. I wish I had been one of those brave and resourceful Israeli air force pilots, but I have settled for my Piper Cheyenne Twin Turbo prop, which I fly almost every weekend."

Helping the Disabled

BY JEANETTE GROSMAN

My abiding love of Israel, heartfelt commitment to the people, and study of the Hebrew language arose because of my relationship with Israel's disabled war veterans – the *chaverim* (members) of Beit Halochem (Aid to Disabled Veterans). The Israel Defence Forces assumes a long-term obligation to its disabled veterans and their families through Beit Halochem centres. There, they can participate in sports, recreational, and rehabilitative activities, and gather with other disabled veterans and their families.

Kobi and David, severely burned; Surin, quadriplegic; Kuti, blind amputee; Eyal, amputee; Shai, serious head and back injury; and Avi, major leg injury. To the reader, perhaps, just a list of names and wounds, but to me so much more. Each was wounded while serving in the Israel Defence Forces, and each of their lives was changed forever. I am privileged to call them my friends and blessed to have had the opportunity of welcoming them into my home through the Beit Halochem group visit program. Through these visits, and my visits with them and their families in Israel, I maintain a connection with Israel that bridges all physical and cultural distances.

Background: Jeanette Grosman welcomes soldiers into her home as part of the Beit Halochem program.

The Benefits of Bonding

BY RUHAMA GEFEN GOLDSTEIN

After completing my military service I left Israel to join my parents in Toronto, where my father, Dr. Aba Gefen, was Israel's consul general. One evening I attended a State of Israel Bonds event, where I met my future husband, Sol, a psychoanalyst and child psychiatrist. When we had children, we hoped they would grow and develop as proud, independent Jews in the Diaspora, while maintaining a strong connection with Israel.

Because of my involvement with State of Israel Bonds, where I served for three years as North American Women's Division chair, our children had the opportunity to join us in attending Bond functions all over North America. They also travelled with us on our yearly family visits to Israel. Today, Benji, Rachel, and David, mature young adults and graduates of the Hebrew Day School system, are an example of how it is possible to combine one's life in the Diaspora with a positive connection with the State of Israel.

Right: The Goldstein family, 1997. Clockwise from upper left: Benji, Rachel, David, Ruhama, and Sol.

The Cost of Conflict

History does repeat itself. Here, on Ben Yehuda Street, Jerusalem 1948, wreckage is being cleared following an explosion that killed fifty-two people and injured at least a hundred others. A similar bombing took place on the same street in 1997.

The Miracle of Life

BY RITASUE FISHER

I hadn't seen Yifat for two years. She'd been married in the meantime, and I looked forward to meeting her husband, Shlomi. Our last phone conversation promised me a "surprise gift." It was the most marvellous gift imaginable. Yifat was eight months pregnant. Tears of joy and amazement streamed down my face, for this pregnancy was a miracle.

I'd first met Yifat nine years earlier, in 1987. It was Sunday at midnight, and I'd had a long day. Simcha Holtzberg and I had already been to several hospitals visiting sick and wounded soldiers. I'd gone from ward to ward with my guitar, hoping my smile and my songs might bring comfort to those who had risked so much. Now I was ready to go home, but Simcha had other plans. "Please, Ritasue," he said, "just one more visit."

Nineteen-year-old Yifat was not yet asleep. Her mother was gently stroking her brow. Despite her pain, Yifat's eyes grew wide with pleasure as we entered the room. I introduced myself and began to sing. It was a simple song, but it seemed to ease the suffering of their unspeakable nightmare. Yifat had been waiting for the bus back to her army base after a visit

home. It was the time of the intifadah uprising. On this beautiful Jerusalem morning, a terrorist had driven his car into the group of civilians and soldiers. Yifat was rushed to hospital, her chances of survival bleak. She did survive, but as a double amputee. Her strength over the next few years became a source of inspiration to friends and family alike. Our friendship grew deeper, and with it, my sense of awe.

July 1997: We are once again with Shlomi and Yifat in their wheelchair-accessible home. When I ask about the beautiful music being played, I learn that Shlomi is an accomplished pianist. I marvel at his virtuosity, but more so at his indomitable spirit. For Shlomi was left blind and without an arm after the Lebanon war.

As I look around the room, I wonder if I'm dreaming. I'm not. There's Yifat, joyfully holding her precious child – little Ma'ayan, now a year old. I thank God for this miracle of new life.

Above: Yifat and Shlomi Zaks, with Ritasue Fisher, centre, holding the "surprise gift," Ma'ayan Zaks, 1997.

Just Another Purse

BY ESTHER MATLOW

I rving and I were married in April 1952. To marry him meant acceptance and adoption of his commitment to Israel. The final part of our extended honeymoon was spent in the new state. Since then I have been to Israel often. And I have led two groups there, both at historic times.

By December 1973, the Yom Kippur War had all but ended. Israel's troops were still positioned on Egyptian soil, but a cease-fire was in effect on all fronts. The casualties had been high; the citizens were demoralized; and tourism was non–existent. Israelis felt isolated and ignored. Toronto Hadassah–WIZO showed leadership and sponsored a tour to show our solidarity, as well as our sympathy for families who had lost loved ones. Each one in our group of ten felt she or he was doing a *mitzvah* (good deed) by going there when others stayed away. We knew that we made a difference to everyone with whom we had contact. It also made a difference to us.

In January 1991, shortly after I had been installed as the national president of Canadian Hadassah–WIZO, I led a tour of thirty–one to Israel. This time the crisis of the Gulf War was heating up. Some were staying one week; others like me, who had family there, stayed longer. The hotels were almost empty.

In the middle of the night, January 17, 1991, we were told by the hotel administration that the war had commenced and that we should come down to the lobby and pick up our gas masks. When we heard the sirens, we were to leave our rooms, take our masks, and go into a special sealed room that the hotel had set aside on each floor in case of chemical attacks. There, we would wait for the all–clear.

The next night, when the sirens sounded, we followed instructions and went into the sealed room, where it was extremely crowded. We were joined by many families from Tel Aviv who had decided it was safer to be in Jerusalem. The sirens sounded again and again; each time, off we traipsed to the sealed room.

The following day Naomi Frankenburg of Vancouver and I had a meeting to attend. We decided to walk there, each carrying a box containing a gas mask. It had become just another purse to us and to Israelis. The carrying cases became a fashion statement. Even though we believed that Saddam Hussein would not fire on Jerusalem, a city holy to the Moslems, we breathed a sigh of relief on our safe return to the hotel.

Above: Esther and Irving Matlow on their honeymoon in Israel, 1952.

The Persian Gulf War

In August 1990 Iraq invaded Kuwait. In January 1991, after Iraq refused to withdraw from Kuwait, UN forces responded with a massive bombing campaign against Iraq. Although Israel was not part of these UN forces, Iraq attacked Israel with Scud missiles. About forty missiles landed in and around Tel Aviv. The Jewish community of Toronto watched and waited anxiously as Israelis tried to protect themselves from a possible chemical attack. The Persian Gulf War ended when Iraq accepted a cease-fire on February 28, 1991.

Following the Yom Kippur War, a Hadassah-WIZO Solidarity tour visited Israel, 1973. Front row, left to right: Irving and Esther Matlow, Belle James, Mirial Small. Back row, left to right: David and Cecily Peters, Roz Mendelson, Bob and Helen Disenhouse, Allen Small.

"**O**n February 4, 1997," writes **Lillian Benlolo**, "my nephew **Emile Azoulay**, who had served in Lebanon by his own choice for over two-and-a-half years in an elite commando unit, was killed in a tragic helicopter collision that took seventy-two other lives. Emile was twenty years old.

"I had always spoken about Emile while teaching my students at Beth Israel Hebrew Academy in Toronto about Israeli life. They knew how much he loved working with animals. As his final high-school project he had completed a scientific study that will have a lasting impact on Israel's agricultural industry by increasing milk production through the regulation of cows' diets. The Israeli agriculture ministry has since accredited Emile's study and now encourages its use by all farmers.

"At Emile's shivah [period of mourning], his friend Dvir said he and his other friends would follow in Emile's footsteps. 'If I won't do it, who will?' said Dvir with a half-courageous smile."

At a remembrance service in Toronto, memorial candles are lit for the seventy-three soldiers killed in the helicopter crash in which Emile Azoulay died in February 1997.

The Intifadah

The intifadah (Arabic for "shaking off") was an Arab uprising in the West Bank and Gaza Strip, beginning in December 1987, in response to Israeli occupation of these areas since 1967. It continued with a series of violent confrontations between Palestinians and Israeli troops in these areas. Violence spread and erupted sporadically until the peace process began in 1994.

"**T**he air was thick with tension on the plane flying back from Toronto," writes **Faygie Zack Schwartz**, pictured here practising with her Gulf War gas mask. "The Gulf War had just broken out, and I was accompanying my daughter Sharon and my three grandsons back to their home in Israel. Properly outfitted with gas masks, including an enclosed protective playpen for the baby, Sharon left the airport for her home in Jerusalem and I set out for Raanana, near Tel Aviv, to stay with my daughter Adrienne. Ten minutes after arriving there, I experienced my first Scud attack. Missiles were falling in Ramat Gan, twenty minutes away — but it sounded as if they were just outside our door. I believe it was a miracle so few lives were lost. G–d was watching over us."

Trying to Stay Calm

BY DAVID BALE

JERUSALEM, OCTOBER 1990. Humour was one way Israelis coped with the tension caused by the Gulf crisis and Iraqi threats of chemical warfare. Another way was to talk about it, and two months after Iraq's invasion of Kuwait, the government of Israel really gave its people something to talk about when it announced that gas masks would be distributed to the public. As a radio reporter I was there to document Israel's readiness. With microphone in hand I wove in and out of the tables of Ben Yehuda's outdoor cafés, doing on-the-spot interviews, recording Israeli attitudes and fears.

For a more soul-searching interview, I spoke to Naomi Laker Nahmias, an old friend and colleague from Israel Radio who had made aliyah from Toronto in 1977. "We carry on daily life but are also getting supplies ready just in case. We're getting our gas masks soon, and are just trying to stay calm." After thirteen years in Israel she may have seemed a bit callous. But in fact she acted more like the sabra who develops a tough surface layer to protect a softer interior. "Without it, everyone would be hysterical and incapable of carrying on."

TORONTO, JANUARY 1991. It was 5:00 AM in Jerusalem when I next interviewed a tired Naomi by phone from Toronto. She told me about the frightening repetition of being woken in the middle of the night by civil defence sirens, gathering the family into the sealed kitchen, putting on the gas masks, and waiting. Even though the first Scuds hit Tel Aviv, all of Israel was on alert. For the duration of the Gulf War this was a daily routine, and at no time were Israelis to be without their masks or further than ten minutes from home. Naomi described the impact of all this on her three children. Her little boy was so frightened one night that he threw up in his mask, probably at the ghastly sight of his own family members wearing theirs. "Once that sun goes down," as Naomi's neighbour said, "and you're closed up in your house, not knowing when that siren is going to go off . . . it's terrifying. You shake."

Israel was more than my beat; it was my home. Sitting in Toronto I now imagined those scenes. For many of us, far away in Canada, that experience was our own kind of horror.

Above: David Bale interviewing Prime Minister Menachem Begin, Jerusalem, c. 1979.

Solidarity

BY HENRY CAMPBELL

As participants in the May 1996 United Jewish Appeal Solidarity mission to Russia and Israel, we had come, somewhat reluctantly, to Israel's north to see for ourselves the human side of the story that the television news rarely seems to cover.

As our bus moved through Kiryat Shmonah and on to Metulla, on the sixteenth straight day of Hezbollah shelling, there was no traffic, no shops open, and the parks were empty.

Not far from Kiryat Shmonah, and out of the range of Katyusha rockets, we visited temporary classrooms set up by the local authorities. Here, children from the evacuated towns and villages of the north continued their studies.

We moved from shelter to shelter to talk with the volunteers and army officers whose job it was to entertain and protect the children, and to talk with the medical professionals dealing with the stress and uncertainty experienced by all the residents of the north.

Late in the afternoon, as we were leaving our bus to visit another shelter, we heard a high-pitched, whirring sound. Before we could react, there was a huge explosion about a kilometre away. The muffled explosions we had heard earlier in the day were now much closer. Once we were safely inside the shelter, we were comforted by the warmth and understanding of those who had learned to take all this in stride.

The children, the volunteers, and the soldiers had all asked, "Why are you here?" The answer: There was nowhere else to be!

Below: In Kiryat Shmonah, during Katyusha bombings from Lebanon, 1996, participants of UJA Solidarity mission from Toronto talk to Israeli soldiers about the tense situation. From left to right: Vicki Campbell, Lorri Kushnir, Marilyn Scharf, and Bonnie Goldstein.

Marnie Kimelman, 1972–1990

BY HAROLD, LINDA, JASON, AND MARC KIMELMAN

An explosive device, planted by terrorists, went off on the Tel Aviv beach on July 28, 1990. Marnie alone was killed. The tragedy of her loss touched hearts throughout Israel and the Jewish world, particularly in Toronto, her home.

Marnie was one of hundreds of Canadian youngsters exploring Israel on a summer program. She was a bright, idealistic, and popular young woman, deeply committed to Judaism and the State of Israel – a leader and peacemaker among her peers.

Despite ongoing pain, we – Marnie's parents, Harold and Linda Kimelman, and her brothers, Jason and Marc – decided to dedicate ourselves to *tikkun olam*, the "repair of the world," to keep Marnie's spirit alive.

Marnie was treated at Ichilov Hospital in Tel Aviv. The state-of-the-art Marnie Kimelman Trauma Unit has now been established within its Rabin Trauma Centre (named for Prime Minister Yitzhak Rabin after his death in the same emergency room in 1995).

In Toronto, many fine projects have been dedicated in Marnie's memory, including a theatre and a teen lounge named Marnie's Rainbow, "like Noah's rainbow in the Bible, a symbol of hope," at the Hospital for Sick Children.

The Marnie Kimelman Cancer Research Fund continues to support the breakthrough cancer-research efforts of a young Israeli scientist, Rinat Eshel, at Tel Aviv University.

Although the tragedy of Marnie's loss will always be deeply felt by her family and many friends, our combined efforts to remember her goodness have resulted in enduring testaments to a young and beautiful woman. May her memory be a blessing.

Above: Marnie Kimelman (1972-1990).

Sharing Their Talents

Hockey Night in Israel

Sitting amidst the shadows of the Hermon Mountains, along the Lebanese border, is the tiny city of Metulla. Settled over a hundred years ago, Israel's northernmost community has enjoyed an inspiring, yet often precarious, relationship with its neighbours. The citizens of Metulla and southern Lebanon strive to co-operate as friends and allies, but the people of Metulla are often forced to scramble for shelter as Katyusha rockets, fired from Lebanon, rain down across the Upper Galilee.

In this uniquely Israeli setting stands the Canada Centre, a sports and recreation complex generously funded by the Canadian Jewish community, which includes among its many facilities: racquet courts, basketball courts, and a swimming pool. But it is Metulla's ice rink that truly gives the centre its Canadian identity. There is a comfortable familiarity as soon as one enters its doors, with sights and sounds instantly recognizable to any rink rat who grew up in the York Mills, Chesswood, St. Michael's, or any other Toronto neighbourhood arena.

The sound of a skate blade carving fresh ice . . . the smell of the dressing room . . . the smile on the face of a first-time goal-scorer. . . . It's the thrill of a winter sport in a land without winter.

How It Came to Be
BY DOROTHY DREVNIG

The idea of building the only Olympic-size skating rink in the Middle East was just the kind of project to appeal to my husband, Bill, a man who throughout his life was known for striking off into uncharted territory. It was the idea of Yossi Goldberg – the charming and energetic mayor of Metulla – to add an Olympic-size rink to the Canada Centre, which already had a well-used but tiny ice rink. Yossi paid a visit to Bill and me on his way to the Skate Canada competition in Calgary in 1994. By the time he left us, his dream of providing a first-rate facility where

Above: Dorothy Drevnig with Prime Minister Yitzhak Rabin in Jerusalem, October 1995, just weeks before his assassination.
Facing page: Jason Kimelman at the Canada Centre, combining his passion in life – hockey – with his favourite place on earth – Israel. Left to right: David Reine, Jonathan Graff, Jeff Budd, Jason Kimelman, and Jeremy Blumes, 1995.

Israeli athletes and the newly arrived contingent of Russian skaters could train for Olympic competition was well on its way to being realized.

On Sunday, October 22, 1995, the William and Dorothy Drevnig Arena in Metulla was officially opened and dedicated. Sadly, Bill was no longer strong enough to make the trip with us, but I was there for the opening ceremonies. What a thrill it was!

An NHL Coach in Israel

FROM A CONVERSATION WITH ROGER NEILSON

M arshall Starkman, the goalie instructor at our hockey camp in Canada, first told me about the rink in Metulla. I've always had an interest in Israel, and I've read many books about it. The hockey camp we ran there in the summer of 1997 marked my third trip to Israel. About twenty kids came over from Canada. We spent ten days there; the camp itself lasted five or six days, and the rest of the time we travelled around the country.

We mixed the Canadian kids with the Israelis, and it worked very well. Although some of the Israeli kids had only been on skates for three or four months, they made very big strides.

One day some rockets were launched from Lebanon. Instead of going on the ice, we hurried to the bomb shelter underneath the rink. All of the kids played Ping-Pong

while we waited out the attack. I think twenty-one bombs landed in the area, but the Israelis said there was a lot more to fear from Israeli drivers than from the Lebanese rockets! The next day President Ezer Weizman came to reassure everybody. I was out walking in my bare feet and he commented that I had become an Israeli pretty quickly!

Skating Through the Sand

BY DANNY ROTH

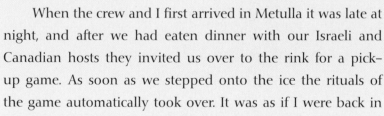

T he thought of hockey in Israel has great appeal. It resulted in my first television documentary, *Skating Through the Sand*, which told the story of Israeli ice hockey and the national hockey team's travels to the world championships in Johannesburg, South Africa, in 1995.

When the crew and I first arrived in Metulla it was late at night, and after we had eaten dinner with our Israeli and Canadian hosts they invited us over to the rink for a pick-up game. As soon as we stepped onto the ice the rituals of the game automatically took over. It was as if I were back in

Above: Danny Roth, centre, with members of the Israeli National Ice Hockey team, Ron Oz, left, and Assaf Evvon, 1995.
Left: Coach Roger Neilson gives instructions at the Canada Centre in Metulla during the Roger Neilson's Hockey Camp in Israel.

Toronto, and yet I was actually playing hockey in Israel! We were "skating through the sand."

The First Israeli at the Winter Olympics:
The Story of Misha Shmerkin

A native of Odessa, Russia, Misha Shmerkin first took to the ice at the age of three. He thought he would have to give up figure skating when he moved to Israel in 1991, but just three years later he became the first athlete ever to represent Israel in the Winter Olympics when he competed at the 1994 Lillehammer Games.

As a youth, Shmerkin had been one of the best young figure skaters in the Soviet Union, but as a Jew he discovered there was a glass ceiling above which anti-Semitic bureaucrats would not let him rise. Finally, in Israel, Shmerkin was able to take his place among the best figure skaters in the world.

Skating is so much a part of Shmerkin's life that he even got married on the ice at the Canada Centre. Combining tradition with his avocation, he smashed the wine glass with his skates. "Without the help of Canadians and the UJA," says Metulla mayor, Yossi Goldberg, "Misha's dream, and the dreams of other talented Israeli athletes, would never come true."

Left: Misha Shmerkin. For the first time ever, the Israeli flag appeared at the 1994 Lillehammer Winter Olympics, carried by Misha.

Mr. Shamir on a Good Day

BY BEN WICKS

I had been warned that the former prime minister of Israel, Yitzhak Shamir, would not be the easiest of interviews. One anecdote had described him as being unhappy during a meeting with U.S. Secretary of State Baker. He was said to have suddenly stood up, left the room, and never returned.

The journalists I met while researching my book *Dawn of the Promised Land* assured me that if my upcoming meeting with Shamir lasted more than five minutes, I could count myself lucky.

I arrived at Mr. Shamir's office with a television crew in tow. A charming, elderly secretary took me by the hand: "It's so nice to meet you, Mr. Wicks."

So far, so good. It was her next remark that caused me some concern.

"You're in luck," she smiled. "You've caught Mr. Shamir on a good day."

I entered, and it was almost two hours later that I bid farewell to this remarkable little man. He was a tough individual, who once headed up one of the most violent of the underground groups: the Stern Gang.

As the camera crew were packing up their equipment, I asked the eighty-year-old survivor of the Holocaust how he was feeling.

"I'm lonely," he answered: a sad reminder that the pain of losing all of one's family in the Holocaust remains even with the toughest of human beings, forever.

Above: Ben Wicks, right, with Monty and Blema Mazin, at his book launch, 1998. Dawn of the Promised Land *was dedicated to Monty Mazin.*

Left: Prime Minister Yitzhak Shamir, right, chatting with Ben Wicks and Robert Ritter, national executive director, Canada–Israel Committee, 1997.

Digging History

BY NATALIE RIBACK ZEIFMAN

When I was a child my parents, my sister, and I made regular visits to my father's family in Israel. I enjoyed the unique advantage of seeing the country through the eyes of a native, when I went with my grandmother to buy bread at the local corner store, picked fruit from my cousins' orchards in the Golan Heights, and walked the streets and markets as if they were my own.

In Toronto I became fluent in Hebrew at Associated Hebrew Schools, where the stories in the Torah and the books of the Prophets dazzled my imagination. Years later, at the University of Toronto, I decided to study anthropology, and through Harvard University was given the opportunity to be part of an eight-week archaeological expedition in Israel. The site, in the Ashkelon National Park, had been excavated for twelve consecutive seasons.

We were uncovering the fallen bricks and floors of a destroyed dwelling dating back to 604 BCE, the time of the Philistines. We also spent time excavating, cleaning, and cataloguing pottery, animal bones, and other objects. We awoke each morning at 4:00 AM and the days were strenuous. Yet every so often we would discover something ancient and wonderful that made the work worthwhile. My most impressive finds were a scarab with a falcon carving on the back and some beautiful clay pots that were almost whole. The age and chronicling of these amazed us all, we felt as if we had peeked into the past. Each moment in the field took me deeper into a world I thought I already knew – my own history.

Below: The dig at Ashkelon National Park, summer of 1994.
Natalie Riback Zeifman is on the far right.

In the spring of 1994, the **National Ballet of Canada** conducted an extensive tour of Europe and Israel, where they were welcomed enthusiastically by audiences and critics alike.

The highlight of their tour was travelling for the first time to Israel and performing in the Roman amphitheatre in Caesarea. The company took time out from their busy schedule to enjoy some of the country's historic and natural beauty. Here, the company poses against the backdrop of the Caesarea amphitheatre, where the National Ballet performed *The Sleeping Beauty*.

Principal Dancer Chan Hon Goh shops in the market place in Jerusalem during the National Ballet of Canada's tour of Israel, 1994.

No Wonder the Map Is Difficult

BY DONIA BLUMENFELD CLENMAN

Donia Blumenfeld Clenman was born in Poland. She came to Canada in 1948 and has lived in Toronto ever since. She is the author of seven books, and many of her poems have been set to music by composers such as Milton Barnes, Sol Chapman, Srul Irving Glick, and Walter Buczynski.

I

I walk and walk
often get lost.
Cannot tell left from right
North from South.
The city rushes at me
a river of memories
      cracks forgotten pride.
I've been away so long
no wonder the map is difficult.

II

In Toronto's right–angled streets
I get lost.
Though kind people would help, I falter.
No map to dispel the darkness.
In narrow–alleyed Jerusalem
I struggle
seem to remember something
a compass–star that with patience
will lead me home.

III

I walk and walk.
A green garden, a living city.
Vines planted in stone.
No marble goddesses
no lofty cathedrals mar my way.
A cracked bell
      tethered
grows children from its cup.
They laugh.
      It sings of peace.

From Older and In Love *by
Donia Blumenfeld Clenman
(Toronto: Flowerfield and Littleman, 1995).*

---

*Background: Liberty Bell Park, Jerusalem, 1993.
Donia Clenman with the bell described in her poem
"No Wonder the Map Is Difficult," which was awarded
the Israel Poetry Peace Prize in 1993.*

"I became an Official War Artist in 1942, commissioned in England by the Royal Canadian Air Force," writes **Aba Bayefsky**. "This commission was the result of winning a forces-wide art competition while I was stationed in Winnipeg.

"One of my assignments took me very close to Belsen concentration camp. I went there and saw for myself the horrors that had befallen the Jewish People. The work that I did in Belsen is now in the Canadian War Museum in Ottawa. After the war I went back to Europe to continue my work in the displaced-persons' camps and holding areas from which Jewish refugees were transported illegally to Palestine.

"My professional work as an artist has been permanently shaped by the events during and after the war. For a while, I thought that anti-Semitism had breathed its last, but now I feel that it has returned in force under the guise of anti-Israel activities. As an artist my only means of speaking out is through art.

"I have completed a very large series of drawings and paintings that express my feelings about Israel, what's going on there, and the difficulties Israel has faced."

Pictured here is *All Quiet on the Western Front*, an oil painting by Aba Bayefsky, shown at a special exhibit at the Canadian War Museum in Ottawa in 1998.

"My family left Iraq and moved to Israel immediately after the Declaration of Independence," writes **Judd Shemesh**. "The transit camp where we lived with other *olim* was where I first encountered European Jews and their variety of languages.

"Now, as a sculptor in Toronto, I find that my background influences my work, as I combine the Star of David with the shapes of art. What could be more appropriate than glass, which retains its original qualities, for Judaic articles such as mezuzahs, menorahs, and candlesticks?"

A Journal of Hope

BY JULIA KOSCHITZKY

On my last trip to Israel, the customs officer was taking an unusually long time to stamp my passport. Finally, he looked up at me and said, "Madam, space in your passport is at a premium. It's time for you to get a new one."

That passport was issued in 1993 and was due to expire in 1998. It was during those five years that I was privileged to be the chairman of the board of trustees of Keren Hayesod – representing the fund-raising campaigns for Israel in all countries outside of the United States. And it was in those years that the Jewish People witnessed one of the great modern miracles, the mass exodus of 700,000 Jews from what was once the Soviet Union to Israel.

For me, those years provided a lifetime's worth of experiences. I personally witnessed how world Jewry enabled this exodus to happen. I visited such storied places as Tashkent, Samarkand, Buchara, Marrakesh, and Casablanca, where I saw how our emissaries were on the spot, in every community, whether they had a hundred Jews or a thousand, to ensure that *"No Jew stands alone."* I saw these people creating some of the most memorable images in modern Jewish history.

In those few years, I also learned that Jewish generosity is one of the great wonders of the world. The photographs on these pages depict that great wonder, and the homecoming of our people to the Promised Land.

ISRAEL, 1992 (*photograph at left*). "I was visiting an absorption centre in Israel, where I met Ethiopians who arrived during Operation Solomon, the miraculous airlift that brought fifteen thousand Ethiopians home within thirty hours. Absorption centres such as this one help to bridge cultural gaps through training and teaching the Hebrew language. This photo brings to mind the fulfilment of Ezekiel's prophesy, 'I will take you from your countries, I will gather you from your nations, I will bring you home.'"

SAMARKAND, UZBEKISTAN, FEBRUARY 1994 (*photograph on facing page*). "I was invited to participate in an American Jewish Appeal leadership mission. We visited synagogues, schools, and *ulpanim* (Hebrew classes). In this particular class, a Jewish boys' choir was singing in Hebrew, '*Hashanh haba'ah b'yerusha-layim*' ('Next year in Jerusalem')."

LOD INTERNATIONAL AIRPORT, TEL AVIV, 1991 (*photograph above*). "This picture was taken during Operation Exodus. It was one of the many times that I was privileged to welcome immigrants from the former Soviet Union. I made a special effort to go over to the frail and elderly, some of whom could neither see nor hear. This woman clutched my hand and said in Yiddish, '*Zent gitte menschen*' ('You are good people')."

MARRAKESH, MOROCCO, JUNE 1992 (*photograph above*). "My daughter Leelah, who joined the Keren Hayesod mission to Morocco, is pictured visiting a Jewish old–age home. This was an opportunity to see how our overseas dollars are translated into miracles for thousands of Jews. This picture calls to my mind the phrase from Psalm 71:9: 'Do not forsake us in our old age.'"

BUCHARA, 1993. "My husband, Henry, always accompanied me on these special Keren Hayesod, United Jewish Appeal missions to the former Soviet Union. Here he is, in the background second from the right, assisting an elderly couple. This picture recalls the well-known Hebrew expression, '*Kol Israel arevim zeh le zeh*' ('All Jews are responsible for one another')."

Toronto and Tiberias: When Stones Talk

BY JERRY S. GRAFSTEIN

In midtown Toronto, on the crest of a small green hill on Roselawn Avenue, is an old, crowded stone garden: the cemetery called the Tree of Life – Eitz Chaim – of the Chevra Shas (Synagogue of the Fellowship of the Talmud). Here, turn–of–the–century Orthodox immigrants lie. My mother's mother, Mirel Etel Bleeman, may she rest in peace, died in 1943 and was buried here. At the top of the Hebrew acrostic poem on her memorial, we read that she was a descendant of the Shelah HaKadosh, the "Holy Shelah."

My early life was replete with stories of the Shelah HaKadosh, the famed mediaeval rabbi and kabbalist whose works deeply influenced the Chassidic movement. Born in Prague in 1570, he was carefully tutored by his father, who was himself a brilliant rabbi and author. The "Shelah" enjoyed a meteoric rise, becoming chief rabbi of Posen, Dubinow, Krakow, and Frankfurt, culminating in his appointment as the chief rabbi of Prague. In 1620 the "Shelah's" wife died prematurely, and in 1621 he decided to emigrate to the Holy Land. He immediately established a yeshivah in Old Jerusalem and was soon elected chief Ashkenazic rabbi of Jerusalem.

Because my mother was in her nineties, and because we endlessly discussed the stories of her roots, I decided that on

my next trip to Israel I would surprise and please her by discovering, if I could, the final resting place of the "Shelah." And so, in August 1995, I found myself in Israel meeting with the late Gerrer Rebbe at a private audience in the book–lined study of his apartment in Old Jerusalem. We spoke of the many problems in Israel, and then I told him of my search for the final resting place of the "Shelah." The Gerrer Rebbe smiled and said, "Don't worry, you will find him. He is in the north." And with a wave of his hand, my audience was ended.

Immediately after that meeting, I hurried to Prime Minister Rabin's office for my appointment to meet with Eitan Haber, Rabin's chief–of–staff. After a thorough and quiet discussion of current events, he asked whom I had visited since arriving in Israel. I mentioned the Gerrer Rebbe. He was astounded. The Ger, he informed me, rarely held private audiences. The Ger was probably the most powerful figure in the Orthodox community in Israel. With a telephone call or two, Haber went on to tell me, the Rebbe could entice thousands onto the streets for any particular cause.

Above: Jerry Grafstein at the tomb of Moses Maimonides, in Tiberias, 1995.

I explained to Eitan Haber that my present mission was to discover, if I could, the final resting place of the "Shelah." Haber mentioned that he, too, was a descendant of a rabbinic line of some renown and was sympathetic to my quest. He made arrangements for me to contact a former soldier in the Golani regiment who was now specializing in trips to the north.

The next morning, my wife, Carole, my son, Michael, and I climbed into a large car with our handsome guide and headed north from Tel Aviv in search of my distinguished ancestor. We began our search in Tiberias in a small cemetery that contained the remains of six or seven famous rabbinical figures. As I walked up the stone path I discovered that this was the resting place of Moses Maimonides, the great Rambam, buried in the twelfth century, as well as of Yohanen Ben Zakkai, buried seven hundred years before the first century. To my surprise and delight, immediately to the left of the Rambam's large tomb was the marble-encased remains of my grandmother's ancestor, the "Holy Shelah."

Apparently, in 1625, after he was elected chief Ashkenazic rabbi of Jerusalem, there was civil unrest, and the "Shelah," as a leader, was imprisoned and tortured. Released after payment of a ransom, he fled north toward Tiberias and Safed, where a great community of scholars resided. It was on the road to Safed, within sight of the Mount of Beatitudes, that my ancestor died and was buried in 1626.

———————

Below: Jerry Grafstein, right, with his son, Michael, at an archaelogical site on their way to Tiberias, 1995.

First Visits

BY ARLENE PERLY RAE

Nothing compares with the enormous excitement – the lump in the throat, the burst of emotion – that greets the traveller who lands for the first time at Lod International (Ben-Gurion Airport). For me that experience came in 1968. Signs of the 1967 Six Day War were still very much in evidence. I remember how easy it was to search out distant relatives. Everyone seemed to know everyone else, or at least where to look. Jerusalem really was golden. It was then, as now, a city that exceeds expectations – vital, complex, and beautiful.

My most recent visit was in 1994 with my husband, Bob, then premier of Ontario, and our three daughters. Immediately upon arrival we went to Yad Vashem (the Holocaust Memorial) in Jerusalem. Although Bob and I had visited before, it was especially powerful to share such a place with our children. They are thoughtful girls. The impact of the photographs, the thousands of names, the floor memorial to those lost in the death camps, the reflecting candles . . . all that and more is permanently etched in our memories. Because the girls were young, while Bob met with politicians such as Yitzhak Shamir, Shimon Peres, and Yitzhak Rabin, we visited museums and many remarkable outdoor sights, including the underground caves at Rosh Hanikra, the market in the Old City of Jerusalem, and the biblical zoo. The children warmed to the power of the land and the vitality and determination of its people. They were fascinated by the diversity of its population and the many challenges to Israel's survival.

One day, our youngest daughter discovered the morning newspaper. Full of concern, she urgently showed us the headline: "Why does Israel want to wipe out tourism?" No, no, we explained, Israel loves visitors. The headline says it is determined to wipe out *terrorism*. Her eyes widened, she thought and nodded, and remarkably, she understood. Another important lesson about Israel had taken place that day.

Above: The Rae family near the Dead Sea, 1994. From left to right: Bob, Lisa, Arlene, Judith, with Eleanor in front.

From Thought to Deed

BY RABBI DOW MARMUR

I made three attempts to live in Israel, but each time I ended up in another country.

The first attempt was soon after the end of World War II. My parents and I had returned from seven years in the Soviet Union to our native Poland. There, we found only Jewish ruins and no family. We were preparing to go to Israel when we located my mother's two surviving sisters in Sweden. They had been rescued from a concentration camp. We joined them in Sweden before the State of Israel was proclaimed.

My second attempt came less than a decade later, when, as the information officer at the Israeli embassy in Stockholm, I visited Israel for the first time. That visit confirmed me in my desire to be a rabbi, so my wife and I went to England to study.

The third time was in 1982, but in Jerusalem I met an officer of Holy Blossom Temple. He invited me to give some lectures in Toronto. That's how we came to live here.

One of our three children, Michael, made it to Israel on his first attempt. After spending a few months at the Hebrew University, he decided to settle in Israel, which he did three years later.

He has been an Israeli since 1984, and is married with

three Israeli-born children. He has just been made dean of the college in Jerusalem that gave him his *smicha* (rabbinical ordination).

It's a special joy for me that my son has turned my dream into his reality. Visiting family in Israel is fundamentally different from going on missions or being a tourist. The romance and the rhetoric of Diaspora existence give way to Israeli realism, which means more frustration – and stronger commitment.

I feel like a participant in the daily life of people at home. Whatever their political and religious views, they are all determined to make Israel safe for themselves and their children, striving to lead a Jewish life that permeates every aspect of their existence. That life promises to be the best guarantor for the future of Judaism. To have a personal stake in it fills me with hope and moves me to ever more enthusiastic involvement.

Above: Happy grandparents in Israel, Rabbi Dow Marmur and his wife, Fredzia, with sabba *(grandmother) and* savta *(grandfather) written all over them.*

Never Again

BY JEHUDI KINAR

As Israel's consul general to Toronto, I am the official link between Toronto and Israel.

I was born in the Netherlands during the Nazi occupation. The Nazis insisted that every Jew take on a specifically "authorized" Jewish name so that any Jewish person would be immediately recognizable in the community. My parents, who had left Germany a couple of years earlier, committed a subtle act of resistance in naming me after a grandfather who was called Jehuda. They changed this to Jehudi (which is not only a biblical name, but means "Jew" in Hebrew).

In December 1942, at the age of sixteen months, I was put into the care of the Dutch Underground. The director of a high school in Amsterdam, who was one of the leading members of the Dutch Resistance, took me on the condition that my parents were not to know to whom I was given (to protect the identity of both the Underground members and the families providing hiding places). Soon after, my parents and sister were taken to a camp in the north of Holland and from there to Bergen-Belsen, which they thankfully survived.

Forty-three of the forty-five Jewish children in the orphanage where I was hiding were rounded up. Only two children were allowed to remain, because of their white-blond hair. I was one of them. The Underground hid me with a woman in a small town north of Amsterdam. I stayed there until the end of the war, when I was taken by the Red Cross to Denmark and Sweden to recuperate. Finally, at age five, I was reunited with my family. It was also around this time that I was first confronted with my Jewishness, insofar as a child of this age can grasp such a concept.

Although I was not yet seven years old, I remember the mass demonstration two days after Israel proclaimed its independence on May 14, 1948. On the Museumplein, opposite the Concertgebouw (Concert Hall), in Amsterdam, thousands of Jews and non-Jews assembled and danced the horah, waving Israeli flags and banners. It was then I decided that never again would I be part of a tolerated minority, even in a country as attractive as the Netherlands; rather, I would be part of the majority that would determine its own destiny.

In 1969 I emigrated to Israel. Five days after arriving, I met my future wife, Ruti. Today we have two children, Yaron and Yael, who over the years have also taken their role as ambassadors for their country very seriously.

Above: Jehudi Kinar at his desk.

Mel **Lastman**, mayor of Toronto, writes, "Israel doesn't just capture the heart; it captures the soul. Israel is our history, our past, and our future. Its physical beauty is surpassed only by the spirit of the land and the security it represents for Jews around the world.

"Israel is of paramount importance. From its founding to the present day, Israel has welcomed us and given us a place of our own, given us protection and security.

"It doesn't matter if it's five thousand, ten thousand, or a million. Without asking how, what, or why, Israel makes room for all Jewish people, even if all they have is the clothes on their backs. Thanks to Israel, they are housed — they are fed, clothed, and helped in their transition.

"During a recent visit, I was most impressed by the links our businesses have formed with Israeli businesses, the economic progress that is being made there, and, particularly, the enthusiasm and friendliness of every person I met."

Connecting with My Sephardi Roots

BY JACQUES BENQUESUS

My younger son, Amram, and I were privileged to be among the first to be shown an ornate and ancient Torah brought back by the Honourable David Levy, then Israel's deputy prime minister and minister of foreign affairs, from his first visit to Egypt. The Torah was given to David by President Mubarak and came from a synagogue that had once been the centre of a vibrant Sephardi Jewish community in Alexandria but had been closed for over forty years.

David Levy and I are from Morocco. As teenagers, David made aliyah to Israel and I moved to Canada. Both of us rose from humble beginnings. Each of us, in his own way, has devoted himself to the loves of his life: Torah, Israel, family, the Jewish People, and our Sephardi heritage.

I first went to Israel in 1968, when I was nineteen, to visit my grandparents, whom I had not seen for eighteen years. For three unforgettable weeks, I connected with the land and the people, with Biba, a school chum from Tangiers, as my guide. Biba eventually became my bride.

At long last I was able to experience everything I had heard about and been taught at home and in school. I relived the stories of the Torah, and travelled to Safed, that great centre of Sephardi Jewish religious and intellectual life, where Joseph Caro and so many others lived. In Tiberias I meditated on the graves of the Rambam (Moses Maimonides) and of Meir Bal Ness, the sainted miracle worker. My mother always gave *tzedakah* (charitable gifts) in his memory whenever she wished something good for us.

When David Levy showed my son, Amram, and me the Torah, it was the beginning of a circle that would be completed one year later, at the opening ceremonies for the Sephardi Kehila Centre in Toronto, with David and his wife, Rachel, in attendance. The former foreign minister carried one of the Torahs from our previous site to the new building and unveiled the cornerstone, which is from the City of David in Jerusalem, thereby dedicating our longtime dream: a Sephardi educational, religious, and cultural centre in Toronto.

Above: Jacques Benquesus, left, with the ancient Sefer Torah brought from Alexandria, Egypt, pictured with the Honourable David Levy and Jacques' son, Amram, in David Levy's office, Jerusalem 1996.

The Old World Gives Birth to New Technology

BY JULIE MORTON

We went to Israel to make the baby that four years of fertility clinics in Canada had failed to produce. As a couple we felt that we were so full of life, and we were desperate to share it with a child of our own. A child, we thought, would only help us to drink more deeply from our cup of life, which already overflowed with richness.

And so we hugged friends and family, and left. We landed in a foreign country, where the citizens spoke in unfamiliar tongues and acted in unfamiliar ways – a foreign country that nevertheless was home. And we hoped.

For the seven months that we lived in Israel, we studied Torah, we met with and then mourned for Yitzhak Rabin, we endured the frightening uncertainty of bus bombs and human torches, we made friends and connections, we celebrated Shabbat, and we concentrated our attention on our repeated attempts to find a way to create a life. We had left our physical world and immersed ourselves in our emotional one. We looked to the Old World for the newest, cutting-edge technologies. We went to a country that has seen its share of war and death to create a new life.

As I sit and write this, my belly swells and moves. Small arms and feet press themselves against the confines of my womb. Our child appears anxious to explore the broader spaces, colours, and sounds that the world has to offer. My husband, Ron, is beside me, his hand upon my growing stomach as he "babysits" our child, and we joyously await its arrival. A year ago I could only wish for this. Today, I know that my wish has been fulfilled.

Postscript: Julie and Ron's son, Jake, was born in Toronto on October 3, 1996.

Above: Julie Morton, joyously awaiting the birth of her child, 1996.
Left: Julie Morton with her husband, Ron, at Jerusalem's City Hall, 1996.

A Tree of Remembrance

BY MIKE HARRIS, PREMIER OF ONTARIO

H aving grown up in Canada, a country whose stabil–ity we so often take for granted, my family and I were unprepared for the flood of emotion that we felt on our first visit to Israel in April 1994.

I believe that my son Mike, who was just nine at the time, was able to grasp the significance of the story of Israel's cre–ation. This was reassuring, because I am convinced that this is something he and all of his generation must know.

We were struck by the way the spirit of progression mixes with the will to remember, and by the tremendous strength that Israel draws from its courage in working to prevent great tragedies from ever again being allowed to occur.

It was with this commitment in mind that we planted a tree of remembrance in the Peace Forest in Jerusalem – a tree that, to us, is a symbol of the growth of Israel, which has offered the security of a permanent homeland for Jews worldwide.

The memory of our visit – and especially that day with my family as we stood together, looking over a desert where life has bloomed, overwhelmed with a nation's emotion – is one that will always affect the course of our lives.

Background: Premier Mike Harris of Ontario, planting a tree of remembrance in the Peace Forest, Jerusalem, while his wife, Janet, and his son, Mike, look on.

A Journey of Sadness and Joy

BY ERNIE RUBENSTEIN

Throughout my life I had heard about the small, and not so small, towns in Poland from which both of my late parents' families came. I became fascinated with constructing a family tree, which meant a trip to Poland in late June of 1997. I was accompanied by my twenty-three-year-old son, Michael, and my seventy-six-year-old uncle, Harry Rubenstein, a man who had fled Poland in 1939 to survive in Russian work camps and ultimately fight the Germans in the Battle of Moscow.

The towns we had set out to discover we saw through my uncle's eyes. In Ostrowiccz I was fortunate enough to obtain a copy of my father's birth certificate. But in all the small towns we visited there were virtually no Jews, nor traces of the lives they led. The tombstones in the Jewish cemeteries in these towns were mostly smashed into rubble to be used for road construction by the Nazi war machine. Although we were saddened, we were glad we had come.

We went on to Israel to attend my cousin's wedding celebration, an outdoor wedding on Kibbutz Nitzanim with a thousand attendees. There was great music, great food, and best of all, you could feel the freedom for Jews. What euphoria we felt standing in the midst of such a celebration in the heart of Israel after having felt such outrage at how the Jewish culture had been eradicated in Poland.

Below: Ernie Rubenstein with his uncle Harry Rubenstein visiting the damaged Jewish cemetery in Ostrowiecz, Poland, 1997.

"**I**srael has been my homeland ever since I was two years old," writes **Francesca David**. "Four decades later, however, as an adult with a family, personal circumstances made us move to Toronto.

"Upon my arrival I was warmly greeted by Shalom Toronto, which welcomes Jewish newcomers from around the world. That is how I was introduced to the vibrant life of Toronto's hospitable Jewish community.

"Soon after, I became a board member of the Jewish National Fund, the Canadian Jewish Congress (Ontario Region), and the Israel Educational and Cultural Institute, which I helped found.

"Yet my major commitment is Toronto's Israeli monthly magazine, published in Hebrew, and to a local weekly Israeli radio show, interviewing many diverse personalities. I devote my time bridging the gap between the Hebrew-speaking community and the community at large. For several years I was one of the hosts at the Jerusalem pavilion at Toronto's International Caravan, where we portray the great diversity of heritage and culture that is Israel."

Francesca David is pictured here interviewing Canada's minister of national defence, **Art Eggleton**, 1997.

The late **Sam Perkell**, an ardent sailor, was very involved with the Island Yacht Club in Toronto. When he passed away, to honour his memory the Perkell family, together with the Island Yacht Club, purchased a training boat for Israeli Sea Scouts that would be used to prepare future officers for the Israeli navy. **Leo Perkell**, Sam's brother, is pictured with the *S. Perkell*, moored near Tel Aviv.

Wanderings

BY ANDY BARRIE

In the spring of 1993, my mother invited me to take her to Israel. She had already been there on several occasions, but it was the first time for me. We rented a car, and at one point I got lost in the middle of the Negev. As we rode around in vast circles, Mom said that the reason the Israelites wandered there for forty years was that the men who led them refused to ask for directions.

For every mile we covered on that drive, I have a different impression, but one of the most memorable stops was at the ruins of the two-thousand-year-old palace of a city once known as Kur-noob. I stood in a room where foot messengers would have been given an audience with their king. Minutes later, and footsteps away, I was sharing my impressions, via satellite, with a radio audience on the other side of the planet.

The word "Diaspora" describes the dispersion of the Jewish People in the first centuries of the Christian era, the centuries of triumphs and tribulations, prosperity and persecution. In the magnificent Tel Aviv Museum of the Diaspora, visitors are

invited to feed a huge computer with whatever they know about their own family's history. Over the years, millions of names have made their way into the database.

And so it was, on the day before our visit, that the Furtweiler family of Switzerland stopped by the computer and learned that some Florida Furtweilers had just entered information: the family tree drawn on the screen revealed that the Florida Furtweilers were the long-lost cousins of the Swiss Furtweilers. Even better, it turned out that their American cousins were still in the building. The family reunion, museum staff told us, was astonishing to see.

The glow of that single computer screen lit my way to understanding what the Diaspora means, and why, when the country called Israel was born fifty years ago, a world full of wandering Jews felt *their* family, at last, had come home.

Above: Andy Barrie and his mother, Mickey, visiting Masada, 1993.

Jordan Recieves Canadian Mission

This UJA Hineni Mission was the first Jewish Canadian group to be invited to the Jordanian royal palace in Amman for an official visit to meet with His Royal Highness Crown Prince El Hassan Bin Tahal, Her Royal Highness Princess Sarvath, and other Jordanian officials. Tea and refreshments were served and a press conference was held, with the prince answering questions from mission participants. This visit, in October 1995, was televised and shown throughout Jordan.

Right: His Royal Highness Crown Prince El Hassan Bin Tahal, and Her Royal Highness Princess Sarvath.

Facing page: Included in this photo, which was taken on the steps of the royal palace, are:

Front row, left to right: Ambassador Michel de Salaberry, Canadian ambassador to Jordan; W. Bernard Herman; Lily Silver; Elisa Morton Palter; Andrew Himel; Rosanne Ain; Malka Green; His Royal Highness, Crown Prince El Hassan Bin Tahal; Her Royal Highness, Princess Sarvath; Gerald Halbert; Rose Wolfe; Tootsie Halbert; Charlotte Steinberg; Jodi Bregman; Steve Ain; Carole Zucker.

Second row, left to right: Mel Wolfond; Shmuel Marom; David Gotfrid; Elaine Rafelman; Gilbert Palter; Harold Soupcoff; Mynne Soupcoff; Caurie Bregman Glickman; Yetta Bregman; Dorothy Drevnig; Murray Menkes; Pauline Menkes; Berta Ovnat; Lewis Steinberg; Karen Morton; Bonnie Goldstein; Julie Morton.

Third row, left to right: Don Rafelman; Nathan Silver; David Goldstein; Wendy Eisen; Elliot Eisen; Lyon Sachs; Dundi Sachs; Manny Kimel; Candice Kimel; Amnon Shinar; Dorothy Nadolny; Lionel Schipper.

Fourth row, left to right: Leslie Diamond; Pam Widrich; Gloria Rosenberg; Bernard Zucker; Herb Nadolny; Lionel Waldman; Sandra Waldman; Avraham Infeld; Debbie Kimel; Shmuel Ovnat; Victor Yagoda; Min Drevnig; Marilyn Gotfrid; Elizabeth Wolfe; Paul Shnier; Paul Morton.

Fifth row, left to right: Arthur Wolfond; Beverley Jones; Alvin Rosenberg; Pedie Wolfond; Renee Rubinstein; Zvi Levran; Esther Glotman; two Jordanian guides.

Sixth row, left to right: Allan Reitzes; Ron O'Brien; Eli Rubinstein; Harvey Drevnig; Warren Kimel; Shannon Belkin.

A group of young Torontonians dance in the courtyard by Jerusalem's Western Wall.

HOPE FOR
THE FUTURE

Affirmation

Norman Blustein, in the foreground, celebrated his bar mitzvah at the Western Wall in 1970, part of the "first wave" of North American bar mitzvahs in Israel after the Six Day War. Norman's family belonged to a Toronto club whose members had an obligation to make yearly family visits to Israel, thus familiarizing each child with the country before his bar mitzvah.

Meeting with a Legend

BY MEL SUFRIN

What's your name?" David Ben-Gurion asked a member of the group who had just spent seven weeks touring Israel. It was the inaugural trip sponsored by the Bar Mitzvah Foundation of Toronto in 1961. "Patricia," was the reply. "What kind of a name is that for a Jewish girl? You should have a Hebrew name."

The same question was repeated a number of times as he worked his way around the Quonset hut in the northern Negev where the group was assembled. Richard, Larry, Howard, Melanie: not names for Jewish children.

Then he spotted a woman standing at the back of the room. "And what is your name?" he asked. "Malcah," she replied. "Is that your real name?" "Yes." "What do they call you? Malcah?"

At that point, the group's guide explained that Malcah Sufrin was one of the Canadian *madrichim* (guides) for the trip. That seemed to satisfy him.

As everyone filed out of the hut, Ben-Gurion said, "Come, Malcah, walk with me. Are you married?" "Yes." "Do you have children?" "Yes." "What are their names?" Without hesitation, her response was, "Akiva, Yehudit, and Mordecai." Fortunately, Ben-Gurion did not go on to enquire how they were known in Toronto: Kerry, Jodi, and Mark.

Below: The first Bar Mitzvah Foundation trip, 1961. Left to right: Larry Tanenbaum, Michael Wise, Prime Minister David Ben-Gurion, Mel Sufrin, and Malcah Sufrin.

What's in a Name?

BY BRYON ISRAEL ALEXANDROFF

I was born four days after the State of Israel, on May 19, 1948. My parents honoured this auspicious occasion by giving me the middle name "Israel."

Before my bar mitzvah in 1961, they enrolled me in the Bar Mitzvah Foundation – the brainchild of Murray Koffler and Rabbi Reuben Slonim, who decided that young people should be given the opportunity to be as inspired as they were by going on a first trip to Israel. Instead of receiving gifts, I received gift certificates from friends and family entitling me to an experience in Israel. When enough certificates were accumulated, they were redeemed for a trip with a group of others also enrolled in the program. If the

amount received was greater than necessary, it was applied to a member whose certificates fell short of the requirement.

I travelled to Israel in the summer of 1964 with approximately twenty-five other fifteen- and sixteen-year-olds. I remember getting off the plane and kissing the ground; it was an emotional time of my life. As a parent, I made sure that my children visited there at a young age. Israel is a part of me, in more than name only.

Above: Planning their 1964 Bar Mitzvah Foundation trip, are, left to right, David Wolinsky, Bryon Alexandroff, Larry Shiffman, and Roy Fisher.

Shoshie Lockshin at her bat mitzvah in April 1993, held in the convention centre at Kibbutz Ramat Rachel near Jerusalem. On the left is her father's mother, **Sylvia Lockshin**, who first visited Israel with her late husband, **Lou**, in 1957. On the right is her mother's mother, **Rita Mendelsohn**, who has made many trips to Israel since her first visit in 1966 with her late husband, **Dr. Robert Mendelsohn**.

Ancient Words Come to Life

BY LIBBY ROSENBERG

When we learned that Rabbi Stuart Rosenberg of Beth Tzedec Synagogue was leading a group of eighty people to Israel in 1969, we seized the opportunity to go with them and celebrate our son Elliot's bar mitzvah in Jerusalem, an unusual arrangement at that time. We thought it would be a valuable experience for Elliot, whose Hebrew education had not been as extensive as we would have wished.

The day before the bar mitzvah, we were being guided through the Shrine of the Book, a unique building near the national Israel Museum. It was erected for a single and unique purpose – to house the renowned Dead Sea Scrolls and

interpret these scriptures written on ancient parchment, which had been found by a Bedouin in 1947 at En Feshqa, close to Jericho and the shores of the Dead Sea.

We were all engrossed in a lecture when suddenly we heard, "Mommy, Daddy, come quick!" We were alarmed and ran upstairs. There was Elliot, in front of the beautiful Isaiah Scroll, reading his Haftorah portion directly from the original, and so beautifully! It was overwhelming. People wept.

We have always felt that our Israel trip made a huge impact on Elliot's life, and we feel truly blessed.

Above: Elliot Rosenberg at his bar mitzvah in Israel, September 1969.

Bar/Bat Mitzvah

When a Jewish child becomes bar or bat mitzvah ("son or daughter of the *mitzvah*"), he or she accepts the religious obligations of adult Jewish life and the laws (*mitzvot*) which govern it. In liberal communities, bar and bat mitzvah ceremonies take place at age thirteen for both boys and girls; in traditional communities, it is at age thirteen for the boys and age twelve for the girls. The boy or girl normally marks the occasion by reading in Hebrew from the Torah, followed by a celebration with family and friends. Some families take their children to Israel to celebrate bar or bat mitzvahs there.

Guess Who's Coming to Dinner?

BY BOB SAVLOV

After my daughter Candace's bat mitzvah at a synagogue in Jeru–salem in March 1994, our family and guests went back to the hotel for lunch. Our guide, David, asked if we would mind having an extra guest join us for lunch. "Would it be all right if Shimon Peres came in to give a *mazel tov* to your daughter, Candace?" he said. I assumed this was a joke. "Sure, David. If Shimon wants to drop in, we won't stop him." I continued celebrating with our guests and forgot about the conversation. At about 1:00 PM, our guide whispered to me that Candace was to come out to the foyer; Shimon would be

there any moment now and would like to meet her. We figured this was some prank David was trying to pull, and we decided to humour him. So out to the foyer we went to see what our guide had in store. The photograph says it all. We were thrilled. And Shimon, if you're reading this, you can come for dinner at our house any time you're in Toronto!

———

Above: Candace Savlov, with surprise guest Prime Minister Shimon Peres, right, and guide, David Bar David, March 1994.

Rabbi **Feldman** with, from left, **Theo Goldstein**, **Lauren Laskin**, and **Jana Lambert**, holding the Torah after reading their portions at Masada, March 1994. Their mothers, **Debbie Goldstein**, **Holly Goren Laskin**, and **Hildi Lambert** write, "Friends since they were three, the girls and their families – from cousins to bubbies and zaydes – came to celebrate this significant rite of passage when the girls affirmed their place as women in Judaism. All of us felt privileged to stand where our ancestors lived and died so bravely, two thousand years ago."

The Group of Forty-two

BY CONNIE KUSSNER

The most awesome experience I have ever had in Israel occurred on Monday, November 29, 1993. On that day, at the age of sixty-two, I celebrated my bat mitzvah with forty-two women from across Canada at a moving and memorable service on Mount Scopus, overlooking Jerusalem. We were divided into groups, each woman reading her portion. (The "portion" is the selection from the Torah reading of the day which the bar or bat mitzvah has prepared to read as part of the service.)

The ceremony took place during Hadassah-WIZO's seventy-fifth anniversary convention. Rabbi Levi Weiman

Kelman officiated at the morning service, and the *b'not mitzvah* (*b'not* is the plural of *bat*, "daughter") led the congregation of over three hundred in song and prayer. A Torah was brought over, especially for this occasion, from the small Jewish community in Yarmouth, Nova Scotia.

For the women who shared this experience, the sights, sounds, and feelings will remain in our hearts and minds forever.

Above: Singing during prayers, left to right: Shoshi Talesniek, Sophie Kettner, Connie Kussner, Mirial Small, and Esther Matlow.

Audrey, Amanda, Gary, and **Evan Taerk** celebrated Amanda's bat mitzvah at the Western Wall among other tourists and Israeli residents in July 1988. What normally is a family affair becomes a public celebration when you are in Israel.

From Generation to Generation

BY JERRY KLASNER

J oseph Klasner, my father, never had a bar mitzvah. He is a Holocaust survivor, the only one in his immediate family to survive.

Born in Poland, Joseph was ten years old when the Nazis invaded. He was on a train to Auschwitz with his family when his father pulled away the barbed wire across a boxcar window and pushed Joseph, his oldest son, through, ordering him to run and hide. Joseph never saw his family again.

After the war Joseph discovered an uncle, Moishe Klasner, who had immigrated to Israel. Moishe died in 1981, and my son Michael was named in his memory.

Moishe Klasner's wife dedicated the writing of a new Torah in his memory. It was donated to the Zion Orphanage in Jerusalem, where Michael and his grandfather Joseph had their bar mitzvahs together in January 1995.

Michael read from this Torah that was dedicated to his namesake. Then he told those assembled, "Most people don't get a second chance, but my zayde did, and I am honoured to share my bar mitzvah with him." And Joseph added, "Sharing in today's ceremonies with my first-born grandson is one of those emotional moments in one's life when memories of the past and hardships endured meld into the excitement of this young man's beginnings."

————————

Above: Grandfather Joseph Klasner and his grandson, Michael, share their bar mitzvahs in Jerusalem, 1995. Much of the family came to celebrate. Front, left to right: Karmela Klasner, Daniel Klasner, Sara Klasner, Adam Klasner, and Katie Klasner. Back, left to right: Rabbi Rakowsky, Eric Solomon, Jerry Klasner, Joseph Klasner, and Michael Klasner.

A memorable occasion, celebrating **Jesse Kaufman**'s bar mitzvah, June 19, 1989, at the Western Wall, with family and friends from Toronto and Israel. Included in this photo are: Ira, Sherry, Lee, and Jesse Kaufman; Morris and Rose Kaufman; Bill and Bertha Savlov; Charles and Ethel Sigel; Skip and Lynn Sigel and family; Michael and Deenna Sigel and family; Chaim and Yael Geron and family; Arieh and Bruria Kaufman; Benny and Hedvah Miller and family; Billy and Shaindy Nathanson; Bryon and Lani Alexandroff and family; Stan and Dorothy Tessis and family; Earl and Ellie Miller and family; Irwin and Elayne Wortsman and family; Tilly and Jack Spears; Dorothy Hendeles and family; Henry Shiner; Mildred Devor; David Bar David; Nathan and Lily Silver; Yehuda Raveh.

Tolerance in Diversity

BY BARRY AND HONEY SHERMAN

In December 1996, our son Jonathon wanted to celebrate his bar mitzvah in Israel. Initially, we thought of holding services at the Western Wall, where his sister Lauren had celebrated her bat mitzvah seven years earlier. However, the *mechitzah* (divider) separating men and women praying at the Wall had since been raised to such a level that we were sure we would no longer feel together as a family if the service were to take place there.

In trying to find an alternative location, we heard from our daughter's friends attending the Hebrew University about the Hecht Synagogue on the Mount Scopus campus, a magnificent setting overlooking the Old City. It appeared we had found the ideal venue for our *simcha*.

But in Israel, there's always another chapter to the story. Imagine our surprise upon arriving at the synagogue the morning of the bar mitzvah to learn that the tradition of the synagogue required women to sit upstairs, separate from the men!

We were suddenly confronted with a real-life example of the impact of differences in Jewish religious practice.

Thankfully, the sensitive and creative Hebrew University staff found a solution. A makeshift *mechitzah* of reasonable height was quickly constructed of beautiful flowers from the outside terrace, dividing the seating on the main floor. Through flexibility and compromise, we managed to overcome philosophical differences and satisfied all involved. The *simcha* was fabulous and proved to be a most meaningful experience for our family.

Above: The Sherman family. Back row, left to right: Lauren, Barry, Honey, and Jonathon. Front row, left to right: Alexandra, Kaelen, and Bubbie Helen Reich.

"**I** t was a historic weekend," writes **Rochelle Florence**. "On Thursday, July 1, 1976 – Canada Day – our family prayed at the Western Wall. My son Ira was called to the Torah at synagogue on Saturday, July 3. During the service the congregation prayed for the hostages held in Entebbe, Uganda.

"On Sunday, July 4, the hostages were freed! People cried tears of joy, danced, hugged, and kissed in the streets, and jets flew overhead skywriting '*kol hakovod l'zavah*' ('Hurrah for the army!').

"At our reception that evening our family and friends happily gathered together on a huge terrace overlooking David's Tower and the ancient wall surrounding the Old City of Jerusalem, to celebrate Ira's bar mitzvah and the rescue of 103 hostages. Fireworks enhanced the festivities as the United States celebrated its bicentennial. It was a glorious weekend, never to be forgotten."

Pictured on a trek through the Sinai desert are, left to right, **Rochelle**, **Ira**, **Michelle**, and **Max Florence**, 1976.

Helping Hands

Sar-El Volunteers for Israel

In the summer of 1982, during Operation Peace for Galilee, Golan Heights agricultural settlements faced the possibility of losing entire harvests because most able-bodied settlers had been drafted into the army reserve and crops had been left unattended.

Dr. Aharon Davidi, director of the Golan Heights community cultural activities, was touched by the settlers' distress. He sent some friends to the United States as a recruiting team. Within a few weeks 650 volunteers were at work. Because of their success, those first volunteers recommended that the project be continued.

In the spring of 1983, Sar-El, the national project for volunteers for Israel, was founded as a non-profit, non-political organization. (Sar-El is the Hebrew acronym for *Sherut Le-Israel*, "Service for Israel.") Sar-El is now represented in about twenty countries, with the largest numbers of volunteers coming from the United States, France, and Canada.

The purpose of Sar-El is to relieve Israeli reservists from duties at home and to perform routine jobs in the military, while providing a way to build lasting relationships between Israeli and Diaspora Jews.

What Was a Grandmother Doing in the Israeli Navy?
BY LILLIAN ANDER

There probably isn't another country that would accept someone my age into their armed forces.

Our group of seventeen Canadians was bused to the Bahad Navy Training Base in Haifa. After a tour of the base, we had to outfit ourselves with two complete uniforms, including boots, socks, hat, and belt. You can imagine how funny this was, trying on sizes *aleph*, *bet*, *gimel*, and *mem* until we had the right sizes. A couple of the men were over six feet tall, and since most of the uniforms were for shorter men, they were pretty unhappy until they got clothes of the right size.

Our day started at 6:00 AM, and you really had to move it. Imagine fifty soldiers washing at the same time! The hardest part was getting into uniform and boots and looking proper for inspection. Breakfast was at 7:00 AM and flag-raising at 7:50. I was chosen to raise the flag the first morning.

Facing page: Lillian Ander with four of the soldiers on her base, December 1991.

Our job was in the main supply building that services the training camp, the navy docks, and various camps nearby. We were to do a total overhaul of this building: reboxing, counting, and folding uniforms and blankets, and checking equipment and all the office supplies. The men mended barbed-wire fences, cleaned guns, and fixed sidewalks.

On or off the base, we were treated like soldiers. Wherever we went, everyone blessed us. I now have enough blessings to last a long time.

Everybody Knew Sandy
BY SANDY POSLUNS

When we first arrived at the Motor Pool Army Base, which functions as a giant garage for the army, the young soldiers looked at us as if we were aliens. I used a little Hebrew and I smiled a lot and laughed with them. Eventually they smiled back and began to kibbitz with me.

I helped Manny in the kitchen. Moshe helped me carry anything heavy, and I taught him English words along the way. Zio quietly asked how to converse with girls on the beach at Tel Aviv. Amnon ran around searching out extra nails and a hammer for me. Soon everybody knew Sandy: *"Boker tov, Sandy!"* ("Good morning, Sandy!"). I had arrived!

The special card we got identifying us as army personnel came in handy when I was leaving Israel. The airport security agent began to drill me about why I had been in Israel alone. But when I flashed my ID, she stood at attention, thanked me for volunteering, and carried my luggage to the check-in counter!

The Sirens Started to Blare
BY PEARL HIMEL BANKS, LOIS VAILE, AND ITCHE HIMEL

Our *madrich* (guide), Shimon, made us welcome and attended to the needs of the mixed group of thirty volunteers: young, old, Jews, non-Jews, men, women. We checked old tank communication gear, sorted nuts and bolts, and made new cases for guns from old U.S. army gun boxes.

On one of the first evenings there was a rainstorm. The power went off, and then the sirens started to blare. The barracks were black, noise came from outside, and the sky was lit with bolts of light. People scurried for the shelters, thinking we were under attack. But it turned out that when the power goes off the sirens blare automatically. The noise and light were, of course, thunder and lightning from the storm!

Above: Itche Himel, Pearl Banks, Lois Vaile, and Shimon Rebibo in the dining hall at their army base, 1989.
Left: Sandy Posluns, with a soldier from the motor pool at the army camp, 1988.

Amy **Mouckley Simon** writes, "I am a second-generation Sar-El volunteer. My parents, David and Eunice, started the tradition. My job was cleaning weapons, specifically M16s and Uzis. This included taking them apart and putting them together again. The work was long and hard, which I loved. On Shabbat I had time to visit with friends and reminisce about past visits."

Sar-El volunteers **Eunice** and **David Mouckley** write, "Our base was a large supply depot. We worked from after breakfast until four in the afternoon — cleaning, labelling, schlepping, and complaining about our dirty job in an old airplane hangar. Early in the morning we assembled for flag-raising. There we were, standing at attention with a hundred eighteen-year-old Israeli men and women as the blue-and-white Magen David flag was raised. Did we cry? You bet we did, every day!"

Anna and **Lou Van Delman** were Sar-El volunteers at Kfar Giladi, a kibbutz situated two kilometres from the Lebanese border. Anna writes, "Our life there was a series of contrasts. The nights brought the terrifying sound of shells, yet we awoke to a serene peace enhanced by a symphony of birdsong. We remember the beauty of spring blossoms growing over bomb shelters; the innocence and vigour of young people carrying submachine guns. The irony was that we were thanked for our 'gift of time.' It is we who owe thanks for an unforgettable experience."

Sar-El volunteer **Elsa Chandler** writes, "Service in the Israeli army has given me a chance to help Israel as Israel helped me, after I was liberated from Bergen-Belsen by the Swedish Red Cross. My road to recovery was made easier with the help of workers from Israeli Youth Aliyah. Under their leadership, many of us child orphans received our first formal education."

Every day, Sar-El volunteers **Lani Alexandroff**, left, and **Susie Goldberg** were bused to the Golan Heights in 1995, where they wired together iron grids that were used to line the trenches at the borders.

Len **Berk**, centre receiving the patch designating him as a *mitnadev* (volunteer) Sar-El, in May 1997. He is flanked by Staff-Sergeant Boris and Base Commander Shimshon. Len writes, "My job was repacking first-aid kits used by army field medics. First we checked the dates of the items to ensure that they were not too old. Then we prepared sets of bandages and alcohol swipes and heat-sealed them. We also tested the flashlights, often by banging them on the worktable. Finally we sealed the kits in plastic bags. The army does this about every two years in order to have an emergency back-up supply."

Canadian and American Active Retirees in Israel (CAARI)

BY ANICE AND ARNOLD STARK

For the past fourteen years, the JNF has called on Diaspora Jews fifty years old and over to "give their love and hand to those that need that love and care." CAARI's goals are to bring people to Israel during the winter vacation to use their talents and skills in social agencies, in the forests, to tour and study all aspects of Israel, and to participate in social and cultural activities. In the forests they plant, trim, and cut trees. In schools, day-care and senior centres, and youth hostels, they teach English or do maintenance work.

The participants commit themselves to working five mornings per week for about three hours. Afternoons and evenings are free for lectures, Israeli dancing, and tours.

Below: These volunteers for CAARI are kicking high with delight at the Dead Sea, February 1995. Left to right: Betty Levitan, Anice Stark, Florence Korbel, Frances Bondarofsky, and Claudette Banon.

Yad BeYad

Yad BeYad is a program of the Canada–Israel Forum and the Israeli Forum that brings English-speaking people to Israel to share their expertise. The Israeli Forum is a non-political organization committed to advancing ties between Jews in Israel and the Diaspora and the social absorption of new immigrants in Israel. Yad BeYad is translated as "Hand in Hand."

One need identified by the Forum was for immigrants to learn conversational English to enable them to find employment in their professions or be retrained for new jobs. Volunteers teach English in classrooms and immerse themselves in an Israeli community. During their stay volunteers meet members of Israeli society and become part of the Israeli way of life. They also participate in Forum-planned mini-tours and hear speakers on key Israeli and Jewish issues.

The Canadian branch of Yad BeYad was established in 1992 by Loretta Helman, a South African immigrant to Toronto. Loretta spent a year living and working as a social worker in Jerusalem during the sixties. She returned from a Jewish Federation of Greater Toronto mission to Israel fired up to do something practical and meaningful – and so Yad BeYad was born.

The program is a four-week summer school, in which volunteers teach daily for three hours in two-week segments. While there, volunteers are "adopted" by Israeli families who have them over for a Shabbat meal and befriend them during their stay.

Participants in Yad BeYad have successfully built a bridge of understanding through language between themselves and Israelis.

Above: Loretta Helman, receiving a certificate in recognition of her work with Yad BeYad from Roni Milo, the mayor of Tel Aviv, 1996.

We Wove Our Faiths into a Fabric
BY FERN WESTERNOFF AND THERESA YOUNG

Travelling together as a Jew and a Christian brought a richness to our Israel journey, but no travel book or article prepared us for the tapestry we wove. As volunteers teaching English through the Yad BeYad program, we used our skills as speech–language pathologists to contribute to the growth of Israel. We also led a daylong seminar sharing mutual areas of clinical concern with members of the Israel Speech, Language and Hearing Association.

Above and beyond our professional interests, we were touched by those we met, beginning with the wonderful people involved in Yad BeYad. Our travels took us to Jewish and Christian sights. Fern realized her dream of reading her haftorah and completing a spiritual bat mitzvah. Theresa's early–morning trek through the maze of near–empty streets to attend Mass at the Church of the Holy Sepulchre was a treasured moment. We walked up the hill on which Jesus delivered the Sermon on the Mount while reading these passages in the Bible. At the Western Wall on Shabbat we were moved to tears amidst the aura of the prayers folded into its crevices. Together we wove our faiths' perspectives into a fabric of biblical stories and historical information, threaded with recollections, connections, juxtapositions that on occasion were deeply moving. The people we met added splashes of colour and texture as our lives fleetingly connected in ways that drew our hearts together. The experience of Yad BeYad framed our weaving with crimson velvet.

I Took My Role Seriously
FROM A CONVERSATION WITH MATILDA BIGIO

I was born and educated in Egypt, where I learned English and French in school, Arabic from the family's servants, and Yiddish from my Romanian–born father. I fled Egypt in the fall of 1956 and came to Canada.

After forty years in Canada, an advertisement for Yad BeYad appealed to me, and in July 1997, by then a widowed grandmother, I went to Israel. I took my role as teacher very seriously. Every morning after breakfast I prepared the lesson for the next meeting. And my commitment paid off. When I took attendance after a few days, I realized that my students had increased from eleven to seventeen. By word of mouth people had heard about me from their friends and decided to give me a chance. I felt I was doing a mitzvah, not only for them but also for myself.

Above: Matilda Bigio, seated at centre, receives an award in recognition of her role as a volunteer teacher, Israel, 1997.
Left: Fern Westernoff, left, and Theresa Young, overlooking Haifa, 1997.

Francie Storm, far left, and **Rifky Gold**, far right, write, "Reflecting on our experience in Israel in 1992 evokes many treasured memories. A highlight was Shabbat lunch at the home of our students, Nora and her mother, Chana. Both of these immigrants from the former Soviet Union are physicians who were seeking to strengthen their English language skills."

Healing Hands

Peace through Medicine

BY ARNOLD NOYEK

Since 1967 I have been visiting Israel regularly to lecture at scientific meetings. While there, I learned of the Israeli medical community's need for contact with international experts.

In 1984 the Canada–International Scientific Exchange Program (CISEPO) was initially set up to encourage scientific exchange between Canada and Israel. In the current political climate, however, the program has already built bridges faster and more effectively in the region than any government could do. The Canadian government has given its support, but all funding comes from private sources.

Peace-building projects led by Canadians are quietly linking Palestinians, Jordanians, and Israelis, drawn together by a mutual concern for children's health, among other issues. As CISEPO's chair, and chief otolaryngologist at Mount Sinai Hospital in Toronto, I know that our projects have an impact. We provide treatment programs for children with deafness, which is a relatively common problem in the Middle East.

CISEPO's programs bring together medical and hearing specialists and administrators from Mount Sinai Hospital and

the University of Toronto with their counterparts from hospitals in Nablus, Nazareth, Gaza City, Tel Aviv, Jerusalem, Beersheba, and Amman. Medicine knows no political boundaries.

The transcending of political divisions is evident in these words of the director of the Atfaluna Society for Deaf Children in Gaza, written to a specialist at Soroka Hospital in Beersheba, Israel: "We look forward to future co operation in the same spirit of friendship, goodwill, and professionalism that is created by your having taken the first step in meeting with us here in the Palestinian Authority."

Even in the midst of tensions, CISEPO doesn't look at the politics of the situation. We focus on bringing peace.

Above: Arnold Noyek, left, with Israeli consul general Jehudi Kinar and his wife, Ruti Kinar, 1997.
Facing page: Some of the children at the Atfaluna Society for Deaf Children, Gaza, Palestinian Authority, who benefit so greatly from the Canadian–International Scientific Exchange Program (CISEPO). Arnold Noyek is in the back row, second from left.

The Gift

BY JUDY KOPELOW

In 1982 I learned that Hadassah was offering a scholarship for nursing and medical students to work in Israel for a summer. I enthusiastically applied; my heart was set on a summer in Israel at the renowned Hadassah Hospital. Finally a letter came saying that I had been chosen!

June in Jerusalem is hot but still fresh. I settled in the nursing residence opposite the hospital. I felt the presence of those before me, the women who had the courage and passion to participate in the birth of Israel. Sunday in Israel meant business as usual. The softness and lingering of Shabbat had ended and the week began. As I dressed for that first day in the deep-blue uniform I had been given, I was bursting with emotion. How I wished that my mother, a nurse who had died when I was a teenager, had known of my experience.

Stationed on the haematology/oncology ward, I was invited to join morning rounds. After rounds, the entire staff had breakfast in their tiny coffee room, leaving the nursing station unattended. At first I was concerned for the patients, but my fears were assuaged when a patient attached to an IV came wavering down the corridor and sat at the nursing desk to answer phones while we ate. I learned that it was beneficial for patients to participate in this way.

One memorable patient was a regal and wealthy Egyptian. Diagnosed with a type of cancer that had a poor prognosis, she had come to Israel for treatment, accompanied by her five daughters who spoke flawless English. There was some Arab/Israeli tension surrounding this woman, as there was with the Bedouin patients who overflowed their rooms with carpets, food, belongings, and extended families. I was in awe of this family's respect and care for their mother. Over the weeks, they became less guarded, and our relationship flourished after they asked about my mother. We cried together as I related my mother's years of struggle with ovarian cancer.

As a nurse in the Critical Care Unit at the Hospital for Sick Children, I take care of many Israeli children who come for surgery and medical attention. In my broken night-school Hebrew I can say, "I am your nurse, my name is Judy, and I worked at Hadassah, Ein Kerem, when I was a student." Their eyes light up hearing my faltering Hebrew. I am grateful that in their time of worry I can comfort them with some familiarity.

Above: Judy Kopelow is a critical-care nurse at the Hospital for Sick Children in Toronto.

Teleconferencing

BY ROBERT FILLER

Toronto's Hospital for Sick Children (HSC) has maintained a relationship with Israeli patients, physicians, surgeons, and scientists for many years. Each year we consult on an average of a hundred Israeli children who have rare or complex conditions. Twenty to twenty-five are admitted for treatment. As well, we train physicians and scientists in paediatric fields, and our staff frequently travel to Israel to participate in meetings and training.

We have established a close relationship with Rabbi Ezriel Reichman of Toronto, who works with leading community advisors in Israel. Together we respond to the health-care needs of individuals in various Israeli communities. This work is aided by Ezriel Reichman's own travel business and his humanitarian instincts, as well as by anonymous benefactors. Ezriel takes personal responsibility for the travel details and the Toronto living arrangements for the child and family. He also serves as translator and ombudsman.

In 1997 HSC donated teleconferencing equipment to Ezra L'Marpeh, a non-profit, non-sectarian medical-aid association headed by Rabbi Meilech Furer, a holder of the Prize of Israel. With this new technology we can now provide medical consultation to Israel by live interactive teleconferencing, and reduce travel requirements, time, and money. With the assistance of Teleglobe Canada, this new electronic link has simplified the consultation process and has greatly reduced delays in treatment. Furthermore, it provides a medium for the easy exchange of information and enables us to assist in the educational objectives of our Israel liaison.

Below: A June 1997 press conference, demonstrating the Canadian and Israeli medical link through live teleconferencing. At the table, left to right: Tommy Shonfeld, Schneider Children's Hospital, Tel Aviv; Itzhak Vinograd, Asaf Harofeh Hospital, Tel Aviv; David Berger, Canadian ambassador to Israel; Rabbi Meilech Furer, Ezra L'Marpeh Center, B'nai Brach. On the TV monitors, left to right: Robert Filler, the Hospital for Sick Children, Toronto; David Berger, Canadian ambassador to Israel.

Exchanging Skills

BY BERNARD GOLDMAN

I had little understanding of Israel until June 1967, when I shared the tense days of the Six Day War with Yair Lieberman, a visiting surgeon from Tel Hashomer Hospital. I was in my last weeks of training at the Hospital for Sick Children. Yair, an Israeli reserve officer, was desperate to get home but was torn by his need to stay in Toronto and complete his graduate work.

Yair was the first of many Israeli surgeons I would meet, either at international meetings or as visitors to Toronto hospitals. I admire these doctors for many reasons: they have excellent facilities and superb training, but they also have relatively poor salaries and the demands of reserve duty. Imagine trying to perform heart surgery, teach students, and do research, knowing that you will be called up to examine terrorists in jail, go on tank manoeuvres, or command a patrol boat. Yet they cope and continue to provide excellent care.

Joseph Borman, chief of cardiac surgery at Hadassah Hospital, has become a close friend and colleague. Through him I have had the opportunity to be a visiting professor and lecturer at Hadassah and a participant at many conferences in Jerusalem.

Professor Borman has also lectured in Toronto as my guest on many occasions, and I have had the pleasure of training some of his residents, first at Toronto Hospital, and later at Sunnybrook, where I now head the cardiovascular surgery unit. Naturally, my wife, Fran, has adopted them and their families during their time in Toronto.

Perhaps the most significant moment in my relationship with Israeli medicine came in 1991, when I was asked to head the new heart centre at Jerusalem's Shaare Tzedek Hospital. After much soul-searching, I decided I was not prepared to make aliyah at that time. However, I became involved in the search for a suitable team. Thus developed a warm relationship between Shaare Tzedek and Sunnybrook, with bilateral visits and shared clinical trials.

At a Shabbat dinner in Jerusalem in June 1996, my wife and I were delighted to be reunited with all the trainees I had met in Toronto, as well as most of the senior surgeons of Israel. They had gathered to honour me for my "contributions to heart surgery in Israel." It was a very emotional evening.

Above: Fran and Bernard Goldman, left, with their friends Joe and Ruth Borman, Jerusalem, 1994.

A Bridge of Friendship

BY HART LEVIN

Our 1967 UJA Mission arrived in Israel only months after the Six Day War. I was proud of the military, social, and cultural achievements of Israel – proud of everything.

During two more visits to Israel, my wife, Marilyn, and I made the decision to buy an apartment in Netanya so we could spend summers there with our children. After a 1973 UJA Mission to Israel, I began thinking about how I could best make a contribution to the country. I decided to organize and lead groups of dentists to Israel. In March 1974 my wife and I led the first Dental Mission, consisting of members of the Toronto branch of the international Alpha Omega Fraternity of dentists. There were forty-four people in the group, and for most of them it was their first trip to Israel. We have now led eleven missions together, bringing over eight hundred people to Israel.

These trips have awakened in people a love of Israel and increased their involvement with the country. For Marilyn and me, it's always a thrill to see Israel through someone else's eyes. In conjunction with the missions, I have organized international symposia with renowned speakers in dentistry to address our groups and the faculties of dentistry in Jerusalem and Tel Aviv. Marilyn and I established an Alpha Omega *gesher*, a bridge of friendship that continues to this day.

Below: Marilyn and Hart Levin in front of the Western Wall, wearing their official Tenth Mission T-shirts, 1987.

THE TORONTO HOSPITAL
(Toronto General Hospital and Toronto Western Hospital)
SHIFF FAMILY MEDICAL EDUCATION ASSISTANCE FUND 1994-1995

The purpose of the Shiff Family Medical Education Assistance Fund is to assist those physicians interested in doing research or obtaining specialized clinical experience at the Toronto Hospital in Toronto. The Toronto Hospital comprises the Toronto General and the Toronto Western Hospitals and is a major teaching hospital of the University of Toronto. The Fund is open to both staff doctors and senior trainees from Israel who wish to come to Toronto for one or two year period or for a sabbatical. Applicants will be expected to have already been accepted by a senior staff member at the Toronto Hospital who would oversee his or her work and who would be responsible for providing the basic salary. Applications for additional financial support should be submitted by November 1, 1993 and should be addressed to: Dr. Abraham Rapoport Toronto Western Hospital MP 11-330, 399 Bathurst St. Toronto, Ontario Canada M5T 2S8

The **Shiff family** in action!

Harold J. Hoffman writes: "At the Hospital for Sick Children (HSC) we have trained six Israeli paediatric neurosurgeons and looked after seventy-five Israeli children. This is thanks to a bequest, in 1989, from Edna Rittersporn, a Torontonian who had lived in Israel for many years and who wanted to do something to benefit Israeli children. The interest from this fund is being used to bring talented neurosurgeons from Israel to hone their skills at the HSC. Whenever I go to Israel to lecture, I visit former patients, their parents, and our Toronto-trained surgeons."

Pictured here, left to right, are Harold J. Hoffman with **Mrs. Abe Sahar**, President **Yitzhak Navon**, and his wife, **Ophira**, 1978.

Something to Smile About

BY ALFRED INTRATER

The Dental Volunteers for Israel's Dental Clinic is located in Mekor Hayim in Jerusalem. It is a modern facility where underprivileged children, referred to the clinic by the social welfare departments of Jerusalem, receive free dental care. Volunteer dentists come to the DVI clinic from thirteen countries.

There is no dental insurance in Israel and preventative dental-care education in schools is limited. Consequently, the level of dental health among poor people is very low throughout the country. Many seek professional care only in emergencies.

It requires persistence to change behaviour and modify poor dietary habits, but, after seventeen years, the DVI clinic is seeing results. The clinic's preventative program is a critical part of its success.

In 1982, after visiting the clinic at the request of David Ariel, the Israeli consul in Toronto, I cancelled my excursion plans and stayed to work at the clinic for three weeks. Eventually, Dr. Max Florence and his wife, Rochelle, and my wife, Genya, and I formed the DVI committee in Toronto. We raise funds for the clinic and collect dental supplies that are sent to Israel with volunteer dentists. Every year six to ten Canadians go to work at the clinic, making a direct contribution to a worthwhile Israeli charity – one that gives young people something to smile about.

– Dr. Alfred Intrater passed away in March 1998.

Above: Alfred Intrater, 1965.

From Generation to Generation

The March of the Living

The March of the Living program was first launched in the spring of 1988. It takes thousands of students from around the world on a two-week pilgrimage to the death camps of Poland and the ancient sites of the Land of Israel.

In Poland, the group's visit culminates on Yom Hashoah (Holocaust Remembrance Day). On this solemn day, thousands of teenagers, representing some thirty nations, walk hand-in-hand along the three kilometres separating Auschwitz from Birkenau.

In Israel, the students experience the homeland of the Jewish People, reborn after two thousand years of exile. On Yom Ha'atzmaut (Independence Day), together with the entire country, the students celebrate the creation of the State of Israel, dancing in the streets of her ancient capital, Jerusalem.

The March of the Living asks students never to give up hope for themselves, their people, or humanity.

Above: Barbara Bank, chair of Toronto March of the Living, 1996–98, listening intently to a speaker at a March ceremony in Poland.

Confronting the Ghosts

BY ELI RUBENSTEIN

When I was a child growing up in Toronto, the Holocaust was an ever-present yet little-discussed subject. We knew people in the community who had somehow escaped the massive destruction that was visited upon two-thirds of European Jewry, but most were silent about their wartime experiences. The pain of recollection, survivor guilt, the difficulty of expressing oneself in a new language, and the prevailing culture of silence mixed with fear and embarrassment, all created an environment in which the Holocaust was not addressed publicly. The little my school friends and I knew about the Holocaust left us fearful, yet curious at the same time.

As we wrestled with the ghosts of our parents' past, embattled Israel was making headlines. In the late 1960s,

Above: Eli Rubenstein, national director, March of the Living.
Facing page: Jennifer Miller, seated, with another March participant at the Valley of the Lost Communities, Yad Vashem Memorial, Jerusalem, 1994.

Israel was still considered by many to be the virtuous David, valiantly resisting the attacks of powerful and hostile Goliaths that surrounded her. Along with a new sense of pride and hope for the future of the Jewish People, the survivors were also developing a growing sense of security as they were integrated into North American society. The Holocaust began to be discussed more openly.

As I entered university, the Holocaust was becoming a recognized academic subject, and the complexity of its nature was being revealed. Yet, with all this academic learning, questions still remained. There was a need to examine the event in its place of origin, and somehow symbolically to practise *tikkun olam* (literally, "mending the world") in the very place where the evil was perpetrated. But this journey had to conclude on a note of hope. Thus began my involvement, and the involvement of many others, in the March of the Living.

The conclusion of the March of the Living journey in Israel is significant. After the emotional intensity of a week in Poland, every site in Israel takes on added meaning, and the privilege of the Jewish People living in their own land becomes even more apparent. The experience in Poland is marked by moments of despair and comforting – but undying hope is the prevailing emotion that characterizes the journey to Israel. To all, Israel is a testament to the ability of a nation to overcome history and geography, hatred and powerlessness, to achieve its most cherished goals.

Judy Weissenberg Cohen of Toronto spoke of her Holocaust experiences to the 1997 participants in the March of the Living student mission. She concluded, "I rebuilt my life in Canada, first with my sister and brother, then with my husband and my children. Still, the memories are there and they will never go away. But I share them with you, so you also know them. They say, when you listen to a witness, you become a witness too."

My Duty Is to Help Others
FROM A CONVERSATION WITH HENRY MELNICK

In the 1996 March of the Living I participated as a *madrich* (group leader). I share my stories of the Holocaust and my times in Israel with young people because I feel that they have to be informed about the past in order to grow up as proud and productive Jews.

I was interned in Auschwitz during World War II, and liberated from Bergen-Belsen in April 1945, when I was in my early twenties. For two and a half years after Liberation, I worked as a volunteer with the Jewish committee in Hanover, Germany, helping with the illegal Aliyah Bet immigration to Israel. I did it because it was my duty to help others.

In 1948 I was finally able to go to Israel myself, along with my wife, Hela. We settled in Tel Aviv, which I remember as a busy place, with shops, cafés, and theatres. But what most impressed me were all the signs in Hebrew. When I saw all those Hebrew letters out in the open, my heart was overflowing with joy.

Shortly after arriving in Tel Aviv, I joined the Haganah, and along with other Holocaust survivors, who had no combat experience and were armed with inadequate weapons, I was sent to the battlefield. I participated with the 7th Brigade in the bloody battle at Latrun, in which we were unable to capture this important Jordanian stronghold to free the road to Jerusalem. When I was in Latrun with the March of the Living in 1996, I looked into the valley and thought, how easy it would have been to take this post, if only we'd had the right weapons.

After seventeen years in Israel, Hela and I came with our children to Canada to be near Hela's relatives. We had lost so much of our family during the war, and we missed being with people with whom we shared a past.

I have returned to Poland twice, once with my family and once with the March of the Living, and each time it has been a deeply emotional experience. I visit Israel often, and am very proud of the advances I see from one trip to the next. Still, my most profound experience in Israel was the day David Ben-Gurion read Israel's Declaration of Independence. We were singing, dancing, and crying in the streets of Tel Aviv. We were so happy that after all our suffering we finally had a homeland. Of course we learned soon enough that the struggle was just beginning.

Left: Henry and Hela Melnick with their children, Eli and Betty, Tel Aviv, 1960.

Reflections on the March of the Living, 1996
BY ROMAN ZIEGLER

I had mixed emotions about revisiting Poland as a *madrich* (group leader). But as a survivor, I have an obligation to tell the story of my life, to pass on my legacy to future generations. So I accepted the invitation of the March of the Living.

Majdanek was the only camp to be captured completely intact. Before arriving there I tried to imagine the effect the sight of this camp would have on me. I reasoned that it had been more than fifty years since the events that happened here; besides, I am involved with Holocaust remembrance and education and often speak to students about my wartime experiences. I believed, therefore, that this place would have little effect on me. I have never been more wrong.

When we entered the camp I was faced with a pile of ashes that had pieces of human bone protruding from it. It was almost like being struck by a bolt of lightning. Several minutes passed before I could move. Overcome by grief and

unable to face anyone, I managed to find a spot where I could light a candle. I wanted to say Kaddish but was unable to utter the words of my prayer, as tears rolled down my face. It took a while before I could regain my composure and rejoin the group.

We continued to explore the chambers of horror, where parents, brothers, and sisters had been brutally murdered. At the conclusion, I was asked to say Kaddish, and again I was so overcome with emotion that I could hardly speak the words.

At Treblinka, Rabbi Smolarcik, who accompanied our group, invited me to say a few words to the students. This is what I said:

> The Talmud teaches us that if you save a life, it is just as if you saved a world. Because each life is a world in itself. Therefore, we can say that if you destroy a life, you destroy a world. . . . Hundreds of thousands of Jews, or hundreds of thousands of worlds, were destroyed here. Not only was this the greatest catastrophe that ever befell the Jewish People, but the world as a whole was a loser.
>
> Rabbi, you call me a survivor. It is true. Physically, I experienced the Holocaust. But morally, every Jew on this planet is a survivor.

The rabbi embraced me and said, "You made me feel really proud by calling me a survivor."

Left: Roman Ziegler, with two March participants, 1996.

I would like to share a story I recount to my family every year at the Passover seder.

In October of 1942 I was imprisoned in Brande, a forced-labour camp. This was the harshest camp I experienced during my thirty-one months of incarceration, and its commandant was cruel and sadistic. His second-in-command was a fellow we nicknamed Zombal ("toothy"), because he had buckteeth. When they were together, they tried to outdo each other in cruelty, but Zombal by himself was, to a degree, endurable.

In December 1942 the commandant went home for the Christmas holidays. On New Year's Eve, we were asleep in our unheated barracks when, shortly before midnight, we were awakened by shouts and the crack of a whip. "Get Up! Roll Call!"

We had just five minutes to dress ourselves, make our beds, and assemble outside in the yard. When we had stood for almost an hour in the freezing cold, Zombal appeared, drunk, to make an announcement: "Tonight is New Year's Eve. I want it to be lively and happy, so start marching and singing!"

Here we were, half-frozen and starved, dumbfounded that he wanted us to behave as if we were happy. Fortunately, our capo, a former yeshivah student named Schoengurt, knew the proper response to Zombal. He said, "Chevra, let's sing *Ve He she'amda* [a chapter from the Passover Haggadah]." We marched and sang for almost an hour, and then were ordered back to our barracks. At the time I did not know the meaning of the words we sang, but a few years later I read them in translation:

This promise made to our ancestors holds true also for us. For more than once have they risen against us to destroy us; in every generation they rise against us and seek our destruction. But the Holy One, blessed be He, saves us from their hands.

Right: Rosemary Goldhar, photographer for the March of the Living, caught in a pensive moment at a Holocaust memorial, Poland, 1996.
Above left: Roman Ziegler, right, donating his concentration camp number, torn from his camp uniform at the time of Liberation, to Gideon Hausner, chair of Yad Vashem and chief prosecutor of Adolf Eichmann. Roman's wife, Miriam, one of the children liberated from Auschwitz, is on the left, 1981.

Part of the Canadian contingent on the 1988 March of the Living, walking from Auschwitz to Birkenau concentration camp.

A young March of the Living participant walking down the train tracks that were used to transport Jews to the death camps.

Jody Schloss, left, and her Israeli friend Sharon, with horses named Honey and Kim, Kfar Yona, 1994.

Kefiada

Since 1995, hundreds of Canadian students have spent their summers in Israel taking part in English-speaking day camps offered in over a hundred communities throughout the country, run by university-aged counsellors from Canada, the United States, Great Britain, Australia, New Zealand, and South Africa. The program is called Kefiada, and its name is derived from the Arabic and Hebrew word meaning a fun, exciting, or "cool" activity.

Anat Kribunets, right, of Toronto and her Israeli counsellor discuss activities during a 1997 Kefiada at Mevot Hahermon.

Israel Loves Young Company

BY SARI GOLDMAN

Since I was five years old, I have travelled several times to Israel with my family and, at age sixteen, with my synagogue youth group. Israel has always been an important part of my life. Although I have had many wonderful experiences there, nothing has ever given me more satisfaction or challenge, stimulation or sense of achievement, than being a counsellor in Kefiada – the Canada–Israel Experience.

I was assigned to a new community centre in Eilat, where my friend and I had to set up the program and literally scour the town to enroll the reluctant kids. I spent four weeks teaching English as a second language to twelve-year-olds, through play. I fell in love with my work, the rambunctious kids, and, once again, Israel. It was hard work, in blazing heat, trying to accommodate the various skill levels of the campers' English, and organizing events that would keep them stimulated. I made new friends and learned once more how to live in Israel, to shop for food, to explore new sights, and to feel I belonged. I hope to go back again, perhaps as a tour-group leader so that others can share my feelings.

There's a poster in my house that my mother brought back in the 1970s, showing teenagers around a campfire near Caesarea, entitled "Israel Loves Young Company." It wasn't until I had travelled the country with my peers at age sixteen that I understood the truth of those words. Only now do I understand the impact on my life.

———————

Below: Sari Goldman, right, in Eilat with her co-counsellor, Lori Alter, 1994.

Joining Hands

BY WILFRED POSLUNS

M y wife, Joyce, and I and our three children, their spouses, and our nine grandchildren, aged five to thirteen, began an exciting journey to Israel in June 1997. All seventeen of us shared and experienced the country's richness and fragility together. We witnessed air-force drills, kayaked on the Jordan river, and took part in archaeological digs. In Tel Hai a special dedication ceremony was held at the Posluns Family Youth Hostel. It was here that our ties to Israel were cemented, literally, for each of us immersed a hand in a wet concrete block. Each block would later be laid beside one of the trees planted around the hostel, as a permanent reminder that we all had a hand in helping support Israel, a tiny parcel of land intrinsic to the survival of the Jewish People worldwide.

Below: Three generations of the Posluns family visit the Posluns Family Youth Hostel, Tel Hai, 1997. Back row, left to right, Lynn Posluns, Ken Crystal, Matthew Brown, Alan Brown, Wendy Posluns, Wilfred Posluns, Joyce Posluns, David Posluns, and Felicia Posluns. Front row, left to right, Brad Crystal, Eric Crystal, Daniel Crystal, Leah Brown, Evan Brown, Stuart Posluns, Julia Posluns, and Aaron Posluns.

The York Wharton Recanati Program

BY KEN TANENBAUM

In 1978 the Wharton School at the University of Pennsylvania and the Recanati Business School of Tel Aviv University established a pilot marketing and management program to assist Israeli businesses with the problems they might encounter while attempting to penetrate the American market. In the twenty years since then, over seventy Israeli companies have worked with over five hundred students, and together they have increased Israeli imports to North America by over one hundred million dollars U.S.

I learned of this program while attending the Wharton School in 1991 and began planting the seeds to develop a parallel program in Canada. But instead of a parallel program, the concept of a triad was taken to David Goldstein (president of the Canada–Israel Chamber of Commerce and Industry),

Len Lodish (co-founder of the program at Wharton), and Dezsö Horváth (dean of the Schulich School of Business at York University). As a result, early in 1992, the Schulich School of Business joined the existing partnership to specialize in technology transfer and implementation of strategy.

The program has been an enormous success. The Canadian content generated by York University's students has not only been well received by the Israeli companies, but has also set a new level of excellence in the development of export markets. Dean Horváth says: "The York/Wharton/Recanati model is international business education at its best: real-world, interactive, multinational, multicultural, multi-disciplinary, hands-on, and relevant. Through it, Canadian, Israeli, and American MBA graduates have truly become 'citizens of the world.'"

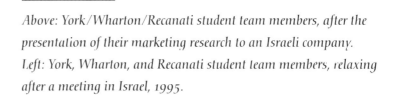

Above: York/Wharton/Recanati student team members, after the presentation of their marketing research to an Israeli company.
Left: York, Wharton, and Recanati student team members, relaxing after a meeting in Israel, 1995.

Liaison to the Foreign Forces

BY SIVAN TAMIR

To my parents' chagrin, I returned to Israel in 1994 to serve my stint in the army, in what turned out to be a very unique place, time, and political situation.

I was chosen to be in the "Liaison to the Foreign Forces" unit of the IDF because of my knowledge of English as well as Hebrew. I was sent to the only spot in the Middle East where the borders of Israel, the Palestinians' Gaza Strip, and Egypt intersect. It was just after the signing of the Oslo Accord, in which Israel and Palestine began implementing Palestinian self government.

The Multinational Force and Observers (MFO), which is the international community's army, was invited by the Israelis and Egyptians to supervise each other. The Oslo Accord resulted in four distinct armies on three lands, Egypt, Gaza, and Israel, each one marching to a different drummer. To prevent collisions it was necessary to communicate with each other so each unit's movements could be co-ordinated.

As the Israeli liaison officer in Rafah, at the Gaza Strip's border, I helped solve any military problems between the Israeli and Egyptian armies, the MFO, and the Palestinian Police (a.k.a. the Palestinian army).

On one occasion I was invited to attend a farewell dinner at the MFO base inside Egypt, for our Israeli commander and his Egyptian counterpoint upon their retirement. Officially, an Israeli soldier is not allowed to be on Egyptian soil. This was the first time regular soldiers were invited inside Egypt. The camaraderie that prevailed during the luncheon quickly disappeared when we returned to our bases, as the Egyptians take their role of protecting their border particularly seriously.

Above: Sivan Tamir (the only woman in the group), with Israeli, Egyptian, and Multinational Force and Observers (MFO) soldiers and officers at a retirement luncheon at the MFO base in Egypt, 1995.

Feeling Lucky

BY TANYA WYMAN

I have travelled to many places in my short lifetime. I have stepped on and off many planes. One thinks of this as an action of habit and necessity. In Israel it is an experience in itself. A moment of hope and love, security and attachment.

Walking back to the El Al airplane after my first visit to Israel, when I was fifteen, I witnessed an exceptional moment. Joe, our family's best friend and a second father to me, was hunched over on his knees, kissing the ground. The diagnosis of cancer he had received three years earlier had made him aware his days were numbered. His first visit to Israel would be his last, and he was savouring the time.

Stepping off the plane in Tel Aviv after spending a week in Poland on the March of the Living was another time of overwhelming emotion. I thought of our friend Joe, who had died two years before, and the millions of Jews who were never able to set foot on this soil.

Finally the time came when I was able to spend a whole year in Israel, in the overseas program at Hebrew University in Jerusalem. Studying the history, exploring the country, and living the life, made me love Israel more and more every day, enough to return the next year as a first-year medical student. I spent my summer in an elective at Shaare Tzedek Hospital in Jerusalem, practising what I had studied for a year by interacting with doctors and patients in Hebrew.

I have lived in Israel, and I will do so again. I am so lucky.

Below: A beautiful sunrise at Masada, enjoyed by Tanya Wyman, right, and her friend Michelle Lackie, summer 1989.

It's Never Too Late for a Bar Mitzvah

BY HARRY GORMAN

W hen I was a child, the land of Israel was a place one read about only in the siddur or the Chumash (the five books of the Torah). I vaguely remember hearing about the Zionist pioneers whose mission it was to create a homeland in Palestine, but I had no concept of what that land looked like nor any idea of how important it would become in shaping my identity.

In the spring of 1948 I was a travelling dress salesman, driving through London, Ontario, in my 1937 Chevy with Sam Brenman, when, through the well–worn speaker of the car radio, we heard the crackling sound of David Ben–Gurion's voice declaring independence for the new State of Israel. What a proud and historic moment that was.

———————

Below: The Gorman family, left to right: Jamy and Michele Rotman, Harry Gorman, Bob and Beverly Benia, Earl and Sari Gorman, Sara Gorman, Debbie and David Sadja.

Since then, I've been to Israel so many times I've lost count. Whether as a tourist or through my involvement with the UJA and JNF, each trip I made has been a learning experience and an opportunity to understand better the country and its people. I've shared *l'chaims* (a toast "to life") with prime ministers and sipped tea with soldiers. I've shed tears with *olim* from the former Soviet Union and danced on the tarmac at Ben-Gurion Airport with those from Ethiopia.

But the most special trip was with twenty-seven members of my immediate family and close friends. The highlight of that trip was the bar mitzvah of my two brothers-in-law, Joe Suckonic and Milt Goodman, some fifty years later than they should have occurred. After the service at the Western Wall, we celebrated atop the new Aish HaTorah, Dan Family Centre, which faces the Kotel (Western Wall). The centre was not yet complete so we arranged to have everything, including the food and the drinks, hoisted up by crane. There, overlooking that holy and sacred place, we as a family renewed our commitments to Judaism, each in his or her own way.

Benjamin Mogil on the campus of the Hebrew University at Mount Scopus, October 1992. "During the school year of 1992–93, I studied at Hebrew University, and then spent the summer on an internship doing government economic research at the Bank of Israel. From the first day, my boss made me feel part of his family and took a genuine interest in my well-being. To me that summer represented Israel, a warm and open family where anything and everything is possible."

Hope for the Future

Serious Friendships and More

BY BRAM BELZBERG

Although I knew that travelling to Israel by myself at the age of fourteen would be a challenge, I was excited to go. I arrived at the Tel Aviv airport feeling all alone. I had no friends and I knew nobody, but I understood that if someone was going to make this experience memorable, it would have to be me. I was right.

The first thing I had to do in Israel in order to be able to get around was to learn the language. Teaching myself Hebrew from scratch in two months is the biggest accomplishment of my life! After I learned to speak the language, I had to teach myself some of the things the other kids in the American Israel Beit Hashita High School Program – all of them extremely smart – already knew, such as politics, music, and literature.

I made some serious friendships during my time in Israel in 1995–96, which I hope will last a lifetime, but there was more to my experience than that. I never believed in that "redeeming the land" stuff until I did it myself. When I put my hands in the soil of my people, I felt a bond with every Jew in the world. I realize that this may be hard to believe, but it's something that only people who have spent time in the homeland can understand. I hold strong feelings for Israel and believe that those feelings will never die. I love the land that we, as Jews, cherish as our own.

_____

Below: Bram Belzberg, right, with his roommate Josh Cohen, overlooking the Jezreal Valley, September 1995.

Racing through the streets of the Old City of Jerusalem are, left to right, Uri Gorodzinsky, Ira Price, Rabbi Mark Drach, Robbie Diamond, and Jonas Diamond, 1994.

The Lay Down Your Arms Story

BY ELI RUBENSTEIN

Doron Levinson was one of those exceptional teachers all of us remember from childhood. He was multi-talented, a spell-binding storyteller, a beguiling magician, a musician and composer.

When I was planning the first national March of the Living, I decided to prepare a tape of Holocaust- and Israel-related music for the students to take with them on the trip. When Doron learned of this, he suggested that I consider including a song he had written based on a biblical text.

This is how the song came about. During the 1973 Yom Kippur War, Doron was commanding a tank battalion when one of his men confided in him his belief that this would be his last battle. Doron calmed the nervous soldier, assuring him they would return from this encounter unscathed. But Doron was wrong. In a fierce tank battle, his gunner was killed and Doron himself was temporarily blinded. During his convalescence, Doron found himself with time on his hands. A piano in the hospital beckoned him and he found his fingers tracing out a melody expressing his anguish over his fallen comrade and over other close friends he had lost in previous battles. Doron set the melody to the Hebrew words in Isaiah 2:4, which state: "They shall beat their swords into ploughshares

and their spears into pruning hooks; nation shall not lift up sword against nation, neither shall they learn war any more." Isaiah's words, written over 2,500 years ago, have spoken to lovers of peace in every generation.

Doron played the song for me. The melody was haunting, the words echoed the prophetic yearning for a world where peace would be the common currency. I immediately agreed to include the song in our collection. A few months later it was recorded in a local music studio by Toronto's Habonim Youth Choir, conducted by Esther Ghan-Firestone.

The song became a favourite of the students on the March of the Living, and was performed throughout the trip. Since then the song has been movingly translated by two Toronto songwriters, Lisa Catherine Cohen and Harry Lewis, into what is now known as "Lay Down Your Arms."

Above: Habonim Youth Choir members, flanked by two admiring supporters. Left to right, back row: Don Green, Rae Brager, Tara Charendoff, Riva de Freitas, and Michael Budman. Front row: Sophie Green, Anthony Green, and Matthew Budman.

LAY DOWN YOUR ARMS

Dear God, please hear us, listen to our prayer,
And help us do Thy will upon this Earth.
Let the children suffer war no more,
And let a peaceful world be given birth.

Every hand that holds a sword can hold a baby.
Every heart can learn to love.
Lay down your arms,
Begin the journey home,
And join the human family.

The road is long and steep.
What we sow, we reap.
Children need you,
Let us lead you,
Promises we make we all must keep.

Somewhere deep inside a soldier there's a dreamer
Dreaming of a world of peace.
Lay down your arms,
Let Time heal every wound,
And Love will someday set us free.

Four organizations are represented here,
in order to give honour to the many organizations
in the Toronto community that have devoted themselves
to Israel's cause over the last fifty years and more.

Row 1:

| Arthur Cohen 1939 | Ben Sadowski 1939–40 | Samuel Godfrey 1939 | Bernard Vise 1941–42 | Charles Foster 1943–44 | Samuel Posluns 1945 | Sam Granatstein 1946 | Frank Godfrey 1947 | Ellis Shapiro 1947 | Gurston Allen 1948 | Arthur Gelber 1949 | William Palca 1950 |

Row 2:

| D. Lou Harris 1951 | Meyer Gasner 1952 | Stephen Berger 1953 | Abe Posluns 1953 | Mark A. Levy 1954 | J. Irving Oelbaum 1954 | Jack Pearlstein 1955 | Samuel Sable 1955/57 | Arnold Epstein 1957 | Leon Weinstein 1958 | Alex Fisher 1958 |

Row 3:

| John Fienberg 1959 | Alvin Rosenberg 1960/83 | Max Tanenbaum 1961 | Noel Zeldin 1962 | Ray D. Wolfe 1963 | Ted Richmond 1964 | Samuel Zeldin 1965 | Morris Kaufman 1966 | Rabbi Stuart Rosenberg 1967 | Philip Givens 1968 | Nathan Silver 1969 | Rabbi Gunther Plaut 1970 |

Row 4:

| Ralph Halbert 1971 | Phil Granovsky 1972/91 | Al Green 1973 | Murray Koffler 1974 | Eddie Creed 1975 | Wilfred Posluns 1976/83 | Joe Berman 1977 | Albert Cole 1978 | Gerald Halbert 1979/83/91 | Gerald Goldenberg 1980 | Irwin Kay 1981 |

Row 5:

UJA FEDERATION

| Allan Offman 1982–83/91 | Lionel Schipper 1984 | Isadore Sharp 1984 | Harry Gorman 1985 | Gerald Shear 1985 | Jack Gwartz 1986 | Adrienne Offman 1987 | Max Handelman 1987 |

Row 6:

| Harold Lederman 1988 | Gerald Sheff 1988/91 | Julia Koschitzky 1989/91 | Don Rafelman 1989 | Marty Goldberg 1990 | Joel Greisman 1990 | Jack Rose 1991 | Schuyler Sigel 1991 | Judy Scheininger 1992 | Paul Morton 1992 | Bernard Ghert 1993 | Neil Nisker 1993 |

Row 7:

| Laurence Fein 1994 | Lawrence Bloomberg 1994 | Wendy Eisen 1995 | Robert Masters 1995 | Charles Gold 1996 | Carol Kassel 1996 | David Goldstein 1997 | Leo Goldhar 1998 | Brent Belzberg 1999 | Lawrence Tanenbaum 1999 |

UJA FEDERATION
Campaign Chairs

The mission of UJA Federation of Greater Toronto is to serve as the city's central Jewish communal organization, dedicated to the preservation and enrichment of Jewish life in the Greater Toronto area and the perpetuation of the community's identification with the State of Israel.

Bert Godfrey
1965–67

Lawrence Shankman
1968–70/1979–80

Morris Kaufman
1971–72

Jack Israeli
1973–74

Norine Daniels
1975–76

Al Latner
1977–78

David Kosoy
1981–82

Herb Green
1983–84

Alex Grossman
1985–86

Allan Silber
1987–88

Kurt Rothschild
1989–90

Harvey Solursh
1991–93

Alex Eisen
1991–93

David Markowitz
1994–96

Mike Florence
1994–96

David Brown
1997–

Jeffery Kaufman
1997–

STATE OF ISRAEL BONDS
Chairs

The goal of the Israel Bonds organization is to increase the number of people
who are linked to the State of Israel through investment in Israel Bonds. The Israel Bonds program
was launched in 1951 by Israel's first prime minister, David Ben-Gurion, to infuse capital into the young nation.
Since the inception of the program, Israel Bonds proceeds have been utilized to build and develop
an important array of industrial, agricultural, transportation, and technological infrastructure projects.

Samuel Kronick*
1949

Senator
David A. Croll*
1952

Edward E. Gelber*
1953

J. Irving Oelbaum*
1954

D. Lou Harris*
1957

Meyer W. Gasner*
1958

Stephen E. Berger*
1959

Wilfred Gordon*
1963

Morris B. Kaufman*
1964

Nathan Phillips*
1965

Bert Godfrey
1966

Nathan Silver*
1967

Philip G. Givens*
1968

Mark & Lillian Levy*
1969

Leon E. Weinstein*
1970

Hon.
John W.H. Bassett*
1971

Joseph Tanenbaum*
1972

Rt. Hon. John G.
Diefenbaker*
1973

Philip Granovsky*
1974

Rabbi
W. Gunther Plaut
1975

James F. Kay
1976

Hon.
William G. Davis
1977

Eric & Esther* Exton
1978

Murray B. Koffler
1979

Rose Wolfe
1980

Theodore D. Richmond*
1981

A.A. (Bucky) &
Madeleine Epstein
1982

Kurt & Edith Rothschild
1983

Abe Posluns*
1984

Donald & Judy Feld Carr
1985

Gerald Halbert
1986

Hon. Edwin A.
Goodman
1987

Douglas G. Bassett
1988

Max & Isadore Sharp
1989

Bernard Weinstein
1990

Harry Gorman
1991

Nathan O. Hurwich
1992

Albert Mandel
1992

Lewis J.E. Moses
1992

George A. Cohon
1993

Joey Tanenbaum
1994

Leslie L. Dan
1995

Hon.
Henry N.R. Jackman
1996

Edward Bronfman
1997

JEWISH NATIONAL FUND OF CANADA
Negev Dinner Honourees

Photographs unavailable for:

Elias Pullan*, 1950, 50th Anniversary of Jewish National Fund, 1951; Dr. Samuel B. Hurwich*, 1955, Jewish Community Centenary, 1956; Morry Wingold*, 1960; Samuel Feld*, 1961; Julius Weiner*, 1962

*Deceased

The objective of the JNF is to improve the quality of life for all the people of Israel through the enhancement and protection of the environment. JNF activities reach well beyond afforestation projects and embrace the construction of reservoirs, tourist sites, dams, scenic lookouts, rural roads, and, generally speaking, develop projects involved with the beautification of Israel's land area. Torontonians can be very proud of the role they have played over the past ninety-six years in helping to protect Israel's environment and in literally making the desert bloom.

Max Goody
1967–71

Max Shecter
1973–77/85–89

Lewis J.E. Moses
1977–81

Melech M. Halberstadt
1981–85

Ruth Leroy
1989–91

Avrom Gossack
1991–94

Tillie Margolis
1994–

Judge Philip G. Givens*
1972–84
National President

Kurt Rothschild
1990–
National President

CANADIAN ZIONIST FEDERATION
Presidents, Central Region

Photograph unavailable for:
Samuel Shainhouse, 1950–71

*Deceased

The Canadian Zionist Federation was established in 1967 as the national umbrella for Zionist organizations
in Canada. It is the official representative of Canadian Zionists to the World Zionist Organization.
It represents a singular vision of a strong and vibrant Jewish life in Canada. The Canadian Zionist
Federation provides programs to educate and nurture young people through such projects as
scholarships to study in Israel and Canadian summer camp programs.

GLOSSARY

Aliyah: (*Heb.*) meaning "ascending" or "going up." The Hebrew word for immigration to the Land of Israel. A Jewish immigrant to Israel "makes aliyah." See page 231 for further information.

Altalena: a cargo ship that set sail from the French port of Marseilles on May 29, 1948. The *Altalena* and its military cargo had been purchased by European supporters of the Irgun led by Menachem Begin. When the ship reached Tel Aviv on June 20, 1948, a confrontation broke out between Irgun activists and the regular forces of the Israeli army, in the course of which the *Altalena* burst into flames. See page 67 for further information.

Amharic: Ethiopian language.

Ashkenazi: term used to describe Jews of western and eastern European background who are descendants of those Jews who lived in German lands ("Ashkenaz") in the early medieval period.

Bar/Bat Mitzvah: (*Heb.*) a Jewish child becoming bar or bat mitzvah ("son or daughter of the mitzvah") accepts the religious obligations of adult Jewish life and the laws (*mitzvot*) which govern it. See page 333 for further information.

Bedouin: nomadic Muslim Arab people who live in Israel and other Middle Eastern countries and in North Africa.

Bubbie: (*Yiddish*) meaning "grandmother."

Bricha: (*from Heb.*) meaning *levroah*, "to flee." A clandestine organization headed by emissaries from Palestine which organized Jews from Eastern Europe after the Second World War and helped them secretly enter Palestine in violation of restrictions on immigration imposed by the British.

Chai: (*Heb.*) meaning "life," symbolized by the number eighteen. Hebrew letters have a numerical value, and in this case the numbers representing the letters in the word *chai* total eighteen.

Chalutz, **chalutziyut** (plural): (*Heb.*) pioneer(s).

Chametz: (*Heb.*) food that is not kosher.

Chanukah: (*Heb.*) Jewish holiday commemorating the victory of the Jews, led by the Maccabees, over their Greek rulers (in 164 BCE).

Chanukiah: (*Heb.*) candelabrum that is ceremonially lit each of the eight nights of the Chanukah holiday.

Chassidism: (*Heb.*) popular pietist religious and social movement founded by Israel Eliezer Ba'al Shem Tov in eighteenth-century Europe. There are large Chassidic communities in North America and Israel.

Chumash: (*Heb.*) the first five books of the Old Testament; Pentateuch (*Greek*).

Diaspora: term used for the Jewish dispersion around the world after the Roman conquest of the Land of Israel in 70 CE.

Druze: a distinct cultural, social, and religious community of approximately one hundred thousand Arabic-speaking people living in villages in northern Israel. While the Druze religion is not accessible to outsiders, one known aspect of its philosophy is the concept of *tacqiyya*, which calls for complete loyalty by its adherents to the government of the country in which they reside. There are also Druze communities in other Middle Eastern countries.

Eretz Israel: (*Heb.*) meaning "the Land of Israel" as distinct from the "State of Israel," which was founded in 1948.

Gevirim: (*Heb.*) meaning "leaders."

Habonim: a Zionist youth movement aimed to foster Jewish culture, use of the Hebrew language, and pioneering in Palestine, founded in 1930 in London, England, and affiliated with the Zionist Labour movement.

Hachsharah, **hachsharot** (plural): (*Heb.*) a Zionist training farm in the diaspora preparing young Jews for life on kibbutzim in Israel.

Hadassah–WIZO: largest Zionist organization in the world, and one of the largest women's organizations in North America, founded in 1912 by Henrietta Szold. In Israel, the organization sponsors medical training, research, and care, along with special education.

Haftorah: (*Heb.*) the *Torah* (Pentateuch) is divided into fifty-four "portions," one of which is read at the synagogue every Sabbath in an annual cycle, beginning and ending shortly after the Jewish New Year.

Haggadah: (*Heb.*) book that tells the story of the biblical Exodus from Egypt, read aloud at the Passover Seder ceremony.

Haganah: (*Heb.*) a small underground force founded in 1920 to protect Jewish life and property against attacks by Arabs; the term *haganah* is Hebrew for "defence." The Haganah was officially transformed into the Israel Defence Forces shortly after independence was proclaimed on May 14, 1948. See page 19 for further information.

Haimish: (*Yiddish*) meaning "homelike."

Haredi, **haredim** (plural): (*Heb.*) meaning "God-fearing." Israeli term for ultra-Orthodox Jews.

Hashomer Hatzair: (*Heb.*) meaning "the young watchman." The oldest existing Jewish youth movement in the world. Founded in Poland (1913/14), Hashomer Hatzair defines itself as a world organization of Zionist youth that strives for personal pioneering fulfillment in Israel. It developed a singular educational ideology and principles that fused scouting, personal example, socialist Zionist fufillment through aliyah, and a collective lifestyle.

Hatikvah: (*Heb.*) meaning "the hope." The title of the national anthem of the State of Israel.

HIAS: acronym for the Hebrew Immigrant Aid Service; formed in New York in 1909 to respond to growing needs of Jewish immigrants from Eastern Europe.

Hora: (*Heb.*) a style of Israeli folk dancing in which a group of people dances in a circle.

Intifadah: (*Arabic*) meaning "shaking off"; Arab uprising in the West Bank and Gaza Strip, beginning in December 1987, in response to Israeli occupation of these areas since 1967. It continued with a series of violent confrontations between Palestinians and Israeli troops in these areas. Violence spread and erupted sporadically until the peace process began in 1994.

Irgun: (*from Heb.* Irgun Zva'i Leumi) national military organization, with the acronym of Etzel. The underground paramilitary wing of the Revisionist Zionist movement, founded in 1925 by Vladimir (Ze'ev) Jabotinsky, later under the leadership of Menachem Begin. See page 19 for further information.

Jewish Agency: founded in Palestine in 1929 as an organization to unite both Zionist and non-Zionist Jewish organizations. In the pre-State period, the Jewish Agency was an "almost government" that dealt with organizing immigration and establishing institutions of Jewish self-government. After statehood was declared, many of its functions were taken over by the Israeli government, but it maintained responsibility for organizing immigration to Israel, absorption of new immigrants, and other activities.

Jewish National Fund (JNF): (*in Heb.* Keren Kayemet LeIsrael) land purchase and development fund of the Zionist Organization, founded in 1901. In the early years the JNF acquired tracts of land in Palestine with funds raised from Jews abroad. After 1948 the emphasis of JNF activity shifted from land purchase to land improvement and development as well as afforestation. Swamps were drained, hills were cleared for agriculture and settlement by stone-clearing and terracing, and new areas for farming were developed.

Joint Distribution Committee: a Jewish organization founded in the United States in 1914, the JDC raised $15 million during the First World War. The funds provided medical assistance, food, and clothing for war refugees and for the *yishuv* (pre-State Jewish community in Palestine). After 1948 the organization became a major partner in financing mass immigration from Eastern Europe and Arab countries. It helped with the aliyah of Yemenite Jews and the integration of immigrants from North African countries.

Judaism, Conservative: trend in Judaism developed in twentieth-century United States, permitting certain modifications of traditional observances in response to the changing life of the Jewish People. The first Conservative institutions in the U.S. were crystallized not in dissent from Orthodoxy but in reaction to the influential Reform movement.

Judaism, Orthodox: term used to designate those Jews who accept totality of historical Jewish religion as recorded in Written and Oral Laws.

Judaism, Reform: trend in Judaism advocating modification of traditional religious observances in conformity with the exigencies of contemporary life and thought. The Reform movement developed in Western Europe and North America in the late nineteenth-century.

Kabbalah: (*Heb.*) term used for esoteric teachings of Judaism and for Jewish mysticism, often developed from the twelfth century.

Kaddish: (*Aramaic*) Jewish prayer for the dead.

Kashrut: (*Heb.*) Jewish dietary laws.

Keren Hayesod: (*Heb.*) main institution for financing the Zionist Organization's activities in Eretz Israel, founded in London in 1920. In 1926, the headquarters of Keren Hayesod moved to Jerusalem. Until the establishment of the State of Israel, Keren Hayesod financed activities of the *yishuv* related to immigration and absorption, settlement, defence, development of water resources, and public works. After 1948, Keren Hayesod concentrated on the financing of immigration, immigrant absorption, and settlement. Membership is composed of representatives from all countries except the United States.

Keren Kayemet LeIsrael: see Jewish National Fund.

Ketubah: (*Heb.*) marriage document recording obligations, financial and personal, between marriage partners. Written in Aramaic, its reading is a major part of a traditional wedding ceremony.

Kibbutz: (*Heb.*) derived from the Hebrew word for "group" and used to describe collective agricultural communities established by Jews throughout Palestine beginning early in the twentieth century. The first kibbutzim were founded by Eastern European immigrants who sought to integrate the ideals of Jewish nationalism (Zionism) and socialism – the goal being to create a new kind of society for a new kind of Jewish People. The first kibbutz, Degania, was founded in 1909.

Kibbutznik: (*Heb.*) a kibbutz member. (See Kibbutz)

Kiddush: (*Heb.*) meaning "sanctification"; the prayer that sanctifies the wine used on ceremonial occasions like the Sabbath or other holiday meals.

Knesset: (*Heb.*) the parliament of Israel.

Kotel: (*Heb.*) the Western Wall; the section of the western supporting wall of the Temple Mount in Jerusalem, which remained intact since the destruction of the Second Temple in 70 CE.

Kristallnacht: (*German*) meaning "night of broken glass"; term describing Nazi anti-Jewish riots occurring November 9–10, 1938, throughout Germany and Austria.

Ma'abara, **ma'abarot** (plural): (*Heb.*) meaning "tent"; an immigrant transit camp.

Madrich (m.) **madrichah** (f.): (*Heb.*) meaning "group leader."

Mahal: (*Heb.*) acronym meaning "foreign volunteers." Term used for volunteers from English-speaking countries, mainly Jews, who enlisted in the Israel Defense Forces and participated in the War of Independence, 1948–49. See page 55 for further information.

Mazel tov: (*Heb.*) meaning "good luck." It is used to offer congratulations.

Mechitzah: (*Heb.*) term for partition screen in Orthodox synagogues, separating men from women.

Menorah: (*Heb.*) candelabrum; seven-branched oil lamp used in the Temple; also eight-branched candelabrum used on Chanukah.

Menucha: (*Heb.*) meaning "rest."

Mezuzah: (*Heb.*) meaning "doorpost." Has come to designate the small rectangular box containing a rolled-up piece of parchment inscribed with biblical passages. The mezuzah is mounted on the right-hand doorposts of all rooms except for bathrooms.

Mitzvah: (*Heb.*) a religiously mandated good deed, also used for general good deeds.

Moses Maimonides, 1135–1204: (Rabbi Moses ben Maimon; Rambam) outstanding rabbinic authority, codifier, philosopher. Born in Spain, he fled persecution to Morocco, and worked as a physician in Egypt.

Moshav: (*Heb.*) a rural village combining some of the features of both cooperative and private farming. Moshavim emerged with the aim of providing more scope for individual initiative and independent management than did the kibbutzim.

Mohel: (*Heb.*) the person who performs the *brit milah*, meaning "circumcision," on male infants (Yiddish pronunciation, "moyel").

Nachal: (*Heb.*) fighting pioneer youth.

Nachla: (*Heb.*) meaning "estate, property, possession, inheritance."

Oleh (m), **olah** (f), **olim** (plural): (*Heb.*) meaning "immigrant(s)" or those who have "made aliyah."

Olah chadusha: meaning "new immigrants."

Operation Exodus: mass immigration of Jews from the Soviet Union beginning in 1989; within several years more than seven hundred thousand immigrants had arrived in Israel.

Operation Moses: a secret effort bringing the Ethiopian Jews to Israel in 1984. Some seven thousand Ethiopian Jews walked hundreds of miles to Sudan, to be airlifted to Israel.

Operation Solomon: effort in which 15,000 Ethiopian Jews were airlifted to Israel directly from Ethiopia in May, 1991.

ORT: Organization for Education Resources and Technological Training; founded in Russia in 1880 for vocational training among Jews. ORT continues to sponsor vocational training in Israel and other countries around the world.

Palmach: (*Heb., abbrev.*) established in 1941, permanently mobilized volunteer striking force of the Haganah and later, until its dissolution, part of the Israel Defense Forces.

Passover: (*in Heb.* Pesach) the week-long springtime holiday that commemorates the biblical Exodus from Egypt.

Rambam: the acronym for Rabbi Moses ben Maimon. (See Moses Maimonides)

Roshei Yeshivot: (*Heb.*) meaning "heads of religious academies."

Sabra: (*Heb.*) literally, the "prickly pear" fruit that is thorny on the outside and sweet on the inside; colloquially used as a term for native-born Israelis.

Shaliach, **shlichim** (plural): (*Heb.*) meaning "emissary." Shlichim representing various Israeli movements, organizations, or institutions are sent to Jewish communities in the Diaspora.

Sephardi: (*from Heb.* Sephard) term for the descendents of Jews who lived in the Iberian Peninsula (Spain and Portugal) before the expulsion of 1492. After the expulsion, Sephardic Jewish communities were established in North Africa, Italy, the Near East, Western Europe, North America, and the Balkans.

Shivah: (*Heb.*) meaning "seven." This refers to the seven-day mourning period observed by Jewish families after a death.

Shoah: (*Heb.*) the Holocaust.

Shochet: (*Heb.*) a person who butchers according to the laws of *kashrut*.

Shrine of the Book: small museum located in the Israel Museum of Jerusalem. This area houses the Dead Sea Scrolls.

Siddur: Ashkenazi term for prayer book.

Simchah: (*Heb.*) meaning "celebration."

Stern Gang: an underground Jewish resistance movement that fought against the British in Palestine in the pre-State period and was responsible for blowing up the King David Hotel in Jerusalem.

Study Mission: an organized tour of Israel to learn about specific aspects of the social, cultural, political, and economic scene.

Talit: (*Heb.*) four-cornered prayer shawl with fringes at each corner. It is worn by men while reciting certain prayers. The *talit katan*, or "small talit," is worn daily by strictly observant Jewish men under their regular clothes.

Talmud: (*Heb.*) compilation of texts of biblical exegesis.

Talmud Torah: (*Heb.*) meaning "study of the law"; term applied generally to Jewish religious study, and used to refer to Jewish religious schools.

Tanach: (*Heb.*) the Hebrew bible, of which the Chumash is a part. The Prophets and Writings comprise the rest.

Tefillin: (*Heb.*) meaning "phylacteries." Two black leather boxes fastened to leather straps, containing biblical passages written on parchment. They are affixed on forehead and arm by adult males during the recital of morning prayers.

Torah: (*Heb.*) meaning "teaching" the Pentateuch for reading in synagogue; term also used to describe entire body of traditional Jewish teaching or literature.

Tzitzit: (*Heb.*) the fringes on prayer shawls.

United Israel Appeal (**UIA**): this organization manages funds that are raised by the United Jewish Appeal for donation to Israel to support social agencies, programs, and institutions.

United Jewish Appeal (**UJA**): the fundraising arm of the Jewish Federation of Greater Toronto. It is the central campaign in response to local communal needs, and its funds support beneficiary agencies, institutions, and social programs. It also raises money for Israel.

Wadi: (*Heb.*) the deepest point in a ravine-like area through which water flows.

Western Wall: see Kotel above.

Yad BeYad: a program of the Canada-Israel Forum and the Israeli Forum that brings English-speaking people to Israel to share their expertise. See page 347 for further information.

Yad Vashem: (*Heb.*) Israel's Holocaust Martyrs' and Heroes' Remembrance Authority. Israel's official authority for commemorating the memory of those killed in the Holocaust; also gives recognition to resisters, survivors, and to "Righteous Gentiles," non-Jews who rescued Jews during this period.

Yeshiva: (*Heb.*) meaning "academy"; name for institutes of Talmudic study.

Yishuv: (*Heb.*) meaning "settlement"; refers to the Jewish community and its institutions in the "Land of Israel" during the pre-State period, before 1948.

Yom Ha'atzmaut: (*Heb.*) Israel's Independence Day, a national holiday.

Yom HaShoah: (*Heb.*) National Day of Remembrance for those who perished in the Holocaust.

Yom Hazikaron: (*Heb.*) National Day of Remembrance for the Fallen Soldiers of Israel.

Youth Aliyah: originally founded in 1933 to rescue Jewish youth from Nazi Germany. Some five thousand teenagers were brought to Palestine before the Second World War and educated at Youth Aliyah boarding schools; followed, after the war, by an additional fifteen thousand, most of them survivors. Today, Youth Aliyah villages continue to play a vital role in the absorption of young newcomers to Israel, as well as offering educational and social programs to assist thousands of dissadvantaged youth.

Zayde: (*Yiddish*) meaning "grandfather."

PHOTO CREDITS

The photographs in this book have been provided by the authors from their personal collections, unless otherwise stated.

INDEX OF CONTRIBUTORS

Shecter, Max, 213

Shedletsky, Benjamin, 33

Sheff, Gerald, B.Arch., M.B.A., 179

Shemesh, Judd Y., 309

Sher, Shimon, 50

Sherman, Barry, B.Sc., S.M., Ph.D., P.Eng., 338

Sherman, Honey, B.A., B.Ed., 338

Sherman, Jonathon, 338

Shiff, Dorothy and Dick and family, 356

Shmerkin, Misha, 303

Shtibel, Adam, 164

Shtibel, Rose, M.Sc., 164

Shulman, Michael G., B.A., C.A., 151

Sigel, Deenna Karen, E.C.E., 132

Sigel, Lynn, 132

Sigel, J. Michael, B.Sc., 132

Sigel, Schuyler M., Q.C., LL.B., 132, 241

Silver, Laura Kaplan, 11

Silver, Lily, 229

Silver, Nathan, 229

Simon, Amy Mouckley, 343

Simpson, Helen, B.A., 119

Skidell, Akiva, B.A., 236

Skolnik, Kenneth, 155

Slavens, Paul, 217

Slonim, Rabbi Reuben, 152

Small, Mirial, 259

Sommerfeld, Uri, 48

Sonshine, Fran, 272

Speisman, Stephen, M.A., Ph.D., 83

Stark, Anice, 346

Stark, Arnold, 346

State of Israel Bonds, 380

Stern, Allen L., A.T.P., C.F.R.E., 150

Storm, Francie, 349

Sufrin, Mel, 331

Susman, Amri, 42

Taerk, Amanda, 335

Taerk, Audrey, B.A., B.Ed., 335

Tamir, Sivan, 370

Tanenbaum, Anne, 138

Tanenbaum, Joe, 193

Tanenbaum, Kenneth M., 369

Tanenbaum, Loretta, 270

Tanenbaum, Max, 138

Taqqu, Rachelle, 124, 125

Teich, Ira, 166

Torgov, Morley, LL.B., D.Litt., 153

the Toronto Symphony Orchestra, 227

Troper, Harold, 146

Tulchinsky, Anne, 256

United Jewish Appeal, 379

Ungerman, Irving, 204

Vaile, Lois, 342

Van Delman, Anna Gold, M.S.W., 344

Van Delman, Lou, 344

Waters, Bruce, B.Sc., 52

Waters, Lisa, B.A., 52

Waters, Philip, 52

Waters, Ruth, 52

Weinberg, Kurt E., 114

Weiner, Harvey Kenneth, 163

Weiner, Lindsay Gold, 157

Weinstein, Isadore (Gus), B.A., 119

Wellisch, Henry, 20

Westernoff, Fern, Ed.D, M.H.Sc., 348

Wicks, Ben, C.M., 304

Wise, Yaffa, 257

Wolfe, Rose, O.C., B.A., 129

Wortsman, Elayne, 254

Wyman, Tanya, M.D., 371

Young, Theresa, B.A., M.Cl.Sc., 348

Zacks, Sam, 220

Zauderer, Dianna Roberts, 96

Zeifman, Natalie Riback, 305

Ziegler, Roman, 362

Zimmerman, Willie, 23

Zimnowitz, Hana, 36

Zweig, Betty, 126

Zweig, Eric, B.A., 126

1949
- Armistice agreements are signed with Egypt, Jordan, Syria, and Lebanon.
- First Knesset (parliament) elections.
- David Ben-Gurion becomes Israel's first prime minister.
- Jerusalem is declared capital of Israel by Knesset.
- Jerusalem is divided between Israel and Jordan, with Jordan controlling the Old City and east Jerusalem.
- Operation *Magic Carpet* begins, bridging Jews from Yemen to Israel.

1956
- Sinai Campaign is launched by Israel, aided by Great Britain and France, following an Egyptian blockade of the Straits of Tiran, and a tripartite military alliance by Egypt, Syria, and Jordan. Israel captures the Gaza Strip and the Sinai peninsula.

1964
- The Palestine Liberation Organization is founded.
- The National Water Carrier is completed, bringing water from the north and centre of the country to the semi-arid south.

1917
- 400 years of Ottoman rule are ended by British conquest.
- Balfour Declaration is issued, pledging the British government's support for the establishment of a Jewish National Home in Palestine.

1948
- David Ben-Gurion declares the establishment of the State of Israel, May 14.
- Israel is immediately recognized by the U.S. and the U.S.S.R., followed by other countries.
- War of Independence begins May 15 as the armies of Egypt, Syria, Jordan, and Lebanon and a contingent from Iraq invade Israel.
- Jerusalem is besieged; Jordan captures Jewish settlements in Northern Dead Sea area as well as the Jewish Quarter of Jerusalem's Old City.
- Mass immigration from post-war Europe and Arab countries begins; in the years 1948–52 immigration brings 687,000 people to Israel.
- The *Altalena*, a ship of the underground defence organization Irgun, is sunk off the shore of Tel Aviv by Israel Defence Forces.

1957
- Israel withdraws from the Gaza Strip and the Sinai peninsula, with assurances of free passage for its shipping through the Suez Canal.

1955
- David Ben-Gurion begins second term as prime minister.

1965
- Teddy Kolle becomes mayor of Jerusalem; his term of office lasts 28 years.

1963
- Levi Eshkol becomes prime minister.

1896
- Theodor Herzl, father of political Zionism, writes *The Jewish State*, asserting that the problem of anti-Semitism can be resolved only by a Jewish state.

1938
- Aliya Bet, "illegal immigration" of Jews from Europe, begins; by 1948 almost 100,000 immigrants will arrive.

1954
- Moshe Sharett becomes prime minister.

1960

1940

1920

1900

1890

1910

1930

1950

1909
- Tel Aviv, first all-Jewish city in modern times, is founded near Jaffa.
- First kibbutz, Degania, is founded by young Jewish pioneers on the shores of Lake Kinneret (Sea of Galilee), combining agricultural settlement with a collective way of life.

1922
- League of Nations confirms British Mandate for Palestine, citing the Balfour Declaration in the preamble of the Mandate.

1939
- White Paper is issued by British government, restricting immigration and the sale of land to Jews.
- World War II begins; some six million Jews, including 1.5 million children, are murdered by the Nazis between 1939 and 1945 (the *Shoa*, or Holocaust).

1947
- The ship *Exodus* is sent back to Europe from Palestine, with 4,500 refugees on board.
- UN votes affirmatively on establishment of Jewish and Arab states in Palestine.
- Arab riots against settlements intensify.

1952
- Operation *Coresh* begins, bringing Jews from Iran to Israel.

1961
- Operation *Yachin* begins, bringing Jews from Morocco to Israel.
- Adolf Eichmann, organizer of the Nazi extermination program during World War II, stands trial in Jerusalem; he is found guilty and sentenced to death for crimes against humanity and the Jewish People.

1968
- The PLO formulates its covenant, which negates the existence of Israel.

1950
- Operation *Ezra and Nehemiah* begins, bringing Jews from Iraq to Israel.
- The Law of Return is passed by the Knesset, granting all Jews the right to come to Israel as *olim* (immigrants) and become citizens.

1969
- Golda Meir becomes prime minister.